Identity Theft and Fraud

Evaluating and Managing Risk

Identity Theft and Fraud

Evaluating and Managing Risk

Norm Archer, Susan Sproule,
Yufei Yuan, Ken Guo and
Junlian Xiang

UNIVERSITY OF OTTAWA PRESS
OTTAWA

University of Ottawa Press
542 King Edward Avenue
Ottawa, ON K1N 6N5
www.press.uottawa.ca

uOttawa

The University of Ottawa Press acknowledges with gratitude the support extended by Heritage Canada through its Book Publishing Industry Development Program, by the Canada Council for the Arts, by the Canadian Federation for the Humanities and Social Sciences through its Award to Scholarly Publications Program, by the EC Innovations company, by the Social Sciences and Humanities Research Council, and by the University of Ottawa.

LIBRARY AND ARCHIVES CANADA CATALOGUING IN PUBLICATION

Identity theft and fraud : evaluating and managing risk / Norm
Archer ... [et al.].

(Critical issues in risk management)
Includes bibliographical references and index.
Also issued in electronic format.
ISBN 978-0-7766-0777-1

1. Identity theft--Canada. 2. Identity theft--Risk assessment--Canada.
I. Archer, Norman P. II. Series: Critical issues in risk management.

HV6685.C3I34 2012   364.16'330971   C2012-903070-8

Contents

Chapter 1
Introduction   1

Chapter 2
Understanding Identity Theft and Fraud   14

Chapter 3
Risk and Trust   43

Chapter 4
Information Sources for IDTF   58

Chapter 5
The Nature and Scope of IDTF   76

Chapter 6
Measuring IDTF   102

Chapter 7
**Managing the Risks of Data Theft, Identity Theft
and Fraud**   122

Chapter 8
A Lifecycle Approach to Identity Asset Protection   154

Chapter 9
Employee Responsibility for Risks to Identity Assets   187

Chapter 10
Consumer and Business Perspectives   204

Chapter 11
Technical Perspectives on Security   226

Chapter 12
**Evaluating and Managing Organizational Readiness
   for Security and IDTF Risks**   259

Chapter 13
A Research Agenda for Identity Theft and Fraud Risks   275

Chapter 14
Monitoring Trends: Indexes of Identity Theft and Fraud   299

Chapter 15
Overview of the Book and a Glimpse of the Future   314

Glossary   330

Index   351

Chapter 1

Introduction

"I don't need to worry about identity theft because no one wants to be me."

—Jay London

The information age has brought many benefits to consumers, organizations and government agencies. We have ready access over the Internet to a huge range of information that can satisfy just about anyone's needs, we can communicate with people and organizations in ways unheard of even a decade ago, and consumers, businesses and governments can transact business over the Internet. But along with the speed and convenience of all these innovations has come an enormous increase in the incidence of related risks, such as identity theft, fraud and cyber-extortion by criminals. These criminals can work in anonymity from any country around the world, shielded from unsuspecting citizens and organizations by sophisticated techniques that continue to evolve constantly. The rapidly expanding availability of information and communications technology (ICT) has vastly increased the amount of confidential information at risk, exacerbating the potential for financial and reputational loss to firms and consumers alike through identity theft and fraud.

Identity theft and fraud (IDTF), whereby criminals use another person's personal identity and other relevant information in unauthorized ways, have become a significant and growing problem throughout the world. There is much public confusion about the definition of identity theft. Because of this, we differentiate between identity theft and identity fraud in this book; the differences are explained in detail in Chapter 2. Briefly, *identity theft* involves the collection of identity information, like birth certificates and credit card identifiers, from the owners of that information. This is not always illegal, so legal systems have only recently started to recognize criminal forms of identity theft. Identity information may also be generated illegally (using fictitious IDs or manipulating one's own ID). This is not identity theft, but it is a criminal activity. The actual use of stolen or bogus identities to commit fraud is defined as *identity fraud*, which is, and has been for many years, a criminal offense.

In the United States and Canada, identity theft and related forms of fraud have reached the level where they affect more than 4% of the population each year. As new methods of IDTF continue to appear, this rate may grow. A major reason for the rise in IDTF cases is the increased use of credit and debit cards, and commercial Internet applications, because of which identity information is more widely used and available in online databases and thus an easy target for criminals. These types of criminal activity have been dramatic and stunningly persistent (Anonymous 2007). Although consumers are entitled to free credit reports annually, credit file errors remain undetected and credit repair scams are growing in number. For many successive years, IDTF has ranked first in fraud complaints filed with the United States Federal Trade Commission (FTC). In 2009, these frauds accounted for 21% of the 721,418 complaints received by this agency. Similar concerns and results have been reported by Canada and other Western nations.

Although IDTF has become one of the top business, consumer and legal concerns of the information age, a more dangerous aspect than fraud is the possibility of physical danger, where terrorists can use identity theft to breach national security. Combating IDTF and thus protecting consumers and society as a whole is of urgent importance in maintaining a healthy economy and a stable social environment. Attacking this problem in an organized and focused manner requires a detailed understanding of the relative risks and costs arising from the many facets of IDTF.

IDTF is far from a new phenomenon, as the impersonation of officials and other individuals for the purpose of committing criminal fraud has plagued society for centuries. Over the ages, smugglers, pirates and other criminals have used aliases to hide their true identities in order to commit crime. For example, in the urban society of seventeenth-century London, England, when there was no photo identification and little by way of documented identification for commoners, people looked at dress, demeanour and symbols of office to determine identity, which gave an advantage to impostors of the day (Hurl-Eamon 2005). That environment eventually gave way to a society where, beginning with the upper classes, everyone had some form of identification available, such as birth certificates or passports. The first forms of identity theft merely involved stealing a person's identity papers. Before the widespread use of consumer credit cards in the 1950s, this usually meant stealing passports, social security cards or other identification.

Credit Cards

Credit cards, reportedly first used in Europe for inter-business transactions in the 1890s, soon spread to other Western nations and were made available by banks to some of their credit-worthy business customers in the 1930s (Bellis 2008). Credit cards are a way to extend automatic credit to customers. In a modern economy, sellers offer goods and services to strangers in exchange for a promise to pay, based on systems that link the buyer to a specific account or credit history. While credit cards do not contain all of an individual's identity information, they do provide access to the owner's credit account, which makes them a frequent target of thieves. Like other entrepreneurs, thieves follow the money. Identity thieves acquire data about another person that enables them to counterfeit the person's identification, so they can access goods and services by fraudulently charging someone else's account. With the increasingly widespread use, by the 1900s, of credit, banking and utility accounts, various types of account fraud followed. Initially, credit cards could only be obtained by applying in person with photographic identification or by being vouched for by a bank manager. This made identity theft infrequent, but obtaining credit was cumbersome (IDTF History 2008).

Credit cards did not become a common source of personal financial information until the early 1980s in the United States, when the Fair Isaacs Organization developed the FICO system of credit scoring (FICO 2009). This system of rating a person's reliability was often supplied in the form of a report that contained other sensitive and private personal and financial information. If an identity thief could gain access to such a credit report, it was a simple matter to access bank and credit card accounts.

During recent decades, credit cards have become easier to obtain. They are often, in fact, mass-mailed to consumers, with college students being a prime target. This has helped fraudsters to avail themselves of credit transactions on the Internet, as well as reap the bounty of automatic teller machines (ATMs). Ironically, a credit card is considered a superior form of identification, for both the legitimate owner and the thief. Hence, if another person has one in his or her possession and can display it to pretend he or she is someone else, then that someone else's identity has been successfully stolen. And the speed with which thieves can reap the benefits of these thefts is legendary: some of us know people whose cards were used to buy diamonds in Brazil, cameras in Monte Carlo or groceries in Los Angeles—all before they knew their cards were missing—even though credit card companies continue to strengthen automatic safeguards to detect and prevent such abuses. It is a simple matter for a thief with a stolen credit card number to open new accounts and go shopping. The thief runs up charges on the stolen cards and returns the goods for cash.

The advent of ATMs and the Internet were the identity thief's dream come true, and identity theft continues to mutate by taking advantage of new technologies. Much of the recent increase in identity fraud has been made possible by modern online payment systems (Anderson & Rachamadugu 2008). The net effect is a negative impact on public trust (Acoca 2008), which dampens enthusiasm for online commerce.

Consumer Identity Digitization

Prior to the existence of Internet support for business and personal transactions, personal identities in the paper world were tied primarily to a single identifier (in the US, the Social Security Number, or SSN, nominally a unique identifier, and in Canada, the Social Insurance Number, or SIN), or sometimes to driver's license numbers. Businesses, governments and other entities in the United States commonly use the SSN for record locators for both identification and authentication. Use of the SIN in Canada as a common identifier is not illegal, but certain federal government agencies (Revenue Canada, Canada Pension Plan, etc.) are specifically authorized to use it (Privacy Commissioner of Canada 2011). Financial institutions and other businesses must also collect SINs because they are required to report certain personal information such as salaries and benefits to the relevant government agencies. In general, SIN use in Canada is not as widespread as SSN in the United States, where many externally provided identifiers like credit card numbers, student ID numbers and employee ID numbers are tied to SSNs. Paper records containing these identifiers could be accessed and stolen, but only by someone physically present where the records were stored. Thus, large-scale theft of these unwieldy paper records was relatively unlikely until widespread access to and use of the Internet became common.

The smash-and-grab burglary of the past resulted in the theft of physical property like cash, jewellery and pieces of personal and financial information like driver's licenses, social insurance cards, credit cards and chequebooks. The burglar became an identity fraudster by using the stolen identification documents to commit fraud on existing accounts or by opening new accounts. Classically, this was committed on a relatively small scale, since only one dwelling could be burglarized at one time, and there was, of course, considerable risk of being caught. Later, theft of other physical identification became possible, like carbon-copy imprints from credit card receipts, PINs (personal identification numbers) obtained by looking over a cardholder's shoulder at the point of sale and digging through discarded office files. All these crimes must be committed in person, which obviously limited the volume of identity theft and fraud.

Then a dream came true for the underworld: digitization. The digitization of paper records and their storage on networked computers, together with ineffective security, greatly increased the likelihood of illegal access and theft of massive files of names, addresses, social security or social insurance numbers, debit card account numbers and PINs, bank account numbers and passwords, mothers' unmarried names, etc. (Schreft 2007).

The risks to individuals whose identity information and other related data are held by third parties, including government institutions and businesses, include both privacy risks and the danger that stolen identity information will lead to fraud. The public is constantly advised not to give out personal financial information, to shred personal papers, and to be generally cautious when doing business online. Compliant as the public may be, these precautions do not protect citizens in the face of database breaches. Criminal tactics have changed, since thieves no longer need to steal single identities but can steal them by the tens of thousands (Schneier 2005) from databases that are managed, and ostensibly protected, by third parties like banks, credit card companies, retail firms and government agencies. This information is often available on Internet sites protected only by passwords, and personal credit histories are stored, controlled and often sold by companies that the identity owners don't even know exist.

Online digital IDTF can be accomplished at very low cost, with a greatly reduced chance of arrest and on a much larger scale as a result of the tremendous advances in technology that have altered the way transactions are made. Computer processing speed has increased exponentially and lowered computing costs accordingly, and improvements in network connectivity and communications have made it possible to transfer data at high speeds with broadband technology. This has enabled a tremendous growth in e-commerce, including business-to-consumer, business-to-business and business-to-government transactions. Regrettably, these benefits have come at the cost of user exposure to database hackers and the interception of transaction data. This is why computer and network security has become critically important to successful e-commerce activity. Traditionally anonymous cash transactions have given way to transactions that involve the transfer of personal identification information to authorize transactions, requiring secure authentication processes to ensure that transactions are valid and preventing the theft of identity information during the process. Consumers now also carry out an increasing number of other activities online, like communicating with acquaintances and searching for information. All these activities have resulted in the creation of new online industries, which have helped to increase market efficiency. At the same time, unfortunately, these activities have also attracted an entirely new class of online crimes and a criminal industry that must be battled constantly to maintain valid electronic marketplaces.

As with other crimes, the costs of preventing identity theft and fraud must be balanced against the benefits of doing so in attempting to limit IDTF to an economically efficient degree. If the amount of IDTF could be limited to a level where markets could still operate efficiently, the government would not have to intervene, but this is not the case (Schreft 2007). Asymmetric information (one party to the transaction, often the seller, has more information than the other party) and economic externalities (consequences of economic activities that are experienced by unrelated third parties) are associated with the transfer and use of personally identifiable information in making payments. This means that the full cost of IDTF is not borne by the organizations best positioned to prevent the theft, giving them little incentive to protect against identity-related crimes. In addition, payment system integrity and efficiency are public goods that markets tend to under-produce even in the absence of IDTF, which further threatens their provision, creating the necessity for increased government intervention and regulation.

Data collection by marketers to use in studying trends and tendencies of consumer purchases has also created opportunities for identity theft and privacy invasion. The use of ICT to monitor everyday tasks through video monitoring and data collection from many different sources such as cash registers and office computers, can generate large amounts of information on individuals, including their opinions and habits (Rauhofer 2008). Large databases containing this information about many thousands of consumers can generate a potential market for data by both private and public organizations. These data can often be purchased and used for a variety of purposes by companies seeking to target specific individuals whose purchasing habits have been identified in these databases for marketing, tracking activities and locations, etc. According to Rauhofer (Rauhofer 2008), the 'market value' of privacy is falling as individuals continue to disclose information about themselves. In fact, there is a balance between individual privacy and public risk, but where this balance should be maintained is a major public policy issue.

Social Media Networks

The recent exponential growth in the use of Facebook, MySpace and other social networking sites draws on a wealth of personal information supplied by users (Grognou 2009) that is increasingly being targeted by cyber-criminals. Data posted on these sites—name, date of birth, address, job details, e-mail addresses and phone numbers—are a windfall for hackers (not to mention online human predators) and have aggravated consumer concerns about privacy protection. For example, the Canadian Privacy Commissioner recently undertook a detailed investigation of Facebook (Bardeesy 2009) due to complaints about consumer privacy from the Canadian Internet Policy and Public Interest Clinic (CIPPIC). As a result, the Commissioner ruled that Facebook was in violation of Canadian privacy legislation and asked for better disclosure, transparency or protection around deactivating and deleting accounts, handling the accounts of users who have died, and collecting the personal information of non-users (Privacy Commissioner of Canada 2007). Facebook has also been faced with other consumer demands to make their policies more transparent and to give users more control over their data. A greater, additional challenge will be to persuade young people that their charming but naïve belief in their invulnerability will not protect them from the villains who surf the Web for victims.

Institutional Identity Theft and Fraud

In addition to harm to individuals through financial and other losses, identity theft and fraud is a threat to institutions. For example, in a survey of 7,600 Canadian businesses in 2007–08, about half of the retail and insurance business establishments surveyed reported that they had experienced some type of fraud in the previous year (Taylor-Butts and Perreault 2009). Note that this study included all types of fraud, and it was not directed specifically to IDTF. However, IDTF of various types is a risk to all institutions. For example, IDTF for the purpose of falsely obtaining social benefits (health, retirement, etc.) has been a problem ever since such services have been provided by government authorities. Tightening authentication procedures for individuals applying for such benefits would alleviate this problem, but governments have been slow to do this. Data breaches of major databases containing confidential records of thousands of customers are also becoming more commonplace. These have developed into major risks for corporations and governments, which have resulted in not only enormous financial problems for citizens, but also loss of consumer confidence and trust which have, of course, left organizations open to very high liability and litigation costs. Many government and media publications warn citizens about the risks of identity theft and discuss steps individuals can take to minimize its danger, but often executives do not appear to realize the devastating effects and major liabilities that this crime can have on their organizations until it is too late and they actually experience such results (Gerard, Hillison et al. 2004). There are, in fact, multiple resources available from consultants, business associations and government agencies (Frappaolo 2006; Brown 2009; Jamieson, Smith et al. 2009) for companies that need detailed advice on how to recognize, manage and control these risks. Planning and implementing such activities is akin to reducing the risk of unsustainable damage from fire by taking out fire insurance. When executives actually recognize the parallels between the threats from identity theft and other risks such as fire, they will take appropriate action and will be less likely to be victimized by identity theft and fraud.

Ultimately, as the public becomes more familiar with security threats, companies that deal online with customers are likely to incur substantial additional costs and to experience a decline in consumer trust, unless they provide a speedy and reassuring response to consumer complaints about security. It is therefore vital to manage the perception of security, as well as actual security (Sarel and Marmorstein 2006). It is also important to assess actual and perceived threats, along with available technical solutions, and to develop a suitable conceptual approach to dealing with security and trust issues. Customer trust depends to a large extent on customer perceptions about a company's approach to handling security.

Identity theft by institutional employees is also a risk that may be fuelled by a lack of management attention or by a perception among employees that organizational management is corrupt. The past few years have included many examples of fraud and breach of trust in corporations like Enron and WorldCom that appear to be the direct results of a relentless drive for bottom-line results. For example, during the 1990s Enron cooked its books through criminal accounting practices and destroying or hiding evidence of negative company performance in an effort to keep its stock price rising. The company filed for bankruptcy in 2001 because its criminal practices were publicized and the company could no longer borrow money. In the year before the scandal was revealed, however, there was a major move by the US government toward deregulation of the energy industry, which helped Enron make enormous profits. This included income from the state of California, as energy traders took advantage of a more-or-less manufactured summer energy crisis. Such extreme approaches by executives appear to encourage employees to act unethically, influenced more by corporate management's attitudes than by their company's official policies. Employees will discriminate between high and low ethical standards only where management communicates corporate values that reward integrity and good business practices (Ghosh 2008).

This Book's Contents

The objective of this book is to highlight the risks of identity theft and fraud to society in general and to all its stakeholders—consumers and businesses, governments and other institutions fall victim to these escalating crimes—and to suggest ways to mitigate these risks and defend against the criminal activities that cause them. In the following chapters, we will further illustrate the various types of IDTF, highlight some recent results obtained from consumer surveys and discuss relevant information sources. We then develop and discuss the ramifications of a general model that demonstrates the interrelationships among stakeholders affected by IDTF, and use this model to evaluate various threats from IDTF to the different stakeholders. In developing secure approaches to defend against these threats, risks to individual and corporate privacy are also an important consideration. We will present statistics that show the extent of IDTF and data breach risks to society and evaluate laws that can be used to prosecute related criminal activities. Since prosecution is an after-the-fact activity, it is far better to mitigate risks to stakeholders through preemptive approaches to fighting IDTF. Discussions in several chapters demonstrate how each of these stakeholder groups is responsible both to itself and others in order to contain the threat of IDTF. We have also included a discussion of some of the technical details regarding the security necessary to minimize organizational risks from IDTF. Finally, we discuss the future of IDTF and what must be done to manage the threats to each stakeholder group and to society in general, as these threats continue to morph into new and challenging criminal attacks.

References

Acoca, B. 2008. "Online Identity Theft." *OECD Observer*, 268: 12–13.

Anderson, J. A., and V. Rachamadugu. 2008. *Managing Security and Privacy Integration across Enterprise Business Process and Infrastructure.* 2008 IEEE International Conference on Services Computing: IEEE.

Anonymous. 2007 (8 January.) "Diagnosis: Identity Theft." *Business Week.*

Bardeesy, K. 2009 (17 July.) "Ottawa Takes on Social Media Giant for Violating Canada's Law." *Globe and Mail.*

Bellis, M. 2008. "Who Invented Credit Cards?" About.com. http://inventors.about.com/od/cstartinventions/a/credit_cards.htm [consulted on January 28, 2009].

Brown, A. 2009. "Why Fraud Happens and What to Do about It." *Accountancy Ireland*, 41: 30–31.

FICO. 2009. "Looking for Your FICO Credit Score?" Minneapolis: Fair Isaacs Corporation. http://www.fico.com/en/Pages/default.aspx [consulted July 5, 2009].

Frappaolo, C. 2006. "Does Your Content Management Strategy Put You at Risk?" *KMWorld, Information Today*, 14: 12–16.

Gerard, G., W. Hillison, et al. 2004. "What Your Firm Should Know about Identity Theft." *Journal of Corporate Accounting and Finance*, 15: 4: 3.

Ghosh, D. 2008. "Corporate Values, Workplace Decisions and Ethical Standards of Employees." *Journal of Managerial Issues*, XX: 1: 68–87.

Grognou, V. 2009. "Cyber-criminals Targeting Social Networking Sites." *The Vancouver Province.* http://www.theprovince.com/technology/Cyber+criminals+targeting+social+networking+sites/1844785/story.html [consulted February 7, 2010].

Hurl-Eamon, J. 2005. "The Westminster Imposters: Impersonating Law Enforcement in Early Eighteenth-century London." *Eighteenth-Century Studies*, 38: 3: 461–83.

IDTF History. 2008. "History of Identity Theft." Identity Theft & Credit Fraud. www.identitytheftcreditfraud.com [consulted January 28 2009).

Jamieson, R., S. Smith, et al. 2009. "An Approach to Managing Identity Fraud." In *Cyber Security and Global Information Assurance: Threat Analysis and Response Solutions.* Hershey, PA: K. J. Knapp. Hershey, PA: 233–48.

Privacy Commissioner of Canada. 2007. "Key Steps for Organizations in Responding to Privacy Breaches." Ottawa: Office of the Privacy Commissioner of Canada. http://www.privcom.gc.ca/information/guide/2007/gl_070801_02_e. asp [consulted April 14, 2009].

Privacy Commissioner of Canada. 2011. "What Is the Social Insurance Number (SIN)?" Ottawa: Office of the Privacy Commissioner of Canada. http://www. priv.gc.ca/fs-fi/02_05_d_02_e.cfm [consulted March 13, 2011].

Rauhofer, J. 2008. "Privacy Is Dead, Get Over It! Information Privacy and the Dream of a Risk-Free Society." *Information & Communications Technology Law,* 17: 3: 185–97.

Sarel, D., and H. Marmorstein. 2006. "Addressing Consumers' Concerns about Online Security: A Conceptual and Empirical Analysis of Banks' Actions." *Journal of Financial Services Marketing,* 11: 2: 99–115.

Schneier, B. 2005. "Risks of Third-Party Data." *Communications of the ACM,* 48: 5: 136.

Schreft, S. L. 2007. "Risks of Identity Theft: Can the Market Protect the Payment System?" *Economic Review,* 92: 4: 5–40.

Taylor-Butts, A., and S. Perreault. 2009. "Fraud against Businesses in Canada: Results from a National Survey." Ottawa: Statistics Canada, 17. http://www. statcan.gc.ca/pub/85-571-x/2009001/aftertoc-aprestdm1-eng.htm [consulted January 2, 2010].

Chapter 2

Understanding Identity Theft and Fraud

"A jury consists of twelve people who determine which client has the better lawyer."

—Robert Frost

This chapter begins the exploration of the concepts behind identity theft and fraud. The basic ideas are presented first, including certain problem domains. Then a comprehensive model of the identity theft and fraud process is introduced, including an explanation of the various components that make up this process model and potential crimes that may result from the criminal activities involved. The legal ramifications of identity theft and fraud are explored briefly from the perspective of criminal law and consumer protection. Finally, a model is introduced that explains the relationships among the stakeholders in identity theft and fraud: the ID issuer, the ID holder, the ID checker, the ID protector and, finally, the ID criminal.

Identity and Identification

In his seminal study "Human Identification in Information Systems," Roger Clarke notes, "human identity is a delicate notion which requires consideration at the levels of philosophy and psychology. Human identification, on the other hand, is a practical matter" (Clarke 1994: 6). Clarke goes on to define human identification as the association of data with a human being.

Socially, we all identify family, friends and acquaintances through memory, matching facial and other physical characteristics, names and contexts like locations or situations. In modern economic dealings, more formal and codified means are required to identify individuals we do not know personally, but who have been given certain authorizations or privileges. Organizations need to be able to identify employees and customers. Governments need to be able to identify their citizens and residents, because these people enjoy certain privileges and must fulfill certain obligations.

Information used to establish one's identity can take three forms. Biometric identity attributes are unique to each individual (fingerprints, DNA profile, hand geometry, facial structure, etc.). Attributed identity consists of attributes given at birth (parents' names, date or place of birth and full name). Biographical identity attributes are details accumulated over time, including life events (details of education or other qualifications, employment history, property ownership and marriage details). Biographical attributes can also include items like benefits claimed, taxes paid, current and past addresses, etc. (Cabinet Office 2002).

Identification is done by matching information that is presented at the current time to information that has been recorded in the past (LoPucki 2001). In the simplest terms, when persons want to be eligible for certain ongoing privileges, they need to first *enroll* themselves with the organization that manages those privileges. For example, when a person wants to be legally entitled to drive a car, that person applies to a licensing bureau for a driver's license. Anyone wanting to open a bank account must make an application to a bank. The issuing organization then puts together a package of information that it will use to identify that individual on an ongoing basis. This information includes names and/ or unique codes that distinguish one individual from another, as well as information that can be used to verify that the person presenting himself or herself in subsequent transactions is the same person that was originally enrolled (these processes are described in detail in Chapter 8). Some sources call the unique identifiers "names" and the verifying information "passwords," however these terms are commonly used for specific instances of these broader concepts. In this book, we will use the generic terms *identifiers* and *verifiers*. For an identification system to work, identifiers can be published, but verifiers must be kept secret (LoPucki 2001).

After an individual is enrolled in a system, each time the individual presents himself or herself to the organization, there is a process of *authentication*. Authentication involves matching the presented identifier and verifier(s) to the identifier and verifier(s) recorded during the enrollment process. Many different types of information can be used as verifiers. A common classification system for such information is as follows:

- Something the person knows. Examples include passwords, personal identification numbers (PINs) or biographical information like birth date, address, mother's unmarried name or a line item from an income tax statement.
- Something the person has. Examples include ID cards, passports, driver's licenses, credit cards, smart cards or data storage devices like CDs and USB tokens.
- Something the person is. This category refers to biometric identifiers, like fingerprints, retina scans, hand vein patterns and facial recognition.
- Something the person does. Such verifiers are unique behavioural patterns that people develop over time, like handwriting, gait or vocalization. While these characteristics may change over time, they are difficult to imitate.

Systems may use more than one type of verifier. Debit or bank cards, for example, require both a card with a magnetic strip (something you have) and a PIN (something you know) before you can conduct a transaction. This practice is known as *multi-factor authentication* (authentication is discussed in more detail in Chapter 11).

The Overall Problem Domain

Many different definitions of identity theft and identity fraud can be found in the literature, and the popular media often use these terms without attempting to defining them. A 2006 survey found that 29% of Canadian consumers agreed with the statement, "I hear a lot about identity theft, but I am not sure what it means" (Ipsos-Reid 2006). In broadest terms, the problem involves activities that surround the creation and use of a *false identity* to obtain benefits or avoid obligations. "A person assumes a false identity if the person pretends to be, or passes himself or herself off as, some other person" (Australasian Centre for Policing Research 2004). The false identity is usually supported by documents or information that falsely attest to the person's identity. A false identity may be used either during enrollment, as when someone applies for a driver's license under someone else's name, or during the authentication process, as when someone uses a stolen credit card to make a purchase.

The model we will use to define Identity Theft and Fraud (IDTF) is a three-stage process model (Sproule and Archer 2007), as demonstrated in Figure 2.1. This model describes the complete problem space that is covered in discussions of IDTF. Each concept in the model is illustrated by examples of activities that may take place during that stage.

Collection of Identity Information

The first stage in this process model is the collection of identity information, which is the act of obtaining personal information relating to another person or persons without their authorization. There are many ways that personal information can be obtained, including,

- Theft of documents like passports, credit cards, driver's licenses, etc.

Figure 2.1: Process Model of the Problem Domain

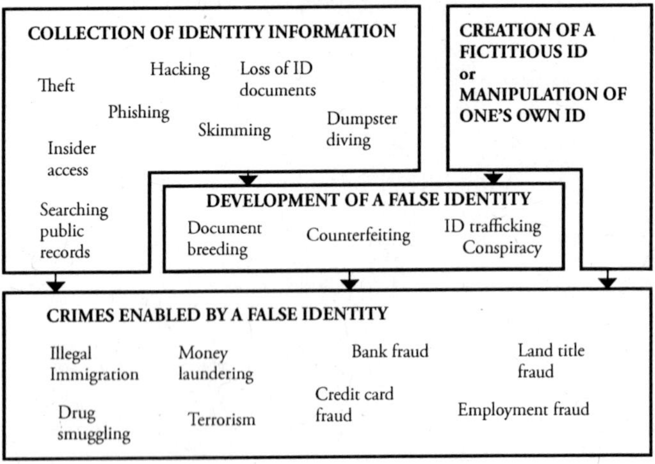

(Sproule and Archer 2007, reproduced by permission of the IEEE)

- Dumpster diving (rummaging through discarded files, papers and other items in the hopes of finding identity information)
- Phishing (fraudulently trying to gather personal information by simulating a trustworthy entity in an electronic communication)
- Insider access to records maintained by an organization
- Hacking into electronic databases where personal information is stored
- Using malware (i.e., spyware or key loggers) to capture personal data that has been entered into a computer
- Shoulder surfing (where someone looks over another person's shoulder) or eavesdropping while personal information is being written, keyed or spoken
- Intercepting wireless data transmissions that contain identity information

- Intercepting or stealing mail, or submitting a change of address so that mail is redirected
- Double-swiping credit or debit cards (skimming)
- Guessing (as in guessing that someone used their birth date or other biographical information as a password or PIN)
- Finding lost documents, like passports, credit cards, driver's licenses, etc.
- Searching public records

Methods of collecting identity information can be classified according to whether the information is obtained physically (e.g., theft or dumpster diving), electronically (e.g., hacking or key logging), through personal knowledge or interactions (e.g., phishing) or through a combination of these methods (e.g., skimming, where the data on a physical card is captured electronically). Methods of collecting identity information can also be classified according to whether they target individuals or many people at a time (Liberty Alliance 2005b). If a method targets a group of people it is sometimes called *identity harvesting*.

Note that some of these activities, such as theft and hacking, are illegal. Some, such as finding lost documents or searching public records, are clearly not illegal in and of themselves. Others, like dumpster diving, lie in areas where the law is not as clear, so prosecution of such activities must be based on offenses, such as fraud, that might arise from them. Laws are constantly evolving to address changing circumstances and technologies. For example, changes to Canadian law in 1998 criminalized the possession of equipment to extract and copy debit and credit card information (Government of Canada Justice Department 1998).

Development of a False Identity

The personal information collected in the previous stage of the process model may be used immediately to commit fraud or other crimes. In many cases, however, the information collected is sold or used further to develop a credible false identity through actions like counterfeiting or document breeding. This is an intermediary stage between the collection of personal information and the commission of a fraud or other crime.

In all but the most opportunistic situations, the identity information that is collected is sold on the black market. Carding forums are websites where stolen information can be bought and sold. Examples of past carding forums were www.shadowcrew.com, www.carderplanet.com and www.cardersmarket.com. These sites offered message posting, tutorials, source code for other types of attacks like phishing attacks, links to hacking tools and blacklists of carders who stole from other carders. A typical carding forum has an organizational structure consisting of administrators, moderators, reviewers, vendors and general members. Administrators oversee the operation, moderators act as subject matter experts or regional managers, and reviewers test products and services for sale. General members who wish to purchase stolen information or other products or services from the vendors must "join" and "sign in" through registration and authentication processes. Vendors post their products and services through public messages and deals are arranged through instant messaging or private e-mail. "Cashiers" are people who take stolen credit or debit card information, produce counterfeit cards, use the cards to make purchases or account withdrawals and then transfer a portion of the proceeds back to the vendors. In 2007, two of the largest carder forums had a combined membership of 20,000 (Kiefer-Peretti 2009).

There are reports that prices for stolen identity information appear to be going down as a result of more efficient markets or a surplus of supply. In 2004, the black market price of an identity was US$ 100–150, while in 2008 it was US$ 14–18. Estimates have the black market economy in stolen identities worth $5 billion and growing 60% per year (Carey 2008).

Counterfeiting develops tokens or documents from the identity information that has been collected. For example, digital information collected from a skimming operation can be used to create counterfeit credit cards. Counterfeiting can also be used to alter or produce new documents. For example, a criminal wanting to adopt a false identity will need to substitute his/her picture for the victim's on a stolen driver's license or passport. This can be done by altering the original document or by producing a new one. Counterfeit documents are also widely available on carder forums.

Using a false identity to enroll in a new system is called *document breeding,* because information or documents supporting the false identity are used to obtain new documents that further support the false identity. Document breeding can also be accomplished by applying to "replace" lost identity documents. This illustrates the layered nature of the identification process (LoPucki 2001). Criminals can also take simple information, such as a name, and use it on sites that help trace ancestry to retrieve other information such as a mother's unmarried name, often used as a verifier in authentication processes.

Criminals often apply for cellular phones using false identities. They can then use such numbers as substantiating information when posing as the victim (ID Analytics 2005). Criminals will also impersonate the victim to request address changes for bank accounts or credit card accounts. Invoices and statements showing fraudulent activity are thereby redirected, and it may be months before the victim notices that something is wrong. This results in what is called *account takeover.*

One of the main difficulties in combating identity theft is that many of the activities in this stage are not classed as illegal; thus, not much can be done to prosecute individuals caught doing them. An example occurred, before the law was changed (in Canada, as recently as 2009), when individuals were in possession of one or more birth certificates that clearly did not belong to them. Had these documents been reported stolen, the individual could have been prosecuted. Otherwise, the documents could have been confiscated, but there was little or no possibility that the individual could have been prosecuted. Such situations are common and were long a source of frustration to police, because they lacked proof that fraud had occurred.

Creation of a Fictitious ID or Manipulation of One's Own ID

An important aspect of the process model is the creation of a false identity that is not based on a real person, thus creating a fictitious (or synthetic) identity. There are sites on the Internet that will generate fictitious identities—with telephone numbers, addresses and zip codes—that will pass routine consistency checks (i.e., by providing a telephone area code and zip code to match a specified city). There is some confusion in the use of the term 'synthetic identities.' A private firm that produces studies of fraud from proprietary data uses the term 'true name' identity theft to describe any case where all of the information presented corresponds to a real person. However, when a real person's information is mixed with fictitious information or information related to other people, these are classified as 'synthetic' identities. According to their definitions, the firm found that only 11.7% of fraudulent new account applications were true name identity fraud. The remaining 88.3% were classified as synthetic identity fraud (ID Analytics 2005). We do not agree with this definition. If a real person's name or other identifier is being used, we would classify the fraud as identity fraud, regardless of what other identifying information is associated with that identifier. In fact, identity thieves often change the address associated with a stolen identity so that the victim does not receive correspondence regarding fraudulent accounts or transactions.

People can have many identities. In fact, manipulating one's identity or adopting a fictitious identity are often seen as good ways to protect one's privacy in the online environment (Mitchison, Wilikens et al. 2004). It is common for married women to continue to use their maiden names at work; actors and authors commonly adopt stage names and pen names. People in certain professions (i.e., espionage, correctional officers) often use aliases

(Clarke 1994). In cases like these, it is not illegal for an individual to have multiple identities, as long as the individual is not committing fraud. However, it is possible for someone to make changes to their own identity that will allow them to commit frauds or avoid prosecution. For example, a man in the UK was charged after it was discovered that he had used twenty-five false names (mostly a combination of his name and his wife's and mother's unmarried names) to avoid paying taxes on dividend payments, rental income and employment income (Cabinet Office 2002).

Crimes Enabled by a False Identity

Again referring to the process model in Figure 2.1, many different crimes, ranging from credit card fraud to terrorism, are committed by criminals using a false identity. In some cases, the false identity is *integral* to the crime. In other words, the underlying crime could not be committed without the use of a false identity. For example, you cannot commit credit card fraud or cheque fraud without posing as someone else. On the other hand, criminals who commit other crimes, like drug smuggling, often use a false identity to avoid apprehension and prosecution. In these cases, however, the underlying crime could just as easily be carried out without the use of a false identity and the use of a false identity is *peripheral* to the primary crime.

Definitions

In this book, we differentiate between identity theft and identity fraud, so each may be discussed in more detail. While Figure 2.1 outlined the overall problem domain, Figure 2.2 shows how identity theft and identity fraud fit within this domain. For our purposes, any illegal methods of collecting identity information are classified as identity theft, along with all of the activities involved in the development of a false identity. The creation of a fictitious ID or manipulation of one's own ID, while they may be classified as criminal activities in some cases, are not identity theft unless the manipulation involves co-mingling identity information of another person with one's own information. Identity fraud includes any crime involving the use of a false identity where the false identity is integral to the crime. Identity fraud may be the aim of perpetrators of identity crimes, but it is usually enabled by identity theft.

Figure 2.2: Identity Theft and Identity Fraud within the Process Model

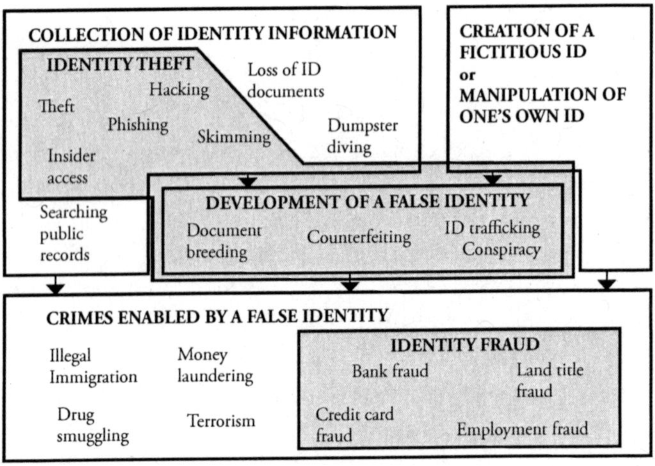

(Sproule and Archer 2007, reproduced by permission of the IEEE)

Note that identity theft can occur without identity fraud. An example would be a case where a hacker has stolen hundreds of pieces of identity information from an organization's database but subsequently uses only a small proportion of the stolen identities to commit frauds. Identity fraud can also occur without identity theft. Examples are when the person to whom the identity belongs is colluding with the fraudster, or when the identity fraud involves the use of a fictitious identity.

The definitions proposed in Table 2.1 separate acts involving the collection of personal information and the development of a

Table 2.1: Definitions

Identity theft	The unauthorized collection, possession, transfer, replication or other manipulation of another person's personal information
Identity fraud	The use of a false identity to obtain money, goods, services, or other benefits, or to avoid obligations

credible false identity from the act of committing a fraud or other crime. From a legal perspective, this separation is useful because historically we have had adequate descriptors and laws for the various crimes that may be committed with a false identity. Current legislative and law enforcement concerns lie primarily in the ways that personal information is collected, trafficked and developed into false identities.

Legal Background

Criminal Law (United States)

In 1935, the US Congress passed the Social Security Act, which established the current system of nine-digit Social Security Numbers (SSNs) for the purpose of administering the Social Security laws for American citizens (Social Security Administration 2010). There has been great concern about the misuse of the SSN, in parallel with concerns in Canada about the equivalent Canadian Social Insurance Number (SIN). There have been attempts to restrict its use as a standard unique identifier for citizens, but this has been difficult to stop. Amazingly, anyone can buy sixty million electronic records from the Social Security Administration—complete with SSNs—for individuals who have died. These records contain important personal identifiable information, including the name, SSN, date of birth, date of death, state or country of residence, ZIP code of last residence and ZIP code of lump-sum payment to the decedent's beneficiary. These records are also accessible at no cost on the Internet at places like ancestry.com (Rotenberg 2001).

In individual US states, the legal situation varies, so for the sake of brevity this discussion will be restricted to federal statutes. In 1998, the United States enacted the Identity Theft and Assumption Deterrence Act (ITADA), which brings identity theft and fraud into the criminal code and includes the following definition, covering activities in the second and third stages of the IDTF process model:

> Whoever knowingly transfers or uses, without lawful authority, a means of identification of another person with the intent to commit, or otherwise promote, carry on, or facilitate any unlawful activity that constitutes a violation of federal law, or that constitutes a felony under any applicable state or local law [commits identity theft].... (ITADA, 1998).

This definition, far broader than any Canadian legislation in place or contemplated, includes the theft of unique physical representations of an individual, such as fingerprints or voice prints (Schreft 2007). An important aspect of the ITADA is that it gives the impersonated person standing as a victim in the courts. Until it was passed, only creditors could claim damages from an identity fraud. Individual victims can now also receive restitution orders from the courts. Unfortunately, reimbursement is difficult to get from perpetrators in other jurisdictions, or from perpetrators who cannot be found, or who have no assets or income. "The chance of these victims actually receiving any compensation from the restitution orders is minimal" (Saunders and Zucker 1999: 189).

The ITADA provided stiffer penalties for crimes involving identity theft and charged the Federal Trade Commission (FTC) to "establish procedures for educating the public, receiving complaints, and coordinating enforcement efforts with various investigatory agencies" (Saunders and Zucker 1999: 189). In 2004, the Identity Theft Penalty Enhancement Act was signed, covering possession of identity information and increasing penalties, including a classification of "aggravated identity theft," when IDTF is associated with other felonies. While the ITADA and the Penalty Enhancement Act provide law enforcement authorities with more powers to act against identity theft and fraud, there is little data on whether law enforcement authorities have been provided the training or the resources to respond to individual reports of identity theft or fraud. Newman and McNally estimate that, in 2004, "of an estimated 9.3 million victims, 9 million of those cases never made it to the criminal justice system" (Newman and McNally 2005: ix).

Pretexting

Identity information and other related personal information can also be obtained by criminal activity through a process called 'pretexting,' which involves a deception whereby the perpetrator acquires personal, often financially related information through false pretences. This may be accomplished by making false statements, through misrepresentation, or by fraud (e.g., telephone calls made to a business or individual pretending to be a particular individual); usually the information is used for monetary gain or to avoid legal process. Pretexting is illegal in most North American jurisdictions. A very public example of pretexting occurred in 2005, when a *Maclean's* magazine reporter was able to purchase a log of the personal telephone records of the Privacy Commissioner of Canada from an American data broker for the sum of $200 (Anonymous 2005).

In New York state, until recently merely giving a fictitious name did not constitute false impersonation. Criminal impersonation was committed when an individual (Abzug 2003) "impersonates another and does an act in such assumed character with intent to obtain a benefit or to injure or defraud another" (N.Y. Penal Law § 190.25). This made it illegal to impersonate a real person but not a fictitious one. That is, if Jane forged Mary's name on cheques made out to Jane so that Jane could cash the cheques, Jane could be guilty of false impersonation—but only if Mary was a real person. New York state recently updated its laws on identity theft through impersonation by enacting a penal law amendment that makes it a crime to impersonate another or pretend to be a public servant by means of online communication (Anonymous 2008).

Most state laws make the impersonation of a public official a criminal act. For example, in Texas, impersonating "a public servant with intent to induce another to submit to his pretended official authority or to rely on his pretended official acts" is a crime (Tex. Penal Code Ann. § 37.11). Depending on the state jurisdiction, the person being impersonated may not have to actually exist. For example, if an identity thief pulls over a driver, displays a fake police badge and tells the driver that a fine can be paid on the spot to avoid arrest, this is a criminal act of false impersonation and/or extortion. Thousands of criminal reports are filed each year in the US by individuals victimized by someone impersonating a police officer.

Criminal Law (Canada)

Canadian legislation on identity theft has lagged the United States in recognizing and penalizing criminal activities involving identity theft. This may be of benefit in some ways, in that Canadian lawmakers can learn from the experience of their southern neighbours and use this knowledge to fine-tune proposed legislation. However, delays in introducing measures to combat IDTF mean that Canadian consumers remain vulnerable to this threat. Until recently, criminal law in Canada did not make reference to identity theft or identity fraud. Offences involving identity theft and fraud were prosecuted under several other *Criminal Code* sections—such as fraud, impersonation, theft, and unauthorized use of a computer—but anyone could possess another person's identity information without penalty (Nurani 2007).

In 2004 and 2006, Canada's Department of Justice conducted consultations on Criminal Code changes related to identity theft. These consultations addressed activities in what we have defined as identity theft, specifically the misappropriation, possession and trafficking of identity information and identity cards with intent to commit fraud or personation. They also considered ways to include a "presumption of intent" when a large collection of identity information was found or when specific identity documents usually kept confidential were found. As a result of these consultations, legislation was proposed in 2009 (Bill S-4 2009) to the Canadian parliament to update relevant laws on identity theft and to give the justice system more power to apprehend and prosecute thieves involved in such activities. This legislation created new offences covering the "obtaining and possessing of identity information with the intent to use the information deceptively, dishonestly or fraudulently." It also covered trafficking in identity information with "knowledge or recklessness toward possible criminal use," "unlawfully possessing or trafficking in government documents that contain the information of another person" and fraudulently redirecting mail (Government of Canada 2009). The bill also criminalized the tactic of pretexting in order to use the information to commit fraud.

This bill received wide attention and support, with a number of agencies submitting briefs to the House of Commons Standing Committee on Justice and Human Rights in support of it, but recommending amendments. It was finally passed into law in October 2009. This bill greatly enhanced the ability of police to prosecute related egregious criminal acts—such as, for example, an identity takeover by a criminal in Chilliwack, BC, who was known to police as the perpetrator but who could not be prosecuted because the statute of limitations had expired, leaving the victim open to prosecution and having to pay off loans, taxes and fines for which he was not responsible (Tomlinson 2009).

There is still room for improvement in Canadian criminal law related to IDTF. The new identity theft and document breeding offences carry maximum jail terms less than those for existing offences for fraud, forgery and impersonation (five years vs. ten years). A brief by the Canadian Internet Policy and Public Interest Clinic (CIPPIC 2008) also pointed out that law enforcement authorities need to be given additional resources that would allow them to prosecute the new offences to ensure that Canadian privacy laws are enforced in the marketplace, and to provide for breach notification to the public in the event of database security breaches, thereby creating greater incentive for security and privacy compliance by businesses, government and public agencies.

Consumer Protection Law (United States)

The US Fair Credit Reporting Act, originally passed in 1970, governs the collection, dissemination and use of consumer information, including the operations of credit reporting agencies. In 2003, it was supplemented by the Fair and Accurate Credit Transactions Act (FACTA). Some of the provisions of FACTA include

- Requirements for the issuing of fraud alerts by credit reporting agencies
- Compulsory truncation of credit card numbers on receipts
- Requirements for card issuers to investigate requests for address changes
- Free annual credit reports to consumers
- Mandatory blocking of identity theft information on credit reports
- Improvements on identity theft resolution procedures within credit reporting agencies

In the opinion of some experts, many of the provisions of FACTA simply require conformance to best practices already in common use. For example, all major credit bureaus had procedures in place to issue fraud alerts on the files of identity theft victims. Similarly, it was already common practice for electronic credit card receipts to have truncated account numbers and hidden expiry dates. While the requirement for credit card issuers to send a notification of a new credit card application to both old and new addresses was, again, common practice, it standardized a process that should help to eliminate a fairly common and easy method of committing identity fraud (Linnhoff and Langenderfer 2004).

The requirement for free credit reports is intended to help consumers detect identity fraud, but it is not clear whether the proportion of consumers who request such reports will increase significantly. Improvements that have been suggested include a coordinated request and response that would include information from all the major credit bureaus in one report, or automatic annual reports sent to the consumer. It is also suggested that future legislation require credit bureaus to notify consumers when negative information is added to their file (Linnhoff and Langenderfer 2004).

Changes to the resolution process and requirements to remove identity theft information from credit reports are acknowledged as major improvements. Once a report of identity theft is received, the credit bureau is required to remove the erroneous information, to notify the organization that provided the information and to ensure that the information does not find its way back onto the credit report. The reappearance of erroneous information related to cases of identity fraud (also known as 're-pollution') had been a major source of frustration to victims (Linnhoff and Langenderfer 2004).

As of 2008, FACTA requires all financial institutions to develop and implement 'red flag' rules to help counteract IDTF. Red flags are indicators that there may be an identity fraud taking place. They include unusual account activity, credit alerts on the consumer's credit report, suspicious applications, etc. Each financial institution must have a program describing the Red Flags and instructing employees how to respond (Federal Trade Commission 2008).

Consumer Protection Law (Canada)

In Canada in 2002, the federal government's Consumer Measures Committee issued a discussion paper exploring a number of options for legislative changes associated with consumer protection and market issues. The paper reviewed applicable federal, provincial and territorial laws and suggested possible actions under three objectives: 1) making it harder for thieves to obtain personal information, 2) making it easier to detect identity theft and 3) making it easier for victims to repair the damage done by the identity theft and fraud. Recommendations to 'stop the leaks' include mandatory truncation of payment card numbers on receipts, verifying the identities of persons and organizations requesting credit reports and discontinuing the use of SINs as identifiers by banks and credit bureaus. To facilitate detection, options included allowing consumers to place alerts and freezes on their credit reports and mandatory notification of data breaches. To assist victims, options include requiring creditors to provide victims with details of the fraudulent debts and requiring credit bureaus to block such information from appearing on the victims' credit reports. The committee also proposed making organizations responsible for informing victims of their rights and making them liable for damages if any of these provisions were not followed. Many of the suggested provisions would duplicate US legislation, primarily the FACTA. However, consumer protection comes under provincial jurisdiction in Canada, and, although the discussions were timely, there has been no concerted effort to enact changes.

The story is better for Canadians when it comes to verifying credit status, which is critical when consumers suspect that identity thieves may have compromised their credit status. In Canada, the two major credit bureaus are Equifax Canada and TransUnion Canada. Although credit reporting legislation differs from province to province, all Canadian consumers are protected from the collection of excessive data by these agencies (Financial Consumer Agency of Canada 2008). Credit agencies may list outstanding debts and payment history, along with current address and employer, but they cannot report information about marital status, etc. Most items on payment history, judgments and collections remain on file for six years, but some provinces allow for longer retention periods. Consumers have the right to obtain a free credit report from a credit bureau at least once a year. If consumers discover that erroneous information has been added to their files, they have a right to have it corrected and/or to have a statement attached to each report issued to loan agencies in the future.

Privacy and Data Protection

In the United States, legislation on privacy and associated data handling requirements has been introduced on a sector-by-sector basis. Some examples of legislation that covers these activities include the Sarbanes Oxley Act, which requires publicly traded companies to maintain adequate security controls on their information systems; the Gramm-Leach-Bliley Act, which requires financial institutions to meet privacy standards related to customer information; and the Health Insurance Portability and Accounting Act (HIPPA), which governs data security of health records (Cavoukian 2005; Oltsik, McKnight et al. 2007).

In contrast, Canada has comprehensive privacy legislation. The Privacy Act, passed in 1983, covers the public sector (Government of Canada Justice Department 1983). Beginning in 2001, and implemented in stages through to 2006, the Personal Information Protection and Electronic Documents Act (PIPEDA) (Department of Justice 2009b) applies to organizations in the private sector, except when provincial laws exist that are substantially similar to PIPEDA. Such provinces include British Columbia, Alberta, Ontario and Quebec. PIPEDA establishes ground rules for how private sector organizations may collect, use or disclose personal information in the course of commercial activities. The law gives individuals the right to access and request correction of personal information such organizations may have collected. Breaches or failure to comply can result in fines of up to $100,000. PIPEDA principles include accountability, identifying purposes, consent, limits to collection, limits to use, disclosure and retention of data, accuracy, individual access, safeguards and openness.

Electronic Signatures

An electronic signature is any type of digital marking used by a party to be attached to or to authenticate a record. In the United States, E-Sign is federal legislation adopted in 2000 for digital signatures in transactions, and many state statutes recognize these signatures as legally binding agreements. Electronic contracts and signatures are beneficial to all participants, since computer systems are fast and accurate and permit businesses to do commercial transactions without human intervention. These contracts are also useful for lower-cost transactions like purchasing airline tickets, since the purchase is legally bound by the agreement; for more complex contracts that may undergo multiple changes, electronic communications assist the parties to confirm the receipt and accuracy of orders immediately, as well as to correct errors rapidly. Non-repudiation of such transactions is supported by reliable records maintained by the underlying electronic system.

Legislation making electronic or digital signatures legal in Canada was created by the Canadian parliament in 2000 (PIPEDA 2000). Provincial legislatures have enacted their own laws, which make digital signatures legal for commerce. Most Canadian organizations, however, have not attempted to use digital signatures, as they find them confusing. Therefore, they still use processes that waste much time and money printing and filing paper documents.

Varieties of electronic signatures may include digitized images of paper signatures, typed notations at the bottom of electronic documents or even addressing notations, like electronic headers or footers (Freeman 2004). Electronic signatures must authenticate the writer's intent, but an important goal is to prevent forgeries and to serve as suitable legal replacements for physically signing a paper document (Freeman 2004). An electronic signature can be any sound, symbol or process attached to or associated with an electronic record by the person who has intended to sign the electronic record. A name on an e-mail, a digital signature system using encryption technology, an indirect affirmation such as a click agreeing to the terms of a new e-mail account, or any reasonable process that seeks to authenticate an electronic record can also be an electronic signature. Such electronic signatures cannot, however, verify that a document has not been altered since it was signed.

For a digital signature to be legal, it must be permanently bound to the document by the use of appropriate software; this is the same requirement for physical pen-and-paper signing. Only digital signatures based upon a public key infrastructure (PKI) system provide signer or document authentication. These signatures identify and authenticate the originator of a document, such that the receiver can determine the sender's identity—whether or not the message has changed since it was transmitted—and verify that all the information has been unchanged since the message was signed.

There are drawbacks to digital documents and signatures. Paper documents provide both parties with a high level of integrity and confidentiality, and they can be locked in a secure location. However, the open nature of e-mail and the Internet imperil this level of privacy, since a transmitted document is subject to Internet hackers, forgers and unauthorized alterations. Electronic contracts also raise questions about the legitimacy of the parties' signatures, since it may not be possible to verify that a particular person actually transmitted the contract, to determine if the sender had the authority to create the contract, or if it was a forgery created by an imposter. E-Sign, the US federal legislation legalizing electronic signatures, does not force consumers to accept electronic signatures. Before electronic contracts can replace written documents, the consumer must have "affirmatively consented, by means of a consent that is conspicuous and visually separate from other terms, to the provision or availability (whichever is required) of such record" (Freeman 2004). If a customer insists on handwritten signatures and retention of a paper copy of the contract, the other parties must abide by these wishes or allow the party to cancel the contract.

Cybercrime Convention

One of the most important characteristics of the Internet is that it crosses international boundaries with ease, allowing communications and transactions to happen between individuals with Internet access almost anywhere on Earth. This is also a drawback when it comes to fighting identity theft and fraud. All the laws that may exist in a province, state or country have little or no effect when attempting to prevent or prosecute criminal activity against its citizens when such activity originates in other jurisdictions. For this reason, an international Cybercrime Convention has been ratified by a number of Western countries, led by the Council of Europe and including Canada and the United States (Council of Europe 2001). This is the first international treaty on crimes committed via the Internet and other computer networks. It contains a series of powers and procedures, such as the search of computer networks and lawful interception of communications believed to involve criminal intent. The main objective of the Convention is to protect society against cybercrime through appropriate legislation and international cooperation. Offenses addressed by the Convention include illegal access, illegal interception, data interference, system interference, misuse of devices, computer-related forgery, computer-related fraud, offences related to child pornography, offences related to copyright and neighbouring rights and violations of network security.

A Stakeholder Model of Identity Theft and Fraud

A theoretical framework that discusses institutional and identity owner interactions in combating identity theft is shown in Figure 2.3 (Wang, Yuan et al. 2006). There are four stakeholders defending against various classes of identity theft and fraud. They are identified as 1) identity owners; 2) identity issuers (e.g., government agencies, credit card companies, banks, etc.); 3) identity checkers (e.g., government agencies, businesses, credit card companies); and 4) identity protectors (e.g., police, lawmakers, the legal system). Figure 2.3 demonstrates the many interactions among these stakeholders and the responsibilities of the defending stakeholders—owner, issuer, checker and protector—to safeguard identities of the individuals, corporations or other identity owners.

Figure 2.3: Combating Identity Theft and Fraud

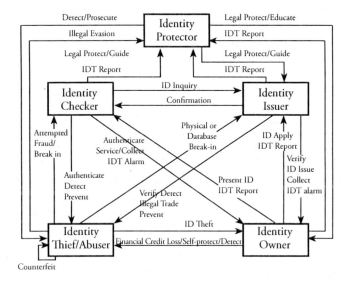

(adapted from Wang, Yuan et al. 2006)

In this framework, the *identity thief* represents an individual or organization that is involved in illicitly obtaining personal information, developing false identities or committing crimes using a false identity. The identity thief may be a "faceless" stranger but can also be a friend or acquaintance of the victim or an employee of an organization where the victim's personal information is stored. The *identity owner* is the person who is truly associated with the identity information or identity documents in question. Identity owners are concerned about identity frauds that result from identity theft; they are not directly concerned about identity frauds based on fictitious identities. *Identity issuers* are trusted institutions (public or private) who issue identity documents or other credentials. Governments issue birth certificates, driver's licenses, passports and other documents that are used to identify the owner of the documents for certain specific purposes. In the same way, banks issue credit cards or banking cards (i.e., debit cards) to individual customers.

The customers then use these cards to identify themselves in future transactions with the banks or associated merchants. An *identity checker* is an individual or organization that verifies that the person presenting the identification document or credentials is the person to whom the identity belongs. For example, a store clerk processing a credit card transaction will electronically transmit the card details to check that the card is valid and should also check the signature on the card to the signature on the receipt to check that the customer is the person to whom that card was issued.[1] Finally, *identity protectors* are individuals or organizations involved with protecting identity owners, issuers and checkers against IDTF. Identity protectors include legislators, law enforcement, security service providers, security solution providers and consumer advocacy groups (Wang, Yuan et al. 2006).

Identity Theft—A Problem of Guardianship

As discussed above, our definition separates acts involving the collection of personal information and the development of a credible false identity from the act of committing a fraud or other crime. For the most part, guarding against identity theft is therefore concerned with preventing the unauthorized collection of personal information. This is a matter of personal and agency guardianship. Identity owners need to manage risks associated with the disclosure of their personal information. This includes decisions about what information to disclose, to whom and how their personal information is stored and transmitted.

Identity issuers and identity checkers maintain records containing identity information for the people they deal with. They are responsible for safeguarding this information and need to manage risks associated with what information they retain, how long it is retained, to whom it is released and how it is stored and transmitted.

---

1 New 'chip and PIN' credit cards use a PIN instead of a signature to verify the identity of the card owner.

The problem of identity theft also deals with trafficking in identity information, counterfeiting, document breeding and other activities involved with the development of a credible false identity. As discussed above, identity issuers must safeguard the identity information they retain, but they also have responsibilities to prevent document breeding and counterfeiting. While we include document breeding as part of the development of a credible false identity, it is also a form of identity fraud. Preventing document breeding requires stringent enrollment and authentication processes when issuing new or replacement documentation. Identity issuers can reduce counterfeiting by adopting new technologies and high-tech materials for the documents and tokens they issue.

Identity protectors are the stakeholders who are primarily involved in preventing, detecting and prosecuting the remaining activities in the development stage, including the possession and trafficking of identity information. Until recently, law enforcement agencies were hobbled by a lack of legislation that addresses many of these activities. The US Identity Theft and Assumption Deterrence Act and recent legislation in Canada (Bill S-4) have addressed these gaps. For many reasons, however, enforcement of these new laws remains a challenge.

Identity Fraud—A Problem of Authentication

Identity fraud involves the use of a false identity to gain money, goods, services or other benefits, or the avoidance of obligations. The false identity used to commit the fraud can be based on a real person or can be a fictitious identity. The main process involved in preventing identity fraud is authentication—establishing whether or not the person who is presenting the identity information is really the person to whom that identity belongs.

Identity issuers and checkers are primarily responsible for preventing identity fraud through adequate enrollment and authentication processes. Identity owners do not play a major role in preventing identity fraud, but they can minimize the damages associated with identity fraud by detecting it early. This and other related issues are discussed in detail in later chapters of this book.

Summary

This chapter introduced and explained the basic definitions essential to an understanding of identity theft and fraud (IDTF), along with two fundamental models that illustrate the processes involved in guarding against IDTF. First, identity and identification were described, and then a three-stage process model was introduced that covers the various ways in which IDTF can occur. Basic definitions of identity theft and fraud, upon which this book is based, were detailed. Some legal background of US and Canadian legislation on IDTF is included, since this prescribes the boundaries that constrain authorities in combating IDTF crimes. Consumer protection under the law is a very important safeguard for privacy and data protection, and this was discussed, along with modern trends in electronic signatures. A stakeholder model was introduced, which briefly described the parties interested in IDTF, including identity owners, identity issuers, identity checkers and identity prosecutors—and, last but not least, identity criminals. The keys to successfully controlling IDTF are guardianship and authentication. These were described briefly as the responsibilities of all the parties engaged in combating identity theft and fraud.

References

Abzug, C. E. A. 2003. *Systems Security Engineering Capability Maturity Model SSE-CMM*. Model Description Document Version 3.0. Pittsburgh: Carnegie Mellon University, p. 340.

ACPR (Australasian Centre for Policing Research). 2004. "Standardization of Definitions of Identity Crime Terms." Discussion Paper, Prepared by the ACPR for the Police Commissioners' Australasian Identity Crime Working Party and the AUSTRAC POI Steering Committee.

Anonymous. 2005. "Commissioner's Phone Records Access Puts Long-Standing Data Broker Problem in the Spotlight." PrivacyScan. http://www.privacyscan.ca/November17,2005.pdf [consulted April 5, 2009].

Anonymous. 2008. "New York Makes Impersonation a crime." *Crime Alert* http://www.hunton.com/files/tbl_s10News/FileUpload44/15889/new_york_internet_impersonation_privacy_alert.pdf [consulted May 31, 2009].

Bill S-4. 2009. *Bill S-4: An Act to Amend the Criminal Code (Identity Theft and Related Misconduct)*. Ottawa: Parliament of Canada. Canada.http://www2.parl.gc.ca/Sites/LOP/LegislativeSummaries/bills_ls.asp?lang=E&ls=s4&source=library_prb&Parl=40&Ses=2 [consulted March 19, 2011].

Cabinet Office. 2002. *Identity Fraud: A Study*. London, UK: Cabinet Office. www.statewatch.org/news/2004/may/id-fraud-report.pdf [consulted March 14, 2011].

Carey, L. 2008. "What's Your Identity Worth on the Black Market?" http://ezinearticles.com/?Whats-Your-Identity-Worth-on-the-Black-Market&id=1498714 [consulted February 8, 2010].

Cavoukian, A. 2005. *Identity Theft Revisited: Security Is Not Enough*. Information and Privacy Commissioner/Ontario, Government of Ontario.

CIPPIC. 2008. "An act to amend the criminal code: Brief submitted by Canadian Internet Policy and Public Interest Clinic (CIPPIC) on Bill C-27 (identity theft and related misconduct)." Ottawa: House of Commons Standing Committee on Justice and Human Rights. www.cippic.ca/uploads/CIPPIC_Brief_C-27_01Apr08.pdf [consulted May 31, 2009].

Clarke, R. 1994. "Human Identification in Information Systems: Management Challenges and Public Policy Issues." *Information Technology and People*, 7: 4: 6–37.

Council of Europe. 2001. *Convention on Cybercrime*. http://conventions.coe.int/Treaty/EN/Treaties/Html/185.htm [consulted March 13, 2011].

Department of Justice. 2009b. *Personal Information Protection and Electronic Documents Act*. Ottawa: Department of Justice. http://laws.justice.gc.ca/en/ShowDoc/cs/P-8.6/20090818/en?page=1 [consulted March 13, 2011].

Federal Trade Commission. 2008. "FTC Will Grant Six-Month Delay of Enforcement of 'Red Flags' Rule Requiring Creditors and Financial Institutions to Have Identity Theft Prevention Programs." Washington, D.C.: Federal Trade Commission. http://www.ftc.gov/opa/2008/10/redflags.shtm [consulted July 8, 2009.

Financial Consumer Agency of Canada. 2008. "Understanding Your Credit Report and Credit Score." http://www.fcac-acfc.gc.ca/eng/publications/CreditReportScore/PDF/CreditReportScore-eng.pdf [consulted March 13, 2011].

Freeman, E. H. 2004. "Digital Signatures and Electronic Contracts." *Information Systems Security*, 8–12.

Government of Canada Justice Department. 1983. *Privacy Act P-21*. http://laws.justice.gc.ca/eng/P-21/page-1.html#anchorbo-ga:s_2 [consulted March 13, 2011].

Government of Canada Justice Department. 1998. *Criminal Code of Canada*. Part IX, Section 342.01: Instruments for copying credit card data or forging or falsifying credit cards. http://laws.justice.gc.ca/PDF/Readability/C-46.pdf [consulted March 13, 2011].

Government of Canada Justice Department. 2009. *Government Re-Introduces Legislation Targeting Identity Theft, Press Release March 31, 2009*. http://www.justice.gc.ca/eng/news-nouv/nr-cp/2009/doc_32347.html [consulted February 8, 2012]

ID Analytics. 2005. *ID Analytics National Fraud Ring Analysis: Understanding Behavioural Patterns.*

Ipsos-Reid. 2006. *Concern Over Identity Theft Is Changing Consumer Behaviour,* Ipsos-Reid on Behalf of Capital One.

ITADA. 1998. *Identity Theft and Assumption Deterrence Act of 1998.* Public Law 105-318 105th Congress http://www.ftc.gov/os/statutes/itada/itadact.pdf [consulted February 8, 2012].

Kiefer-Peretti, K. 2009. "Data Breaches: What the Underground World of 'Carding' Reveals." *Santa Clara Computer & High Technology Law Journal*, 25: 375–413.

Liberty Alliance. 2005b. *Liberty Alliance Whitepaper: Identity Theft Primer.* Liberty Alliance Project.

Linnhoff, S., and J. Langenderfer. 2004. "Identity Theft Legislation: The Fair and Accurate Credit Transactions Act of 2003 and the Road Not Taken." *The Journal of Consumer Affairs*, 38: 2: 204–16.

LoPucki, L. 2001. "Human Identification Theory and the Identity Theft Problem." *Texas Law Review*, 80: 89–136.

Mitchison, N., M. Wilikens, et al. 2004. *Identity Theft: A Discussion Paper.* Italy, European Commission, Directorate-General, Joint Research Centre.

Newman, G. R., and M. M. McNally. 2005. *Identity Theft Literature Review.* Washington, D.C.: US Department of Justice. Document No. 210459.

Nurani, F. 2007 (6 July.) "Identity Fraud Legislation Long Overdue." *The Lawyer's Weekly.* http://www.lawyersweekly.ca/index.php?section=article&articleid=507 [consulted April 5, 2009].

Oltsik, J., J. McKnight, et al. 2007. *Research Report: The Case for Data Leakage Prevention Solutions.* Enterprise Strategy Group for Vericept.

PIPEDA. 2000. Personal Information Protection and Electronic Documents Act. Ottawa: Department of Justice. http://laws.justice.gc.ca/en/P-8.6/index.html [consulted March 19, 2011].

Rotenberg, M. 2001. "SSNs and Identity Theft." Subcommittee on Oversight and Investigations. http://epic.org/privacy/ssn/testimony_11_08_2001.html (Jan 28 2009) [consulted January 28, 2009].

Saunders, K. M., and B. Zucker. 1999. "Counteracting Identity Fraud in the Information Age: The Identity Theft and Assumption Deterrence Act." *International Review of Law, Computers & Technology*, 13: 2: 183–92.

Schreft, S. L. 2007. "Risks of Identity Theft: Can the Market Protect the Payment System?" *Economic Review*, 92: 4: 5–40.

Social Security Administration. 2010. "Detailed Chronology of United States Social Security." http://www.ssa.gov/history/chrono.html [consulted March 13, 2011].

Sproule, S., and N. Archer. 2007. *Defining Identity Theft.* Eighth World Congress on the Management of eBusiness, Toronto, IEEE.

Tomlinson, K. 2009. B.C. Identity Theft Victims Say They Can't Get Justice. CBC News, September 28, 2009. http://www.cbc.ca/m/touch/canada/british-columbia/story/2009/09/28/bc-identitytheft.html [consulted February 8, 2012].

Wang, W., Y. Yuan, et al. 2006. "A Context Framework for Combating Identity Theft." *IEEE Security & Privacy*, March/April: 24–32.

Chapter 3

Risk and Trust

"A word to the wise ain't necessary—it's the stupid ones that need the advice."

—Bill Cosby

Risk is an extremely important aspect of the process of protecting against identity theft, because the level of perceived risk from the threat of identity theft determines how much time, effort and money should be spent to reduce this risk. If the risk is perceived to be low, then the resources that should be expended to address the threat are less than if the risk is perceived to be high. This chapter explores different aspects of risk as they pertain to identity theft and fraud, including definitions, perceptions, impact and likelihood of risky events, risk mitigation and, finally, the implications of identity theft on trust.

Risk, Identity Theft and Fraud

Risk is defined as a state of uncertainty where some of the possibilities involve a loss, catastrophe or other undesirable outcome (Hubbard 2007: 46). In turn, uncertainty is defined as the lack of complete certainty, or the existence of more than one possibility of occurrence, and the 'true' outcome is not known in advance. It is possible to have uncertainty without risk, but not risk without uncertainty. Risk may be measured or estimated where there is a set of possibilities, each with quantified probabilities and quantified losses. An example: based on a statistical survey, there is a probability of 0.0001 that a consumer will experience some sort of identity fraud in the next year. If such an event occurs, the consumer will spend an average of twenty hours trying to clear the problem. That is, a consumer runs a 0.0001 probability of losing twenty hours due to identity theft during the next year. Assuming that time is worth $20 per hour to the consumer, the cost of such an event would be $400. Multiplying together the probability of the event and the amount lost if the event occurs gives an expected risk of $0.04 (just four cents). Technically speaking, this is the expected dollar loss to a consumer from identity fraud this year. This number seems small to a consumer until it actually happens to the individual; then it looms much larger. But this number is meaningless unless it is compared with the same values calculated for other identity risks that might also occur at the same time. With reference to other possible risks, the larger this product is, the more attention should be paid to reducing (mitigating) it.

Although people cannot always determine whether a potential negative event will in fact occur, we increasingly seem to feel that we must act as though we can. As Schneier (Schneier 2003) explains, "People worry about airplane crashes not because we cannot stop them, but because we think as a society we should be capable of stopping them (even if that is not really the case)." Our perceptions of risk, combined with our desire to manage risk, are factors that help to make decisions that are designed to prevent any actual or perceived harm.

Risk perception is often very different (either more or less so) than actual risk in the view of the public. There are a variety of reasons why this is so (Gilbert 2006; Schneier 2003: 26-27):

- People overreact to intentional actions and underreact to accidents, abstract events and natural phenomena (e.g., terrorist threats using biological warfare, with annual death tolls near zero, as compared to the normal incidence of influenza, which annually kills thousands).

- People overreact to acts that they feel are offensive, such as political corruption, whereas they might not react at all to small acts of income tax evasion by common people, even if they cumulatively amount to much greater losses to the government.
- People overreact to immediate threats and underreact to long-term threats. This is what leads to managers insisting on diligently searching out and blocking physical threats to a computer centre, while giving less attention to long-term but low-probability online security threats that could ultimately bankrupt the company if they actually occurred.
- People underreact to changes that occur slowly and over time. As the number of identity thefts and frauds increases slowly over the years, management begins to recognize that there is a potential threat to the organization, but may decide against providing the level of security needed to defend against the threat—until, of course, a critical database is hacked (see first reason, above) causing an overreaction.
- People have trouble estimating risks for anything not exactly like their normal situation. The risks of computer crime are generally believed to be greater than they are because computers are still relatively new and the risks are unfamiliar.
- People underestimate risks they willingly take and overestimate risks in situations they can't control. Commercial airplanes are perceived as riskier than automobiles because the controls are in someone else's hands, even though they are actually much safer per passenger mile. People worry about airplane crashes because we think as a society we should be capable of stopping them.
- People overestimate risks that are being talked about and remain an object of public scrutiny, such as cross-border security.

Figure 3.1 is a conceptual diagram of variation in probability of occurrence of an event and the loss that would occur if the event actually occurred. If the potential loss is large but the probability of occurrence is very low, then there is no need to take more than minimal precautions against loss (e.g., mortgage theft, where losses to homeowners can be devastating, but occurrence rates are low, assuming that banks granting mortgages probe applicants' backgrounds carefully before granting mortgages (CISC 2007)). If the probability of occurrence is higher but the accompanying loss is low (e.g., credit card fraud, where any fraudulent losses are covered by the credit card company, provided that the cardholder notifies them immediately in the case of stolen or lost cards), the potential event should be of less concern, with only normal precautions taken. However, if the probability is moderately high and loss is also moderately high, then this becomes an event that needs considerable attention, with care taken to reduce either or both the probability and the loss due to that event. A good example arises for tourists traveling in a foreign country who might inadvertently leave their passports lying on a table in their hotel room while they go out for the day. The probability of theft in such a

Figure 3.1: Conceptualizing the Need for Risk Mitigation

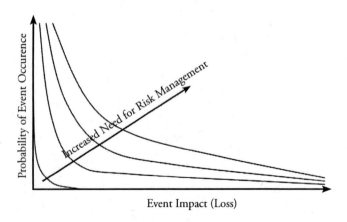

case is much higher than it would be if they left their passports on a table in their home. And the potential loss from theft is much larger, because they would have to go through the extensive hassle of getting replacement passports before they could continue their travels, and the stolen passport might be altered by criminals for illegal purposes, potentially implicating the original document owner indirectly in criminal activities. It is very clear that carrying passports concealed on one's person while traveling is the best and simplest way to mitigate this risk. People who have experienced thefts like this lose not just time and money, but they also experience the lasting psychological impact of such an event, which is not possible to quantify.

Risk Mitigation

Risk mitigation or reduction is an attempt to reduce to an acceptable threshold the probability of an event's occurrence and/or the impact of an adverse risk event. Especially for high-risk events, this is usually far more effective than trying to repair the damage resulting from an actual adverse event. The cost in time and money of risk mitigation should be balanced against the resulting reduction in risk from that event, should it occur. The need for risk mitigation increases as the risk increases, as demonstrated in Figure 3.1. Although it is usually impossible to eliminate all risk of a possible event occurring, determining the sources of risk and dealing with the largest risk events is usually a good investment of time and resources.

Each consumer has his or her own perception of risk, and some are more risk averse than others. For example, some individuals refuse to purchase products or services online for fear of fraudulent use of their identity information. These same people may freely share their identity information with a salesperson via a telephone call (Sproule and Archer 2008b), not realizing that the risk of identity theft through the telephone call may actually exceed that of purchasing the item online. That is, some people are willing to balance higher levels of risk with improved convenience, while others prefer to take measures like securing identifying documentation and not giving out such information to organizations they do not have reasons to trust, thus reducing the risk that such an event will occur.

The risk mitigation situation is different with organizations, which are in a better position to quantify risks and to develop a process for listing, categorizing and taking steps to mitigate those risks that may have the most serious impacts on the organization.

Table 3.1 lists the stakeholders from the framework for combating identity theft that was shown in Figure 2.3 (Chapter 2), along with their related roles, risks and responsibilities.

Specific risks to consumers due to identity theft include loss of privacy, financial losses, need to spend resources (both financial, time and emotional) recovering from theft, identifying miscreants so that police can intervene to bring them to justice and stop problems associated with an IDTF incident. The psychological damage experienced by individuals who may never fully recover from such incidents is certainly not the least of potential consumer concerns.

In almost every situation where individual or organizational privacy must be safeguarded, it is necessary to balance privacy and security in protecting individual interests. The general public has come to expect, based on public policy influences, laws, regulations and standards, that any technology used for commerce, entertainment and governmental applications will enhance security while preserving privacy. The resolution of the appropriate balance between privacy and security must be developed through appropriate tradeoffs, while at the same time recognizing how privacy and security need to co-exist in harmony. Bagby (2009) proposes that personally identifiable information can be regarded as a form of property that flows along an "information supply chain" that originates at its collection and follows through its storage, analysis and use in decision making. Bagby proposes a conceptual framework for balancing privacy and security through a public

Table 3.1: Stakeholder Roles, Risks and Responsibilities

	Identity Theft			Identity Fraud		
	Roles	Risks	Responsibilities	Roles	Risks	Responsibilities
ID Owner	Prevent	Privacy	Limit access to identity information Secure documentation	Detect	Property Reputation	Monitor accounts and credit reports Report discrepancies
ID Issuer	Prevent	Data breaches	Secure systems Background checks	Prevent Detect	Exposure to fraudulent use Reputation	Strong authentication Activity monitoring
ID Checker	Prevent Detect Investigate	Data breaches	Secure systems Background checks	Prevent Detect Investigate	Exposure to fraudulent use Financial losses Reputation	Strong authentication
ID Protector	Detect Investigate Prosecute	Insufficient legal authority		Investigate Prosecute		

policy foundation that safeguards individual rights, the economy, critical infrastructures and national security. On the other hand, Acquisiti (2004) takes a behavioural approach that uses behavioural economics to explain the dichotomies between privacy attitudes and behaviour to develop an understanding of individual decision-making processes with respect to privacy in electronic commerce. This approach suggests that self-control problems and immediate gratification offer realistic descriptions of the decision process and are more consistent with currently available data than an explanation based on individual rationality. This leads to a suggestion (Acquisti 2004) that individuals who may genuinely want to protect their privacy might not do so because of psychological distortions that have been documented in the behavioural literature. These behaviours may affect both naïve and sophisticated individuals and may occur when individuals perceive significant risks when their privacy is not protected.

Risk Mitigation in Organizations

In an organization, a strong risk management process is critical to cut down on surprises or unexpected risks by avoiding, eliminating or mitigating these risks. A process where risk events are listed and categorized, using their probability of occurrence, along with the expected loss should they occur, is the first step towards reducing risk from unexpected events. The focus in risk mitigation is on avoiding negative risks, where there will be a loss if the event occurs. Such potential events are referred to as threats. There may be many sources of threats, and it is important to recognize and list those events that might occur. Together with a relative estimate of the probability of occurrence and the loss, should a specific event occur, gives some guidance on where to focus efforts and resources towards the mitigation of those potential events that have high risks. This allows potential problems to be recognized early and steps taken to address these problems. To produce dependable, low risk, and viable IT solutions, each critical attribute needs to be specifically addressed and prioritized. However, in many case these attributes possess interdependencies, making it more difficult to analyze and address the relative risks. Moreover, the risks may be highly application dependent and dynamic (Croll and Croll 2007). Risk management policies need to be flexible and updated on a regular basis, and new applications and procedures need to be analyzed thoroughly before being implemented.

In the case of a corporation or institution, the likelihood of a specific event occurring, such as unauthorized access to or theft of an entire database of confidential client information, may be very low. However, it is in the interests of the organization to keep the likelihood as low as possible to prevent the loss of information to unscrupulous criminals. In some cases, these events could result in serious direct financial losses or even in lawsuits from affected customers that are so severe as to bankrupt the corporation. At the very least, when such events become known to the public—and to customers particularly—they damage the firm's reputation and the trust that firms work so hard to establish with their customers. A corporation that recognizes such risks may be willing to devote large amounts of resources to securing databases and other employee and customer information from unauthorized access. If it is possible to estimate the likelihood of such an event, along with the losses that would result, it would be straightforward to determine the size of the resource commitment needed to balance that risk. Estimation of either of these quantities is very difficult, however, given an absence of much solid information on either the likelihood or probability of the event or the loss that would occur as a result. A certain level of risk may be acceptable if the likelihood of attack is low or if the cost of prevention is higher than the cost of recovery. Considering security and privacy assurance, the return on investment (ROI) calculation must consider cost avoidance related to the potential impact of security compromises and/or liabilities from information disclosures (Anderson, Durbin et al. 2008).

Implications and Impact of Identity Theft and Fraud on Trust

Perceptions of risk have an influence on decisions and behaviour (Siegrist, Gutscher et al. 2005). People who are afraid of flying might, for example, always take the train when it is possible to do so. Perceived risks can also influence the acceptance of new technologies like sterilization of food with radiation. Perceptions of activities as risky or not have important practical implications. Past research has focused on why various hazards are perceived differently (Slovic 1987), yielding results that help to understand risk perceptions. It is known from daily experience that people differ considerably in their risk assessments, and these depend upon individual personality traits of trust and confidence (Siegrist, Gutscher et al. 2005). Confidence is the expectation of not being disappointed (Luhmann 1988). General confidence is the conviction that everything is under control, and uncertainty is low. For example, normal expectations of someone who is a regular user of the Internet are based on the experience that one can access the Internet and search for information on products or services that are needed for personal or business use.

General trust is the belief that other people can be relied on, but trust is associated with a decision in a situation of risk (Siegrist, Gutscher et al. 2005). Actually purchasing an item advertised on the Internet is based on trust that it is not a scam, that the online payment will be processed as indicated and that the advertised product or service will be delivered. This exposes the purchaser to risk. Whether trust or confidence occurs in a given situation depends on a person's perception and attribution, so both trust and confidence may influence one's perception of hazards (Siegrist, Gutscher et al. 2005). Since trust is the willingness to make oneself vulnerable to another based on a judgment of similarity of intentions or values (Rousseau, Sitkin et al. 1998), this emphasizes that trust is based on social relations, group membership and shared values. Confidence is based on experience or evidence that certain future events will occur as expected. Trust involves risk and vulnerability; it is important when familiarity is low. Confidence, on the other hand, is based on high levels of familiarity. The objects of trust are persons or person-like entities, but confidence can be had in just about anything (Siegrist, Gutscher et al. 2005).

"Swift trust" is "to trust and to be trustworthy within the limits of a temporary system [and] means that people have to wade in on trust rather than wait while experience gradually shows who can be trusted and with what" (Kramer and Tyler 1996: 170). An example of swift trust in e-commerce is the purchase of an item online through the website of a company with which the purchaser is unfamiliar. Swift trust may play a role in the formation of semi-formal, goal-oriented groups with limited lifespans and low expected recurrence, where control mechanisms are not normally available. Swift trust has been studied in relation to group formation in situations where a certain outcome is expected and barriers to confidence are higher than typical interactions with strangers (Lewicki and Bunker 1996). It is likely to involve small groups of people who have similar professional interests and backgrounds and it results from a superposition of three different phenomena: existing relationships, imposed confident behaviour and domain-based confidence (Cofta 2007: Ch. 5).

Trusted third parties (TTPs) may play a significant role in online interactions, particularly those involving service and product transactions. TTPs usually combine technical and social domains. TTPs do not build trust, but they help to manage relationships by acting as trusted intermediaries between human and technical domains. Trust that is vested in a TTP by all the parties involved is a prerequisite to the acceptance of policies and credentials issued by the TTP (Cofta 2007: Ch. 15). Parties that have already assumed the TTP role include certificate authorities (CAs) for the public key infrastructure (PKI) that approve relationships between certificates and the entities that own the corresponding private keys. Financial institutions that issue credit cards are also TTPs, since they act as intermediaries between customers and merchants. Equivalently, the companies that issue SIM (Subscriber Identity Module) cards found in cellular phones are TTPs for mobile phone companies and their cellular phone customers.

A significant fraction of consumers are reluctant to go beyond browsing for products and services on the Internet to making actual online purchases. There are a variety of reasons for the related anxiety and reluctance (Kierkegaard 2008), and these are mostly tied to perceptions of uncertainty and risk. For example, a consumer's willingness to buy online is positively influenced by the dependability of the online store, reduction of uncertainty and online experience (Teo and Yu 2005). The most common concept of perceived risk for online shopping defines it in terms of perceptions of uncertainty. The uncertainty, which can result in consumer anxiety, can be about the outcome or about the adverse consequences of buying a product (or service). The most effective route toward reducing risk, and thus consumer anxiety, appears to be through establishing trust. Attributes that appear to be fundamental to building perceived trust include perceptions of payment security, product quality, fulfillment reliability, quality of service and privacy and confidentiality of personal information (Kierkegaard 2008). Since it is essential for online e-commerce retailers to build trust with users, some online shopping and auction sites have focused on doing just that, so people will not be reticent about entering their credit card information and shipping information (name and address) into the site. A 2005 *Consumer Reports* study (*Consumer Reports* 2005a) found that the majority of Internet users were at least somewhat trusting of both online stores and online auctions. 78% of online users said they trusted sites (38% "a lot" and 40% "somewhat") where products could be bought. The trust in auction sites was somewhat lower, as 61% said they trust online auction sites "a lot" (24%) or "somewhat" (37%). The Internet is a relatively new marketplace, and trust takes time to build up, particularly when transactions take place across borders and recourse in the event of fraud is unclear (Acoca 2008). Such incidents make online ID theft particularly difficult for its victims and make the public skeptical whenever they are given the opportunity to shop online, particularly across borders.

Banking and financial sites have generally earned the trust of users, although those who use the sites trust them far more than those who do not. At financial sites, users can set up automatic bill payment, check credit history and score, buy and sell stocks or mutual funds, or apply for mortgages and loans. In a 2005 *Consumer Reports* survey (*Consumer Reports* 2005a), 93% of those who do online banking said they trust such sites, including 70% who said they trust online banking sites a lot. But only 48% of those who do not use online banking said they trust such sites.

A strategy that has been used to increase consumer trust in online sites is participation in third-party certification programs. One study (Jiang, Jones et al. 2008) has shown that consumer perceptions of third-party logos are related to intensity of seal exposure, importance of trust factors in online shopping and disposition toward third-party certification. Website certification can reassure potential customers and increase the probability of purchase. It also appears that consumer trust in online shopping is transferred from certification to online e-marketers. Validating third-party trust seals that appear as logos on a website may also increase transfer of trust, depending on the type of logo.

Summary

Perceptions of risk govern the behaviour of consumers and organizations when viewing the possibility of certain events. People do not always behave rationally when faced with choices involving risk, giving rise to behaviours that depend on the individual. For example, some people may not want to shop through the Internet but are at ease ordering goods over the phone. In managing and mitigating risk, each stakeholder involved in combating identity theft must take on particular roles and responsibilities. This ranges from the consumer (the ID owner), who must take ordinary precautions when shopping, to ID issuers who must carefully evaluate the background and documentation of consumers claiming to qualify as recipients of ID. Mitigating risk in organizations is more likely to be a subjective analysis of the likelihood of a risky event, combined with a good estimate of the loss if such an event occurs. Finally, trust plays an important role in everyday interactions with other entities, including banks, retail stores and personal physicians. It is very important to earn and maintain a reasonable level of trust if continuing interactions of organizations and people in society are to lead to successful and productive outcomes.

References

Acoca, B. 2008. "Online Identity Theft." *OECD Observer*, 268: 12–13.

Acquisti, A. 2004. *Privacy in Electronic Commerce and the Economics of Immediate Gratification*. Proceedings of the 5th ACM Conference on Electronic Commerce, ACM.

Anderson, K. B., E. Durbin, et al. 2008. "Identity Theft." *Journal of Economic Perspectives*, 22: 2: 171–92.

Bagby, J. W. 2009. "Balancing the Public Policy Drivers in the Tension between Privacy and Security." *Cyber Security and Global Information Assurance: Threat Analysis and Response Solutions*. Hershey, PA: K. J. Knapp.

CISC. 2007. *Mortgage Fraud and Organized cCime in Canada*. Strategic Intelligence Brief, November 2007. Criminal Intelligence Service Canada—Central Bureau. http://www.cisc.gc.ca/products_services/mortgage_fraud/document/mortgage_e.pdf [consulted April 5, 2009].

Cofta, P. 2007. *Trust, Complexity, and Control*. Chichester, UK: John Wiley & Sons.

Consumer Reports. 2005a. "Leap of Faith: Using the Internet Despite the Dangers." *Consumer Reports Webwatch*. http://www.consumerwebwatch.org/pdfs/princeton.pdf [consulted January 29, 2009].

Croll, P. R., and J. Croll. 2007. "Investigating Risk Exposure in E-health Systems." *International Journal of Medical Informatics*, 76: 460–65.

Gilbert, D. T. 2006. *Stumbling on Happiness*. New York: A. A. Knopf.

Hubbard, D. 2007. *How to Measure Anything: Finding the Value of Intangibles in Business*. New York: John Wiley & Sons.

Jiang, P., D. B. Jones, et al. 2008. "How Third-Party Certification Programs Relate to Consumer Trust in Online Transactions: An exploratory study." *Psychology and Marketing*, 25: 9: 839–58.

Kierkegaard, P. 2008. "Fear of E-shopping: Anxiety or Phobia?" *International Journal of Technology Transfer and Commercialisation*, 7: 1: 83–90.

Kramer, R. M., and T. R. Tyler. 1996. *Trust in Organizations: Frontiers of Theory and Research*. Thousand Oaks, California: Sage Publications.

Lewicki, R. J., and B. B. Bunker. 1996. "Developing and Maintaining Trust in Work Relationships." In *Trust in Organizations*. Edited by R. M. Kramer and T. R. Tyler. London, Sage Publications.

Luhmann, N. 1988. "Familiarity, Confidence, Trust: Problems and Alternatives." In *Trust: Making and Breaking Cooperative Relations*. Edited by D. Gambetta. Oxford: Basil Blackwell, pp. 94–107.

Rousseau, D. M., S. B. Sitkin, et al. 1998. "Not So Different aAter All: A Cross-discipline View of Trust." *Academy of Management Review*, 23: 393–404.

Schneier, B. 2003. *Beyond Fear: Thinking Sensibly about Security in an Uncertain World*. New York: Copernicus Books.

Siegrist, M., H. Gutscher, et al. 2005. "Perception of Risk: The Influence of General Trust, and General Confidence." *Journal of Risk Research*, 8: 2: 145–56.

Slovic, P. 1987. "Perception of Risk." *Science*, 236: 280–85.

Sproule, S., and N. Archer. 2008b. *Measuring Identity Theft in Canada: 2008 consumer survey*. McMaster eBusiness Research Centre Working Paper #23. Hamilton, Ontario: DeGroote School of Business, McMaster University.

Teo, T. S. H., and Y. Yu. 2005. "Online Buying Behaviour: A Transaction Cost Economics Perspective." *Omega*, 33: 5: 451–65.

Chapter 4

Information Sources for Identity Theft and Fraud

"I have traveled the length and breadth of this country and talked with the best people, and I can assure you that data processing is a fad that won't last out the year."
—editor in charge of business books, Prentice Hall, 1957

Human identification is the basis of all studies involving identity theft and fraud. This chapter explores this feature in some detail, then applies it to the credit industry, where identification is managed by a variety of identifiers and verifiers. Personal credit and finance revolves around the credit reporting system, which is intimately associated with identity and its management. Related issues are explored, including current issues surrounding databases, brokers and data breaches. Finally, data collection and dissemination practices are discussed in some detail.

The Basics of Human Identification in Information Systems

Roger Clarke describes how human identification, in the context of information systems, is a process "used to link a stream of data with a person" (Clarke 1994: 8) and outlines the needs and bases for the formal identification of humans in systems. Noting that organizations increasingly rely on information systems to conduct the process of identification, Clarke describes the desirable characteristics of a human identifier. These characteristics include

universality of coverage, uniqueness, permanence, indispensability, collectability, storability, exclusivity, precision, simplicity, cost,
convenience and acceptability.

The characteristics of *universality* and *uniqueness* mean that
every relevant person must have an identifier, each of those persons should have only one identifier, and no two persons should
have the same identifier. Names, while universal (i.e., everyone
has one), are not unique since many people may share the same
name. That is why individuals are often assigned codes or numbers for identification.

Permanence means that the identifier should not change over
time, and *indispensability* means that each person should have
and retain the characteristic used as the identifier at all times. The
identifier should be *collectable* by anyone on any occasion, and it
should be able to be *stored* in both manual and electronic systems.
Biometric characteristics observable through such procedures as
iris scanning or fingerprinting are often thought to be good identifiers because they are permanent and indispensible. However,
their collection usually requires sophisticated equipment. While
some biometrics like fingerprints have been historically collected
and stored manually, most new biometrics identifiers are designed
for electronic collection and storage.

Exclusivity means that no other identifier should be necessary,
and *precision* implies that each person's identifier is sufficiently different from all other persons' identifiers that mistakes will not be
made. The systems used to record, measure and store the identifier
should be *simple*, *cost efficient* and *convenient*. The identifier must
also be *acceptable*—meeting societal norms and standards. An
example of an unacceptable identifier would be number tattoos,
because of their historical reference to Nazi concentration camps,
in addition to the fact that the very thought of being tattooed is
repugnant to many people.

Clarke evaluates various common identifiers against these criteria and concludes, "there is no basis for identification that fulfills
all desirable characteristics" (Clarke 1994: 23). Introducing the

idea of risk, he suggests that organizations need to evaluate their specific needs and design a system "with a degree of accuracy commensurate with the gravity of the information or the action (to be taken)" (Clarke 1994: 25). For example, the UK government has proposed four levels of authentication, which correspond to four different levels of risk that may be associated with government services provided over the Internet (Cabinet Office 2002).

Clarke finishes the paper with a discussion of multi-purpose identification schemes, such as inhabitant registration schemes commonly found in European countries. He observes that objections to these identification schemes are based on the potential for discrimination, the need for multiple identities in some cases and the invasiveness and stigma associated with some biometric identifiers. Primarily, however, objections are based on how identification schemes allow organizations to exert power over the individual, pointing out that there is a history of abuses related to such schemes when in the hands of totalitarian regimes (Clarke 1994).

A Discourse on the Credit Industry

By the end of the twentieth century, there was a lot of media and public policy interest directed at the problem of identity fraud and it was widely being reported as the fastest growing financial crime in the United States In 2001, LoPucki used Clarke's work as a starting point to address the specific problem of identity theft, and extended it with five additional observations (LoPucki 2001):

- *Identification is person to person.* While Clarke talks of linking data stream communications to a person, LoPucki argues that the "larger task" is to link a person observed at one time to a person observed at another time.

- *Identification is a matching of characteristic values.* When the identity checker wants to make an identification, the checker is comparing two observations. These observations (either direct or through a data record) require noticing or determining certain characteristics. Each characteristic is a variable and can take on many values. He explains, for example, that eye colour is a variable and that it may be observed to be brown, blue or green. The identification process tries to find matching variables in the two observations. If the values of the variables are different in meaningful ways, we conclude that the two observations are of two different persons. If the values of the variables are sufficiently the same, we may conclude that the observations are of the same person. Both the rarity of the values of the variable and the number of variables used in the matching process can determine what is "sufficiently" similar. For example, facial characteristics, sex and height help to narrow down the identification possibilities far more than just one variable (such as height) would on its own.

- *Identification is layered.* Identity issuers rely on previous identification processes to enroll someone in a system. To obtain a passport, one must present a birth certificate. To obtain a credit card in a store, one is asked to show a driver's license. Thus, "[t]he accuracy of each layer of identification depends on the accuracy of preceding layers" (LoPucki 2001: 98).

- *Characteristic values must be present on both sides of the match.* LoPucki uses the example of police finding DNA at a crime scene to illustrate this point. If there was no previous observation where a DNA sample was made available, the police cannot use that variable to identify the suspect. In financial systems, millions of people take part in matching processes each day, and any identifying characteristic must be present or recorded on each observation. Because of the great volume of the matches that must be made, LoPucki argues that efforts to keep this identifying information "secret" are "doomed to failure" (LoPucki 2001: 94).

- *Characteristics perform two distinct functions.* Here, LoPucki builds on the idea of identifiers (names) and verifiers (passwords). Characteristics used as identifiers should be unique and not subject to change between observations. These identifiers must be made available to all identity issuers and identity checkers. Characteristics used as verifiers, such as passwords or PINs, must also be known by both the identity owner and the identity checker, but should be able to be changed readily. There are problems when distinctions are not made between these two functions (LoPucki 2001: 100).

Both Clarke and LoPucki examined the history and use of Social Security Numbers in the United States, where there has been widespread use of them as identifiers in universities, the military, government agencies, credit bureaus and the private sector. Unfortunately, knowledge of a person's SSN is also commonly used as a verifier. Since SSNs are widely distributed as identifiers, when they are used as verifiers they provide "only a weak inference that the [person providing the information] is the person to whom the SSN was assigned" (LoPucki 2001: 100).

Credit Reporting Systems

LoPucki examines identification systems used in the consumer credit system and makes a number of observations about consumer relationships with creditors and credit-reporting agencies. "The problem is not that thieves have access to personal information, but that creditors and credit-reporting agencies often lack both the means and the incentives to correctly identify the persons who seek credit from them or on whom they report" (LoPucki 2001: 94).

The credit-reporting system in North America is run by a handful of companies. In the United States, Experian, Equifax and TransUnion are the primary credit-reporting agencies or 'credit bureaus.' They keep records of the credit histories of all American consumers. Anyone who extends credit notifies the credit bureau of each instance and provides a history of repayment, or lack thereof. The credit bureau compiles this information into a credit record for each individual consumer, assigns credit scores based on this record and then distributes this information to creditors on request. LoPucki observes that creditors are therefore both suppliers and customers of the credit bureaus. The only influence that the consumer has over the credit bureaus is that which is provided by legislation, such as the Fair Credit Reporting Act and the Fair and Accurate Credit Transactions Act in the United States.

Credit bureaus are under provincial jurisdiction in Canada, where the primary credit reporting agencies are Equifax Canada and TransUnion Canada. Although the relevant consumer laws differ slightly from province to province, all Canadian consumers are protected from the collection of excessive data by these agencies (Financial Consumer Agency of Canada 2008), and consumers have the right to request a credit report from these credit bureaus at least once a year.

There are three types of services provided to victims of identity theft: credit monitoring looks for suspicious activity; a fraud alert advises lenders that there may be a problem and tells them to confirm the identity of the person applying for credit; and a credit freeze locks down the potential victim's credit file so that lenders and creditors will not have access to it.

LoPucki points out that the credit reporting system handles large numbers of transactions daily and is highly automated. In statistics, medical testing and other areas of study, there is often a trade-off between two types of errors—false positives and false negatives. Figure 4.1 shows how this trade-off appears in the credit industry, where a false positive would tell a potential creditor that the person applying for credit is creditworthy, when in fact, he or she is not. A false negative would tell the potential creditor that the person applying for credit is not creditworthy, when in fact he or she is. Identity fraud causes false negative errors, as the perpetrator has destroyed the victim's credit rating, without the victim's knowledge.

Because creditors are the main customers, the system is designed to ensure that any errors have a minimal effect on the creditors. In the credit industry, we therefore have a situation where the number of errors that will be bad for creditors (false positives) will be minimized. This comes at the expense of a higher rate of errors that will be bad for consumers (false negatives). Victims of identity theft often only find out there is a problem when creditors start collection procedures or when the victim is refused credit because of a poor credit record. The victim faces a number of challenges when trying to convince creditors that an identity fraud has occurred (LoPucki 2001):

- The victim's indentifying information is the same as the identifying information that the fraudster provided. There may have been differences in addresses or phone numbers, but the victim is required to prove that those addresses and phone number are not his or hers.
- The victim's assertions are seen as self-serving. Creditors may suspect that the victim is just trying to avoid his or her obligations.
- The creditor has little incentive to pursue an investigation. If there was an identity fraud, the creditor is not likely to be able to recover its losses. The creditor may continue to put pressure on the victim, hoping that the victim will decide that restoration of credit privileges is the only way to fix his or her credit score.
- If the creditor refuses to investigate, the victim's only recourse is to complain to regulatory authorities or to take the creditor to court. The former is 'not much of a threat,' as these authorities rarely act on individual complaints. The latter is expensive and time-consuming and subject to all of the previous problems of proof.

Figure 4.1: Types of Errors in Credit Reporting

		Credit report says that consumer's credit is...	
		Good	Bad
In truth, consumer's credit is...	Good	Accurate (positive) report	False negative
	Bad	False positive	Accurate (negative) report

LoPucki points out flaws in many suggested solutions to the identity fraud problem and proposes a system where consumers would have control over the release of their credit information.

Daniel Solove observes that "LoPucki's profound contribution to the debate over identity theft is his recognition that identity theft stems from problems in identification that emerge with creditors, credit reporting agencies, and other entities using SSN's and other personal data as passwords [i.e., verifiers]" (Solove 2003: 35). While applauding LoPucki's proposed solution for allowing individuals to participate in their identification, Solove argues that the onus for action is still misplaced on the individual consumer. "I contend that the prevailing approach toward dealing with identity theft—by relying on increasing criminal penalties and by depending upon individuals to take great lengths to try to protect themselves against their vulnerabilities to identity theft—has the wrong focus.... The underlying cause of identity theft is an architecture that makes us vulnerable to such crimes and unable to adequately repair the damage" (Solove 2003: 23).

Solove argues that many privacy problems are systemic in nature, not just isolated incidents that occur to unfortunate or careless individuals. The traditional model for protecting privacy is reactive and requires individuals to initiate action. In the modern world, however, we are faced with the compilation of 'digital dossiers' of personal information from various sources (what Solove calls the "aggregation problem") and extensive trade in personal information between private sector and even public sector organizations (Solove 2003).

Aside from the credit bureaus, other "data brokers" collect information from various sources and supply 'digital dossiers' on individual consumers to organizations as varied as marketing firms, law enforcement, private investigators and employers. ChoicePoint, Acxiom and LexisNexis are examples of major data brokers (see below). Solove and Hoofnagle note that the information that these data brokers collect far surpasses the amount of information that government is allowed to collect under US law. Law enforcement and intelligence agencies can, however, contract to obtain this information from the data brokers. These agencies operate under exemptions from privacy protection laws that would otherwise require them to implement access, accuracy and correction rights (Solove and Hoofnagle 2006).

Databases, Brokers and Breaches

Many of the databases that contain individual identification information have been created by legitimate companies (banks, retail organizations, etc.) and by governments with the consent of the identity owners. Others are data brokers, companies that exist strictly for the purpose of amassing personal data on large numbers of consumers. Data brokers purchase personal identifying information from credit reporting agencies and other entities, combine it with information acquired from online public records, organize the information and resell it to companies or government agencies seeking to conduct background checks or otherwise to verify identities. The Internet has allowed the data brokerage industry to thrive (Schreft 2007). These brokers rely on both public and private organizations for their information sources, which often have few restrictions on their ability to resell the data. In the US, one common source of such information was state motor vehicles offices, but the Drivers Privacy Protection Act of 1994 ended such sales once the US Supreme Court upheld the ban six years later. United States regulations adopted in late 2007 under the Fair and Accurate Credit Transactions (FACT) Act of 2003 also allow customers to opt out of a financial institution's use of information received from an affiliated company to market its products and services to customers. Most of these bans are effectively locking the barn door after the horse has escaped. Incidentally, non-financial businesses are not subject to these laws.

A data breach is a security incident in which sensitive, protected or confidential data is copied, transmitted, viewed, stolen or used by an individual unauthorized to do so. An identity thief who obtains electronic records containing a customer's name and phone number or ZIP code from a retail establishment's computers, even if the credit or debit card number were not stored, can use the reverse look-up feature of electronic telephone books to match the phone number or ZIP code with the customer's address. Online directories also identify addresses and telephone numbers for people whose names appear in newspaper announcements of births, marriages and deaths. All of this information can be used to organize relatively complete databases of individual identity information for large numbers of individuals. The theft of a few pieces of non-sensitive data, like names, e-mail addresses and telephone numbers, can put victims at greater risk of having financial frauds committed in their names and with their various accounts in the future. The inclusive definition of identity theft contained in the US *Identity Theft and Assumption* Deterrence Act (ITADA) of 1998 is appropriate for prosecuting such incidents (Schreft 2007).

The Privacy Rights Clearinghouse is an organization that tracks data breaches reported in the US (PRC 2011). For the years 2006 to 2010, they reported a cumulative total of 2,136 reported data breaches with a total of 459,217,337 records exposed. This is very depressing information, given that organizations have known for some time that they must keep their databases secure from unauthorized access. The many high-profile data breaches, lost laptops and other losses of personal information have resulted in legislative pressures to pass stricter laws governing how data are controlled, with more emphasis on security and the notification of affected individuals. However, a recent study in the US (Romanosky, Telang et al. 2008) indicates that data breach disclosure laws have no measurable effect on cases of identity theft and fraud. The research evaluated data from states that had passed legislation governing data breaches from 2002 to 2006 and took into account income, urbanization, strictness of law and interstate commerce. The researchers had some concerns about the quality of secondary data they used and the possibility of reporting bias. They suspect that the lack of an impact might have been due to the small number of identity thefts from this cause as compared to the total number of identity thefts.

Hackers, both individually and in organized crime, can break into databases and either use the personal identifiers illegally to gain access to online accounts or use online markets to sell personal information at low cost and on a large scale. This gives identity fraudsters access to information with which to ply their criminal trade. As of 2007, bank account data on an individual was selling online for up to $400 per person, credit card details for up to $5 each, passwords for up to $350 each, e-mail addresses for between $2 and $4 per megabyte, and "complete identities" were available for $10 to $100 each (Schreft 2007). Financial account information, including passwords, allows direct access to accounts. For brokerage accounts, the balance available can be quite large. In contrast, credit card information is easily obtained and is often sold in bundles (such as the bundles of 10,000 card numbers from the TJX intrusion—see Chapter 5—that the perpetrators were offering for sale).

There is little or no control over who can buy this information, which can clearly be used to commit fraud on existing financial accounts or on accounts opened with the information. Identity theft has been a feature of financial markets for as long as alternatives have existed to cash transactions. The existence of the Internet has allowed this type of theft to balloon to an extraordinarily large scale, as data breaches can involve the apparent loss or acknowledged theft of the personal identifying information of thousands, or even millions, of people. This results in risks not only to individual consumers but also to the integrity and efficiency of the payment system. In this way, identity theft can interfere seriously with the marketplace since it can, if it continues on the scale we are beginning to see, cause a loss of confidence in the security of e-commerce and an unwillingness on the part of both consumers and businesses to participate. Ultimately, this can result in a switch to less efficient methods for commercial transactions, leading to a loss of efficiency in the economy (Schreft 2007).

Data Collection and Dissemination

When processes of data collection and dissemination are not properly controlled, a generalized condition for harm exists. Solove uses architecture as the metaphor for his view of privacy: "Architecture emphasizes that legal and social structures are products of design" (Solove 2003: 12). Individuals often have little choice in handing over their personal information and no control over who has access to that information after it has been disclosed. "If we see the problem architecturally, we see an *architecture of vulnerability*, one with large holes, gaps and weak spots." (Solove 2003: 33). In the same way that building design can enhance physical safety, we need to design systems that enhance the security of our information.

As a basis for a new architecture, Solove adopts the Fair Information Practice Principles introduced by the United States Department of Housing, Education and Welfare in 1973 and refined by the Organization for Economic Cooperation and Development (OECD) in 1980. The eight Fair Information Practice Principles are shown in Table 4.1. Solove argues that applying these principles to the credit bureaus would help solve the problem of identity fraud. In a later paper, Solove and Hoofnagle develop a "model regime" that extends the application of Fair Information Practice Principles to other data collection and reporting companies (Solove and Hoofnagle 2006).

In general, they argue that people should be required to opt-in to the data collection process and that they should have regular and free access to their records. They also suggest that consumers should be informed about any changes or unusual activity on their records and that organizations that collect personal information should be responsible for any inaccuracies in the information (Solove and Hoofnagle 2006).

Sovern continues the discussions initiated by LoPucki and Solove by examining the problem of identity fraud in terms of loss allocation rules (Sovern 2004). Loss allocation rules are used as a decision-making aid in civil law. The general principle behind loss allocation rules is that the loss should be borne by the party who has the best and least expensive way to avoid the loss. Sovern reiterates that, within the credit industry, businesses have few incentives—and often have disincentives—to prevent identity fraud. At the same time, consumers suffer losses yet have no capacity to prevent identity frauds. Sovern looks at which parties bear the losses associated with identity theft and which parties have the best opportunities to avoid these losses (Sovern 2004).

As LoPucki (2001) points out, credit bureaus primarily serve businesses, not consumers, and they suffer no losses associated with cases of identity fraud. In fact, Sovern correctly forecasts the widespread introduction of identity theft protection services offered by the credit bureaus and other businesses. "Thus, credit bureaus profit from the sale of a service designed to prevent a harm to consumers that the credit bureaus themselves make possible" (Sovern 2004: 236).

Table 4.1: Fair Information Principles (adapted from Solove 2003)

Principle	Description
Collection limitation	Data should be collected lawfully, with the individual's consent.
Data quality	Data should be relevant to a particular purpose and be accurate.
Purpose specification	The purpose of data collection should be stated at the time of data collection and the use of the data should be limited to this purpose.
Use limitation	Data should not be disclosed for different purposes without the consent of the person.
Security safeguards	Data should be protected by reasonable safeguards.
Openness principle	People should be informed about the practices and policies of those handling their personal information.
Individual participation	People should be able to learn about the data that an entity possesses about them and to rectify errors or problems in that data.
Accountability	The entities that control personal information should be held accountable for carrying out these principles.

As opposed to credit bureaus, creditors do suffer losses and therefore should have some incentives to reduce identity fraud. "Lenders have two opportunities to prevent the losses consumers suffer from identity [fraud]: first, when they approve the loan, and second, when they report the … default to a credit bureau. Most of the consumer's suffering occurs only after the lender reports the default, thereby damaging the consumer's credit standing" (Sovern 2004: 236).

It is in the interest of both consumer and lender to improve the loan approval process, but the competitive nature of the credit industry tends to incent lenders to provide quick and easy access to credit. Lenders are willing to suffer some fraud losses in order to keep customers from turning to competitors who offer a less onerous and less time-consuming identification process. The consumer's losses are not considered in this cost/benefit analysis. Once the loan has gone into default, there is no advantage to the lender to do a follow-up identification. Such a follow-up would cost money and, if a fraud were found, the lender would lose the opportunity for collection. Lenders, therefore, invariably proceed to file a default report with the credit bureaus without any investigation—and the consumer's problems begin (Sovern 2004).

Loss allocation rules dictate that efficient solutions will match the costs of identity fraud to the costs and the benefits of preventing it. "In short, the goal is to give those who have the greatest power to prevent identity theft and the most knowledge about systems for granting credit the incentive to prevent identity theft, and allow them to come up with a solution to the problem. If they cannot create such a solution, then they will bear the losses generated by identity theft until they can" (Sovern 2004: 239). As we will see in a later chapter, few legal responses to identity theft and fraud have taken this approach, and there are many ways in which identity theft is enabled by poor stewardship of public records. For example, the open availability of SSNs and other identity information in the United States of people who have died is an open encouragement to identity thieves to create fictitious IDs for the purpose of opening fictitious bank accounts, applying for social benefits, etc. A substantial amount of information is collected on consumer preferences through the ubiquitous 'loyalty cards' used by retail stores. When these cards are swiped at the time of a purchase, they may reduce the price charged to customers, but they also accumulate more information on customers: what products they prefer, when and where they shop, etc. Data brokers purchase this data and match it to other information obtained elsewhere in order to create personal dossiers of value to other companies. Legitimate uses of such information include credit checking, background screening and claims histories.

ChoicePoint provides an example of a well-known data broker and its activities. It is a US company that sells information in three markets: insurance, business and government, and marketing. ChoicePoint was spun off from credit rating company Equifax in 1997 (EPIC 2008). In February 2005, ChoicePoint announced that it had sold personal information on more than 145,000 Americans to a criminal ring engaged in identity theft. California police reported that the criminals used the data for unauthorized address changes of at least 750 people, and it is believed that personal information of up to 400,000 people nationwide may have been compromised due to the incident. The data broker business, including ChoicePoint, has been consistently in the news over sales practices, due diligence in investigating potential customers for its data, and the perceived lack of privacy protection for individuals on whom it has amassed dossiers. Many of these individuals are not aware of such activities concerning their personal information and frequently have no way of correcting errors that their files contain. In fact, in the 2005 ChoicePoint incident, the Electronic Privacy Information Center (EPIC) urged the company to make available to those people whose personal information was negligently disclosed by the company the same information made available to the crooks.

Data brokers are still largely unregulated (Otto, Anton et al. 2007) and they can exclude consumers from every aspect of their operations, leaving them little access or control over their own personal information. With the exception of medical and financial information, data brokers aren't required to obtain permission from consumers before collecting, processing and transmitting information, and consumers can't protect themselves against the type of data breach that is described above.

Summary

This chapter explores human identification in some detail concerning how its various facets become the basis for identity theft. The financial and credit industry plays a substantial role in everyone's life. Identification is key to the successful management of this role and the presentation of identity as a variety of identifiers and verifiers. Personal credit depends highly on the ability to identify an individual and that individual's financial situation, which has given rise to the credit reporting system upon which we rely. Related current issues are explored, including data breaches that plague databases and the brokers that manage these systems. Practices relating to the collection and dissemination of data relate closely to identity theft, and these have been discussed in some detail.

References

Cabinet Office. 2002. *Identity Fraud: A Study*. London, UK: Cabinet Office. www.statewatch.org/news/2004/may/id-fraud-report.pdf [consulted March 14, 2011].

Clarke, R. 1994. "Human Identification in Information Systems: Management Challenges and Public Policy Issues." *Information Technology and People*, 7: 4: 6–37.

EPIC. 2008. ChoicePoint, Electronic Privacy Information Center. http://epic.org/privacy/choicepoint/default.html [consulted March 29, 2009].

Financial Consumer Agency of Canada. 2008. "Understanding Your Credit Report and Credit Score." Ottawa: Financial Consumer Agency of Canada. http://www.fcac-acfc.gc.ca/eng/publications/CreditReportScore/PDF/CreditReportScore-eng.pdf [consulted March 13, 2011].

LoPucki, L. 2001. "Human Identification Theory and the Identity Theft Problem." *Texas Law Review*, 80: 89–136.

Otto, P. N., A. I. Anton, et al. 2007. "The ChoicePoint Dilemma: How Data Brokers Should Handle the Privacy of Personal Information." *IEEE Security & Privacy*, 5: 5: 15–23.

PRC. 2011. "2011 breach list." Privacy Rights Clearinghouse. http://www.privacy-rights.org/data-breach [consulted April 29, 2011].

Romanosky, S., R. Telang, et al. 2008. "Do Data Breach Disclosure Laws Reduce Identity Theft?" *Seventh Workshop on the Economics of Information Security*. Hanover, NH: Tuck School of Business, Dartmouth College. http://weis2008.econinfosec.org/papers/Romanosky.pdf [consulted January 15, 2009].

Schreft, S. L. 2007. "Risks of Identity Theft: Can the Market Protect the Payment System?" *Economic Review*, 92: 4: 5–40.

Solove, D. J. 2003. "Identity Theft, Privacy, and the Architecture of Vulnerability." *Hastings Law Journal*, 54: 1227–73.

Solove, D. J., and C. J. Hoofnagle. 2006. "A Model Regime of Privacy Protection." *University of Illinois Law Review*, 2006: 357–404.

Sovern, J. 2004. "Stopping Identity Theft." *The Journal of Consumer Affairs*, 38: 2: 233.

Chapter 5

The Nature and Scope of Identity Theft and Fraud

"The difficulty lies, not in the new ideas, but in escaping from the old ones, which ramify, for those brought up as most of us have been, into every corner of our minds."
> —John Maynard Keynes, The General Theory of Employment, Interest and Money, 1935

This chapter is a detailed discussion of the characteristics of identity theft, including its definition, how it may occur, how identity thieves physically acquire identity information in various ways, and the nature of criminal social engineering activities like certain types of phishing. The electronic acquisition of identity information is also described, where profiles of identity thieves underscore how this type of criminal activity continues to grow like a cancer in society and the sensitivity and value of the personal information that can be stolen. Data breaches are a rapidly growing form of identity theft, and this is discussed in considerable detail, including how these breaches may or may not be connected to fraudulent activities, the growing pressure for public notification when they occur, and their direct and/or intangible cost to consumers and organizations.

Identity Theft

Identity theft is the unauthorized collection, possession, transfer, replication or other manipulation of another person's personal information. It is the first step in the identity theft and fraud process model that was discussed in Chapter 2. The problem of identity theft is the problem of safeguarding people's personal information. All individuals are responsible for safeguarding their information when it is in their possession. We cannot live in today's society, however, without entrusting our personal information to others. As discussed in Chapter 4, this information is collected, transmitted and stored by numerous government agencies, financial institutions, businesses and other organizations. There are always risks of unauthorized access and use of the information, but we trust that these organizations are keeping our personal information secure and not releasing it without appropriate authorization.

As we have defined identity theft and identity fraud, identity theft can occur without identity fraud. There are generally three types of victims of identity theft:

1. Victims who are unaware that an identity theft has occurred;
2. Victims who are aware that their personal information has been accessed, but who have not yet been victims of an associated fraud; and
3. Victims of identity fraud (who often are not aware of the identity theft before the fraud occurred).

Victims who are unaware that an identity theft has occurred may have had their personal information taken by someone, such as a family member, roommate, neighbour, contractor or employee, with access to the information while it was in their possession. However, the overwhelming number of victims in this category has had their information accessed through a data breach within an organization that was entrusted with this information. People whose information has been compromised as part of a data breach will know that there is a problem only if they are notified by the organization responsible for its security or if a subsequent fraud occurs that brings the theft to their attention. Legislation requiring organizations to notify individuals of breaches has been introduced in almost all US states.

In Canada, voluntary guidelines that deal with breaches were published in 2007 by the federal privacy commissioner—but these guidelines are not legally enforceable. The province of Ontario's Personal Health Information Act (PHIPA), however, enacted in 2004, has mandatory data breach notification—and Alberta has required data breach notification through its updated Personal Information Protection Act (PIPA) since 2010. The Canadian government introduced Bill C-29 in May 2010, which if enacted would update its Personal Information Protection and Electronic Documents Act (PIPEDA) to include data breach notification. The proposed PIPEDA changes were relatively weak in that organizations have the right to determine whether even to disclose a breach based on the type of information stolen, the number of customers affected and whether the organization believes that there is a real risk of significant harm to the individuals affected. A later section in this chapter discusses data breaches and notification laws in detail.

A Canadian consumer survey in 2008 asked individuals if they were aware of any case where there had been unauthorized access to their personal information without a subsequent fraud. This is the second type of victim. At the time, there were only voluntary guidelines on notification. The survey asked whether people who had not yet experienced a fraud were aware of any circumstances where their personal information had been accessed as part of a data breach or a fraud operation. The survey found that 3% of consumers were aware of an instance of identity theft involving their information within the previous twelve months (February 2007 to January 2008) yet had not experienced an identity fraud of any kind (Sproule and Archer 2008b).

Approximately half of these victims said that their information was accessed at a store where they had shopped in person. This timeframe includes the discovery and publicity surrounding a large data breach at a popular retailer (TJX, including its Canadian chain of Winners and HomeSense stores). This was a very large breach, so only a small proportion of victims of this breach would have experienced a fraud at this point in time. Seventeen percent of these 'IDT without IDF' victims said that the access to their information happened at a financial institution. A second data breach that received significant attention during this timeframe was the loss of a disk containing customer information by the CIBC's Talvest mutual funds. Affected customers were notified, but the loss was believed to be accidental and therefore the risk of fraud was slim. Other methods of access to personal information (i.e., e-mails, insurance, schools, employment, medical) accounted for less than 10% of the 'IDT without IDF' cases (Sproule and Archer 2008b).

For the third type of victim, where there has been a case of identity fraud, most consumer surveys try to determine how the personal information used in the fraud was obtained. These answers can help us understand something about the nature and incidence of different methods of identity theft, although many fraud victims do not know how their personal information was accessed or stolen. The original 2003 FTC survey in the United States found that 46% of identity fraud victims did not know how the fraudster got their information. According to Javelin surveys, also in the United States, this percentage has risen, year by year, to 65% in 2009. As a result, any data about the nature of IDT that has been collected through these surveys has a large degree of uncertainty associated with it.

How Does Identity Theft Occur?

The following sections describe the various ways that identity theft can occur. While they focus on illegal activities, it is important to remember that there is much personal information that can be obtained legally. A telephone directory will give you names, addresses and phone numbers for listed numbers and online directories allow for reverse look-ups, providing name and address from a query on just the phone number. Many government records and databases are required to be available to the public, and some of these databases are now online. In an experiment by researchers at Indiana University, online access to birth and marriage records resulted in the determination of mothers' unmarried names for tens of thousands of individuals. With such easy access to this kind of public information, biographical verifiers like mother's maiden names should not be used as (secret) verifiers in authentication processes (Griffith and Jakobsson 2005).

There are also numerous instances where sensitive information has been made available online through negligence or incompetence. In 2007, for example, an online applicant for a Canadian passport discovered that by changing one number in the URL of his application form, he could retrieve pages that contained the information of other applicants (Wallace 2007). In another example, in 2005, the state of California imposed a $200,000 fine on Kaiser Permanente, a healthcare management company, for having 150 patient medical records on a test portal that had been publicly accessible through the Web for four years.[1] Because there is so much information online, it is not efficient to search for it page by page. The practice of 'scraping' websites involves automated software that roams the Web identifying and collecting data from webpages. Scraping was originally developed for spammers to collect e-mail addresses, but it can also be used to sniff out Social Insurance Numbers or other identifying information.

There are three primary ways by which personal information can be accessed: physical acquisition, electronic acquisition and social engineering. We discuss each of these ways in more detail in the following three sections. There is much concern and attention focused on large-scale data breaches; such breaches may result from any of these methods or from a combination of them. A later section in this chapter is devoted to a discussion of data breaches.

1 http://attrition.org/dataloss/2005/03/kaiser02.html

Physical Acquisition of Identity Information

Most victims of identity fraud do not know how their information was accessed, but when they do, for every person who says their information was accessed online, there are five who say their information was accessed through physical means (Javelin 2005). Of physical means, the most common method of access was stolen wallets or mail, accounting for about 15% of all cases. Wallets and purses are typically stolen from homes, cars or other places thought to be safe, like gym lockers or office drawers.

Together, stolen mail or garbage accounts for just less than 5% of cases (Javelin 2009). Garbage is a potential source of information for identity thieves if people are not properly disposing of sensitive information; surveys show, however, that most consumers now use paper shredders. Mail can be a rich source of information for identity thieves. Monthly statements for credit cards and utility accounts provide names, addresses and account numbers, as well as billing details, which identity checkers may use to verify the customer's identity. It is common for thieves to use the information gained from stolen mail to impersonate the victim and have future mail redirected. A move to electronic statements and billing has meant that mail theft is becoming less of a problem. In the past, pre-approved credit card applications and replacement credit cards were lucrative targets, but credit card companies have discontinued pre-approved applications and have introduced new authorization processes for replacement cards.

Stolen wallets, mail and garbage are low-volume identity theft operations. These methods are most commonly associated with new account frauds and cheque forgery (Litan 2007). One high-volume identity theft operation that requires the physical co-location of thief and victim is card skimming. In a credit card skimming operation, the identity thieves run the victim's credit card through a device that captures the information contained on the card's magnetic strip. Counterfeit cards can then be encoded with the magnetic strip information. Gas stations and restaurants, where it is common for the server to take the card out of the customer's sight, are popular skimming sites. Skimming devices are small and can be handheld.

In skimming operations targeting debit cards, the thief must not only capture the information from the magnetic strip, but also the customer's PIN. These thefts involve a skimming device, together with a very small camera positioned above the keypad. Skimming devices can be very sophisticated and have included entire false fronts to ATM machines. The skimming device is typically installed at a location for only a short time. The magnetic strip and video camera information can be transmitted over a wireless connection to the fraudster, who sits in a nearby vehicle. More recently, the use of skimming devices and cameras has extended to point-of-sale (POS) terminals. In these cases, the fraudsters gain access to the terminal, often by distracting the employee. In some cases, where fraud rings have infiltrated cleaning services, entire POS terminals have been replaced with skimming devices during off-hours and retrieved the following night.

Social Engineering

The second way that identity thieves get information is through social engineering. Social engineering attacks generally involve the thief misrepresenting himself or herself as someone who should be entitled to the information. In jailhouse interviews with identity thieves, Copes and Vieraitis (2007) found that these individuals possessed good social and intuitive skills, allowing them to read and manipulate situations. Identity thieves also understand how organizational processes and systems work and can quickly identify vulnerabilities (Abagnale 2001; Copes and Vieraitis 2007). Even though most identity fraud victims do not know how their information was accessed, about 3% of victims tell us that their personal information was accessed in response to a telephone or e-mail query (Sproule and Archer 2008b).

The most familiar type of social engineering attack is phishing, where the identity thieves send an e-mail that looks as if it is from a legitimate organization. The e-mail provides a link to a website that also looks as if it is from a legitimate organization. In keeping with the pun on fishing, the e-mail message is sometimes referred to as the 'lure' and the website as the 'hook.' In a typical phishing operation, subjects receive an e-mail that looks like it is from their bank. The e-mail states that there is a need for the subject to verify his or her login information. The purported reason is often related to "security measures" and subjects are told that they will lose access to their account if they do not respond. The link provided in the e-mail connects to a site that looks just like the bank's login page, but the site is really operated by the identity thief. When subjects key in their login information, it is captured by the software on the site.

The number of phishing attacks rose dramatically in the first few years of this century, despite media attention and public education. The rate of increase has recently leveled off somewhat, and security experts credit this improvement to earlier detection and much earlier takedown of fraudulent sites. The Anti-Phishing Working Group maintains statistics about phishing attacks, coordinates research, advises on policy and provides public education and victim assistance. See www.antiphishing.org for details. In surveys, approximately 3% to 5% of consumers report that they have responded to e-mail phishing messages (Gartner 2004; Sproule and Archer 2008b).

Some newer variations on phishing are 'vishing' and 'smishing,' which use Voice Over Internet Protocol (VoIP) or Short Message Service (SMS) in place of e-mail and the Web. VoIP or SMS can be used as lure or hook or both. For example, a phishing e-mail (the lure) may give a telephone number to call (the hook) rather than a link to a website. When subjects call the telephone number, they are asked to key in certain information. In a smishing attack, subjects receive SMS messages (the lure) that tell them to go to a website (the hook). While the figure of 3% to 5% mentioned above may seem low, it means that if a phisher can send one e-mail to one million people, the phisher will receive sensitive account information on 30,000 to 50,000 individuals.

The costs and traceability associated with traditional telephone service meant that telephone frauds were typically limited to a geographical area and short-term operations—the 'boiler-room' scams of the past. With VoIP telephony, there is no physical location associated with the telephone numbers used to commit the fraud, so the costs associated with telephone calls are negligible. While people are becoming more cautious about revealing personal information when using the Internet, vishing takes advantage of the trust that users have in the telephone system and their familiarity with automated phone validation systems. Vishing also allows identity thieves to prey on people who do not have e-mail (Ollman 2007).

'Spear phishing' refers to highly targeted phishing attacks. In the early years of phishing, attacks were primarily aimed at large banks and other financial organizations. Recipients of a phishing 'lure' will only respond if they have a relationship with the organization being impersonated, so organizations with larger customer bases would result in a higher proportion of responses. Since then, phishing has received a lot of media attention, there have been large public education programs, and banks and other institutions have advised their customers that they will not contact them to request information via e-mail. We are now seeing phishing attacks aimed at smaller financial institutions, such as small, local credit unions, especially where the potential customer base can be identified.

The effectiveness of phishing lures is also enhanced if the recipient believes that the message is from someone that they know. An experiment at Indiana University showed that university students who received phishing messages that appeared to be from a 'friend' of theirs were four and a half times more likely to respond by clicking on the link than those who received the same e-mail message from a stranger. ('Friendship' was determined by participation in a popular social networking site.) In fact, the response from men who received the message from what looked to be a female friend was 68%, versus 53% when the message came from a male friend (Jagatic and Johnson 2007).

Other types of social engineering can involve deception over the phone or in person. The perpetrator generally claims to be someone in authority or someone with a right to access certain information. As mentioned earlier, this practice is called 'pretexting' and can be used to enable many different types of crimes or frauds. In a high-profile scandal in 2006, it was revealed that the chairperson of Hewlett Packard (HP) had hired private investigators to find out how confidential information was being leaked to the media. The investigator used pretexting to gain access to the phone records of HP's board members. A typical example of pretexting related to identity theft is when the identity thief calls someone at work and pretends to be from the information technology group. The caller informs the employee that there is a problem with their access to the system and asks for the employee's login and password. Pretexting can also be used to gain physical access to offices or secure areas in order to steal hardware or media.

Electronic Acquisition of Identity Information

Digital information can be accessed electronically in many different ways. Identity thieves use hacking tools and processes to gain access to systems, then often install malware to monitor activity on those systems, capture targeted information and open a 'backdoor' through which information can be passed back to the thief at a later time. Some hackers are also adept at covering the electronic trails that are used to detect intrusion.

Electronic acquisition enables high-volume attacks, often involving thousands, and in some cases millions, of victims and are most often associated with cases of credit card fraud and existing account frauds (Litan 2007). In Javelin's latest consumer survey, only 4% of victims knew that the method of access to their information was online (Javelin 2009a). Many experts, however, believe electronic acquisition accounts for most of the 65% of cases in which the method of access is not known. This means that electronic access may account for anywhere between 4% and 69% of cases. Also, many people believe that it is risky to conduct financial transactions online and many experts are afraid that this belief and the fear of identity theft will slow the growth of online banking and commerce. Consumer surveys support this proposition (*Consumer Reports* 2005; Sproule and Archer 2008b).

Who Are Identity Thieves?

Studies that have looked at demographic characteristics of identity thieves show a very diverse group. The CIMIP (Center for Identity Management and Information Processing) study of US Secret Service cases showed that the largest proportion of offenders (44%) was between 25 and 34 years of age and that one third were female. Interestingly, 71% of offenders had no arrest history. A study of 2008 media reports of identity theft found similar numbers, with 40% of offenders being women and an average age of 33 (Dupont and Louis 2009). In a smaller study in Florida, the average age was 32, but women accounted for 63% of offenders (Allison, Schuck et al. 2005).

The psychographic categories of criminals that deal in IDTF can be described as 'opportunistic,' 'lifestyle/shoppers,' 'vocational' and 'enterprise' (ID Analytics 2005). The 'opportunistic' criminal is generally someone close to the victim, who is trusted or has access to the necessary identity information. This type of fraud is sometimes called familiar fraud or friendly fraud, although there is nothing 'friendly' about it. Surveys show that, in as many as half of the cases in which the victim knows who took their information, the thief was someone closely connected to the victim. CIMIP's study of US Secret Service cases found that 16% of all cases involved a family member or friend.

The likelihood that the thief is someone close to the victim increases in new accounts fraud, as these types of frauds require more detailed personal information about the victim. A family member, friend or relative often knows the biographical details of the victim's life and has access to mail and documents that contain account information and other details used to verify identity. While overall reporting rates for IDTF are low, the reporting rates for familiar fraud are even lower. Victims may be embarrassed that a close friend or relative has taken advantage of them, or they may be trying to protect the perpetrator from prosecution.

The 'lifestyle/shoppers' category includes criminals who are usually gainfully employed but resort to identity theft and fraud to support a lifestyle that is beyond their legal means. Most often, this type of identity thief has access to personal information as part of their job. Surveys show that when the victim knows the identity of the thief, between 10% and 20% of the time it was an employee of a company that they did business with. Insiders may develop the false identity and commit identity frauds themselves, or they may sell the information to others.

The 'vocational' criminal is generally unemployable, often because of drug dependencies. IDTF is their primary source of income to provide for basic needs and to support their habits. Links between identity theft and drug addicts are well known (Kiefer-Peretti 2009). Hackers also fall into the vocational category, when identity theft is their primary occupation.

In its study of US Secret Service case files, CIMIP found that 20% of the cases involved organized group activity with between three and forty-five offenders (Gordon, Rebovich et al. 2007). The 'enterprise' category includes everything from small, loosely organized groups of criminals to highly sophisticated fraud rings and traditional crime organizations. They may be engaged in the collection of information but often concentrate on trafficking the information purchased from vocational criminals. The administrators and management of carder forums are enterprise thieves. These criminal rings may also 'place' employees into positions in organizations where identity information can be collected (ID Analytics 2005). Law enforcement authorities believe that criminal organizations are behind much of the growth of identity theft and fraud. With low risks and high returns, identity theft can fund other criminal activities and is known to have been used to fund terrorism in at least two cases (Kiefer-Peretti 2009).

At the enterprise level, identity theft is often global in scope. Prosecution of the top-tier operators in one carder organization (Shadowcrew) involved law enforcement agencies from the United Kingdom, Canada, Bulgaria, Belarus, Poland, Sweden, Ukraine and the Netherlands. One of the administrators (the top level in the organization) was from Russia and another from Argentina. A second carder forum (CarderPlanet) had ties to Russia, Ukraine and the United Kingdom (Kiefer-Peretti 2009).

Sensitivity and Value of Different Kinds of Personal Information

There are many different kinds of personal information that are subject to unauthorized access. A useful high-level categorization divides this information into 'account level' and 'identity level' information (ID Analytics 2006).[2]

Account level information consists of a person's name and account information such as account numbers, PINs and passwords. Account level information can be easily changed; consumers can change their passwords and PINs on a regular basis, or whenever they think there might be a problem. Credit card companies routinely close accounts, open new accounts and issue new credit cards when account level information is compromised. Account level information is often sufficient to commit credit card fraud or existing accounts fraud.

Some identity level information, on the other hand, is difficult or impossible to change. It includes name, biographical information (e.g., date of birth, mother's unmarried name) and federal gov-

---

2 Similar distinctions are sometimes made via use of the terms 'personally identifying information,' for identity information that can be used to establish new accounts, and 'means of identification,' for account information (Government Accountability Office 2007).

ernment-issued identity information (e.g., driver's license numbers, SSNs or SINs). However, some identity information may change from time to time, including names (in case of marriage), addresses and health card numbers (when one moves from one province to another in Canada, or when moving to a different insurer in the United States). Identity level information is required to open new accounts or to commit other non-financial frauds. Frauds involving identity level information are more costly, of longer duration and more difficult to resolve (ID Analytics 2006).

Canadian consumer surveys asked victims about the type of information accessed. Between one-quarter and one-third didn't know what type of information had been accessed. Of those who did know, approximately 60% of the thefts involved account information only, between 25% and 30% involved both account level and identity level information, and 10% to 20% involved identity level information only (Sproule and Archer 2008; Sproule and Archer 2008b).

The difference in value of each level of information can be seen in studies of the black market in personal information. An IBM study considered three types of information packages available for sale on the black market:

1. *Credit card packages* contained name, card number, issue/ expiry date, CVV2 code (the three digit number on the back of a credit card) and magnetic strip data.
2. *Standard identity packages* contained name, address, phone number and date of birth.
3. *Complete identity packages* contained name, address, phone number, date of birth, mother's unmarried name, bank account number and account password.

Of equal value were packages of two thousand credit card records, forty standard identities and five complete identities (Ollman 2007). Another law enforcement expert on black market prices says that credit card information sells for $0.50 to $5.00, bank account information for $30 to $400 and full identity information for $10 to $150 (Kiefer-Peretti 2009). In this case, the bank account information is the most valuable, probably because existing account fraud is less risky and less time consuming than new accounts fraud, even though new accounts fraud can be more lucrative. Because people tend to reuse the same logins and passwords on many sites, this information is also valuable on the black market. A batch of seven thousand logins, passwords and e-mail addresses from a porn site was valued at US$ 250 (Ollman 2007).

Data Breaches

"Secure information typically walks out the door in one of three ways: hackers grab it, employees steal it or companies lose it—through incompetence, poor gatekeeping, bad procedures, or some combination of the three" (Roth and Metha 2005: 68).

One of the hazards of our 'information society' is the data breach, where information kept by organizations ends up in the wrong hands. While data breaches involving personal information can lead to identity theft, data breaches can also involve unauthorized access to trade secrets, customer lists and other proprietary or confidential information. In any case, data breaches can be costly—and not only from a financial perspective. Competitive positioning and a company's reputation can also be harmed.

People believe that an increase in data breaches is a major contributor to the rise in IDTF. Because of this belief, many governments have passed legislation requiring organizations to notify individuals whose personal information has been accessed as part of a breach. Below are some examples of large data breaches that have made the news. There are three websites that provide a wealth of up-to-date information about data breaches: DataLossDB (formerly Attrition), Identity Theft Resource Center and Privacy Rights Clearinghouse.[3]

---

3 http://datalossdb.org/, http://www.idtheftcenter.org/artman2/publish/lib_survey/ITRC_2008_Breach_List.shtml and http://www.privacyrights.org/ar/ChronDataBreaches.htm, respectively.

Examples of Data Breaches

The following cases give an idea of the diversity and scope of data breaches and the personal information that has been compromised:

- While we associate data breaches with computers and digital information, organizations were keeping records of personal information long before the information age. According to DataLossDB, a 1986 breach involving Canada Revenue Agency microfiche records containing information on sixteen million individuals is still one of the ten largest breaches on record. The microfiche was stolen by an employee who was planning to start a business tracking down dormant bank accounts. The employee turned himself in to the authorities once the theft was discovered.

- Data aggregator ChoicePoint was spun off from the Equifax credit bureau. In February 2005, it was discovered that perpetrators had set up fake businesses with ChoicePoint accounts and bought full digital dossiers on 163,000 people, including SSNs and credit reports. As a result, ChoicePoint was fined for failing to provide proper authentication processes and for selling information to businesses that had no legitimate reason to acquire the information. The FTC identified eight hundred victims of identity fraud as a result of this breach.

- In 2006, a laptop was stolen from the US Department of Veterans Affairs that contained the personal records of twenty-six million people. The stolen laptop was recovered with no evidence that any of the data had be used or further dispersed, but this data breach initiated a broad examination of laptop security and encryption within government and in the business community in general.

- TJX, a US retailer, was the victim of hackers in late 2005. It is believed that the hackers intercepted wireless transmission signals at two stores in the Miami area and were able to access eighty gigabytes of data. The breach went undetected for eighteen months and was only discovered in January 2007. Initial estimates were that the records of forty-six million customers had been accessed, but final estimates reached as high as ninety-four million. (It is believed that up to two million customers of TJX's Canadian stores, including the Winners chain, were affected.) The data accessed was mostly account level, but some customers' driver's license numbers were also exposed. An investigation found that TJX was not compliant on nine of twelve required security controls under the Payment Card Industry Data Security Standard (PCI DSS). By late 2007, TJX estimated its related pre-tax costs to be $216 million. A year later, it reported $250 million in costs, including $40 million in restitution to banks for the cost of issuing new cards. Soon after the data breach was disclosed, some people were caught using stolen card data, but the hackers themselves were not identified until 2009.

- In April 2007, Affiliated Computer Services, a contractor handling healthcare claims for the City of Atlanta, lost a computer disk with information on three million patients.
- On October 18, 2007, the UK tax and customs service found that it was missing two unencrypted disks containing the personal information of all citizens receiving child benefits. This was twenty-five million people, or about half of the population of the United Kingdom. The files contained individuals' names, addresses, phone numbers, national insurance numbers, dates of birth, child benefit numbers and, in some cases, bank account information.
- In February 2008, *Bell Canada* announced that information about 3.4 million customers was found in the home of a Montreal man. The data were for sale.

- In March 2008, the information system at the Hannaford Bros. supermarket chain was hacked, gaining the hackers access to the credit card information of 4.2 million customers.
- In June 2008, the Canadian Canola Growers Association disclosed that a laptop with the bank accounts and SINs of 32,000 farmers had been stolen in a 'smash and grab' theft. The farmers had applied for an advance payments program. The data were not encrypted, but the laptop had strong password authentication and a fingerprint reader.
- In January 2009, Heartland Payment Systems became the current data breach record holder when it announced that 130 million credit card accounts had been accessed by hackers. Malware had been installed in 2007. Heartland discovered the breach in 2008 and asked the Secret Service to investigate. In August 2009, Miami resident Alberto Gonzalez and two Russian men were indicted for the Heartland case. Gonzalez was also arrested for the TJX and Hannaford Bros. cases. He pled guilty on December 30, 2009.

As these and other examples show, intentional breaches include hacking, insider theft, physical theft of equipment and access through pretexting. Negligence or accidental breaches include lost hardware or media, unintentional exposure of data on the Web and improper disposal of data.

The *DataLossDB* website, administered by the Open Security Foundation, is a treasure trove of data breach information.[4] Table 5.1 shows the number of reported breaches and the number of exposed records for the years 2000 to 2010, according to this website. The increase in breaches reported over these years can be attributed to two factors: 1) increased data collection and a resultant increase in the value of this data to identity thieves, and 2) the adoption of reporting requirements in many US jurisdictions. To date,

4 http://datalossdb.org/statistics

the peak number of breaches occurred in 2008, at 791, and the peak number of records exposed occurred in 2009, at over 221 million.

Table 5.1: Reported Data Breaches and Record Exposed (2000–10)

Year	Reported data breaches	Number of records exposed
2000	10	374,075
2001	19	200,363
2002	7	268,998
2003	16	7,061,950
2004	25	3,717,590
2005	142	55,988,256
2006	538	51,251,706
2007	512	165,262,288
2008	791	87,027,908
2009	621	221,694,058
2010	486	28,278,683

(Source: DatalossDB, http://datalossdb.org/reports)

The DataLossDB website reports that stolen laptop computers make up the largest proportion of data breaches. Hacking was the second-most common cause of breaches, and exposure through the Web was third.

According to DataLossDB, almost two-thirds of breaches were caused by someone external to the organization. Where insiders were responsible, most cases were accidental exposures and not intentional theft. Other studies provide a range of estimates for the proportions of breaches caused by external and internal agents.

- In a business survey, IT managers said that insiders were behind the largest proportion of breaches (Ponemon 2008).

- A survey of five hundred breaches investigated by the Verizon Business RISK team found that 73% of breaches were external and 18% were internal[5] (Baker, Hylender et al. 2008).
- Another study found that 44% of breaches were caused by an external attack, 41% by insiders and 11% by a combination of the two. Causes in the remaining cases were unknown (Oltsik, McKnight et al. 2007).

The Verizon study also found that business partners were implicated in almost four out of ten cases. Sometimes these were cases of collusion, but more often a vulnerability in the partner's system was exploited, giving an external hacker access to the victim company's systems (Baker, Hylender et al. 2008). At least two studies have found that the proportion of breaches involving third parties increased significantly from 2004 to 2005 (Baker, Hylender et al. 2008; Ponemon 2009) and that breaches involving third parties result in a greater number of lost records than those that do not involve third parties (Ponemon 2009).

Prevalence of Data Breaches

A number of surveys have asked businesses about their data breach experiences. A survey of security professionals at 206 US and Canadian companies found that nearly one third had experienced at least one data breach in the previous twelve months. Another 10% did not know whether they had experienced a breach (Oltsik, McKnight et al. 2007). A survey commissioned by security software firm McAfee found that 60% of companies had experienced a data breach in the last year (McAfee Inc. 2007). Still another survey found that one in three businesses experienced at least one security breach in the last three months (CMI 2007).

As disturbing as these figures are, these surveys also reveal that many respondents are not confident that their organizations have

---

5 It also may be the case that insider attacks are handled internally, in which experts like Verizon might not be called in to investigate.

a good handle on data security. In one survey, only 6% of respondents stated that they are sure that they have not had any "data leakage" (McAfee Inc. 2007). In other surveys, 40% of respondents said that they did not have procedures in place or "do not know if databases are monitored for suspicious activity" (Ponemon Institute 2007), while 31% are not confident that all data breaches will be detected by their organization (IDExperts 2008).

Connection to Fraud?

An extensive study by the US Government Accountability Office (GAO), and its report to Congress, found that determining the link between data breaches and identity fraud was difficult because identity fraud victims often do not know how their information was stolen and because there can be years between the theft of information and its use in a fraud. Often, the only case where a link can be established is when an insider committed the breach. Law enforcement also believes that once a person has been notified about a breach, they attribute any mistakes or compromises to that breach, even in the absence of supporting evidence. With large breaches (in the millions of dollars) it is very difficult to identify resulting frauds. In a study of the twenty-five largest breaches between 2000 and 2005, the GAO found evidence of credit card or existing accounts fraud in only four cases and evidence of new accounts fraud in only one case (ChoicePoint) (Government Accountability Office 2007).

ID Analytics has completed two studies of publicly available information on eighty-two data breaches. Breaches were classified as accidental loss, incidental theft and intentional theft, and the information exposed in the breach was classified as account level or identity level. The riskiest type of breach is intentional theft of identity information. The least risky breach is accidental loss of account information. In the first study, four cases were examined in detail. In three of the four cases, ID Analytics concluded that the risk of fraud was not significantly increased by the breach (ID

Analytics 2007). In the second study, a dozen breaches were analyzed in detail, involving more than ten million identities. All of
the breaches were intentional theft and all showed some suspicious
activity. The rate of victimization ranged from 0.01% to 0.5%
and was inversely related to the size of the breach. While frauds
related to a breach may extend over years, misuse of any single
identity typically lasted no more than two weeks (ID Analytics
2007). Other sources estimate that there is a 1% to 5% probability of a breached account resulting in fraud (CIPPIC 2007;
IDExperts 2008).

Disclosure and Notification

The many high-profile data breaches, lost laptops and other losses
of personal information have resulted in legislative pressures to
pass stricter laws governing how data is controlled, with more
emphasis on security and notification of affected individuals. The
justification behind disclosure/notification requirements is two-
fold: 'right to know' and 'sunlight as disinfectant' (a phrase coined
in the 1930s by Justice Louis Brandeis). The first disclosure law
came into effect in 2003 in California. Since then, many states
have followed suit, with various interpretations of what needs to
be disclosed, to whom, how and when. Some of these laws also
require companies to cover victims' costs associated with credit
monitoring or credit freezes. In the United States, businesses have
many problems dealing with this multitude of state requirements,
and federal legislation is expected.

Although there is no explicit legislation, some provisions of
PIPEDA might be interpreted to require notification. In fact,
"Privacy Commissioners across Canada have released a number
of decisions that suggest, in certain circumstances, existing privacy laws may already require data breach notification" (CIPPIC
2007: 5). In a 2006 survey by EKOS Research Associates, 68% of
Canadians believe there should be a requirement for both individuals and privacy officials in governments to be notified of a

data breach, and an additional 19% believe that just the individual should be notified (Saravanamuttoo 2006).

Canada has had the opportunity to learn from the US experience. On the plus side, notification requirements should increase the attention that companies give to security, particularly encryption, and incident response plans (Bergman and Verlet 2006). With notification, it is also argued that affected consumers can be more vigilant in detecting identity frauds, but others argue that this "shifts the burden from the responsible parties to the innocent data subject" (Romanosky, Telang et al. 2008).

On the negative side, there is the issue of over-notification where notification thresholds are set too low. Over-notification can lead to panic and de-sensitization in consumers. In one US survey, 62% of consumers had been notified of a breach in the previous year (Ponemon Institute 2007). In another survey, 55% of respondents said that they had been notified of two or more data breaches in the past two years, while 8% had four or more notifications (IDExperts).

The risk associated with a data breach is affected by many factors, including whether the breach was intentional or accidental, whether the data was protected by passwords or encryption, whether there is specialized hardware required to access the data, and the number of records accessed. Large breaches have a greater chance of at least one fraud victim, but less risk to any individual victim. In general, the risk associated with a data breach can be evaluated on four dimensions:

1. How sensitive is the information? Was the information account level or identity level?
2. What was the extent of protection provided? Was the data encrypted?
3. How did the breach occur? Was it targeted, opportunistic or accidental?
4. Has any misuse of the information occurred to date?

Most new guidelines and legislation for breach disclosure and notification contain 'serious harm' or 'serious risk' thresholds

(Maurushat 2009). For example, Canadian guidance is to consider if the disclosure was to an "unknown party or to a party suspected of being involved in a criminal activity" (Cate 2008).

Costs of Data Breaches

A number of studies have considered the costs of data breaches. Costs can include the costs of detection, notification, response, liabilities to other parties (e.g., banks and credit card companies) and lost business. Overall, recent estimates of the costs of breaches range from $90 per record (Gartner 2003) to $203 per record (Ponemon 2009). Notification costs account for between $50 and $70 per record and credit monitoring can cost another $20 to $40 per customer. Lost business is thought by some to be the highest part of data breach costs (Ponemon 2009). In one study, 31% of consumers notified of a breach said that they terminated their relationship with the company (IDExperts 2008). While there is often a dramatic short-term impact on stock prices, studies have shown mixed results as far as the long-term effects of data breach notices on a firm's financial performance and market value (Romanosky, Telang et al. 2008).

Summary

This chapter has highlighted the bewildering array of identity theft activities with which both consumers and organizations are faced in modern society, an array that is constantly shifting and evolving as defenses are raised and criminals develop new ways to defeat these obstacles to crime. The threats that face consumers are in some ways similar to those facing organizations, ranging from physical activities to social engineering that directly impacts consumers to the growing problem of data breaches that affect both organizations and consumers. Effective organizational responses to IDTF are discussed in some detail in following chapters, as are consumer defenses against the types of identity theft attacks described in this chapter.

References

Abagnale, F. W. 2001. *The Art of the Steal: How to Protect Yourself and Your Business From Fraud—America's #1 Crime*. New York: Broadway Books.

Allison, S. F. H., A. M. Schuck, et al. 2005. "Exploring the Crime of Identity Theft: Prevalence, Clearance Rates, and Victim/Offender Characteristics." *Journal of Criminal Justice*, 33: 1: 19–29.

Baker, W. H., C. D. Hylender, et al. 2008. *2008 Data Breach Investigations Report*. Verizon Business RISK Team.

Bergman, A., and A. Verlet. 2006. "Security Breaches: To Notify or Not to Notify—That Is the Question." *Network Security*, May: 4–6.

Cate, F. H. 2008. *Information Security Breaches: Looking Back and Thinking Ahead*. Washington, D.C.: The Centre for Information Policy Leadership. Hunton & Williams LLP.

CIPPIC. 2007. *Approaches to Security Breach Notifications*. Ottawa: Canadian Internet Privacy and Public Interest Centre, University of Ottawa.

CMI. 2007. *Canadian Security Technology Readiness Intelligence Report*. Canadian Advanced Technology Alliance: 18. http://www.cata.ca/Media_and_Events/Press_Releases/cata_pr06070701.html [consulted July 3 2009].

Consumer Reports. 2005a. "Leap of Faith: Using the Internet Despite the Dangers." *Consumer Reports. Webwatch*. http://www.consumerwebwatch.org/pdfs/princeton.pdf [consulted January 29, 2009].

Copes, H., and L. Vieraitis. 2007. "Identity Theft: Assessing Offenders' Strategies and Perceptions of Risk. *Technical Report*. Washington, D.C.: National Institute for Justice.

Dupont, B., and G. Louis. 2009. *Les voleurs d'identité. Profil d'une délinquance ordinaire*. Montréal: Université de Montréal

GAO. 2007. *Data Breaches Are Frequent, but Evidence of Resulting Identity Theft Is Limited; However, the Full Extent Is Unknown*. United States Government Accountability Office. GAO-07-737: 1–50.

Gartner. 2003. *Gartner Says Identity Theft Is Up Nearly 80 Percent*. Stamford, CN: Gartner Research.

Gartner. 2004. *Gartner Study Finds Significant Increase in E-mail Phishing Attacks*. Stamford, CN, Gartner Research.

Gordon, G. R., D. J. Rebovich, et al. 2007. *Identity Fraud Trends and Patterns: Building a Foundation for Proactive Enforcement*. Center for Identity Management and Information Protection.

Griffith, V. ,and M. Jakobsson. 2005. "Messin' with Texas Deriving Mother's Maiden Names Using Public Records." *ACNS*, 91–103.

ID Analytics. 2005. ID Analytics National Fraud Ring Analysis: Understanding Behavioural Patterns, ID Analytics.

ID Analytics. 2006. *National Data Breach Analysis*. ID Analytics Inc., pp. 2–36.

ID Analytics. 2007. *U.S. Identity Fraud Hot Spots*, ID Analytics.

IDExperts. 2008. *Ponemon Institute Examines Consumer Response to Data Breach Notification*. Traverse City, Michigan: Ponemon Institute.

Jagatic, T. N., and N. Johnson. 2007. "Social Phishing." *Communications of the ACM*, 50: 10: 94–99.

Javelin. 2005. 2005 *Identity Fraud Survey Report (Complimentary Overview).* Pleasanton, CA: Javelin Strategy & Research.

Javelin. 2009. *2009 Identity Fraud Survey Report: Consumer Version.* Javelin Strategy & Research.

Javelin. 2009a. *Latest Javelin Research Shows Identity Fraud Increased 22 Percent, Affecting Nearly Ten Million Americans: But Consumer Costs Fell Sharply by 31 Percent.* San Francisco: Javelin Strategy and Research. http://www.idsafety. net/Javelin2009IdentityFraudSurveyPressRelease.pdf [consulted February 18, 2010].

Kiefer-Peretti, K. 2009. "Data Breaches: What the Underground World of 'Carding' Reveals." *Santa Clara Computer & High Technology Law Journal,* 25: 375–413.

Litan, A. 2007. *The Truth Behind Identity Theft Numbers.* Gartner, Inc.

Maurushat, A. 2009. "Data Breach Notification across the World from California to Australia." *Berkeley Press Legal Repository.* Berkeley: Berkeley Electronic Press.

McAfee Inc. 2007. *DataGate: The Next Inevitable Corporate Disaster?* Santa Clara, CA: McAfee Inc.

Ollman, G. 2007. "IDs Sell for Much More than Credit Card Numbers in Underground." *Computer Fraud and Security.*

Oltsik, J., J. McKnight, et al. 2007. *Research Report: The Case for Data Leakage Prevention Solutions.* Enterprise Strategy Group for Vericept.

Ponemon Institute. 2007. *Database Security 2007: Threats and Priorities within IT Database Infrastructure.* New York: Ponemon Institute LLC, sponsored by Application Security Inc.

Ponemon, L. 2008. *2008 Study on the Uncertainty of Data Breach Detection: Report of IT Practitioners in the United States.* Traverse City, Michigan: Ponemon Institute.

Ponemon, L. 2009. *Fourth Annual US Cost of Data Breach Study.* Traverse City, Michigan: Ponemon Institute. http://www.ponemon.org/index.php [consulted February 19, 2010].

Romanosky, S., R. Telang, et al. 2008. "Do Data Breach Disclosure Laws Reduce Identity Theft?" *Seventh Workshop on the Economics of Information Security.* Hanover, NH: Tuck School of Business, Dartmouth College. http://weis2008. econinfosec.org/papers/Romanosky.pdf [consulted January 15, 2009].

Roth, D., and S. Metha. 2005. "The Great Data Heist." *Fortune,* 151: 66–75.

Saravanamuttoo, M. 2006. *Identity Theft & Identity Management: Looking through the eyes of the Canadian public.* 7th Annual Privacy and Security Workshop. Toronto: Eckos Research Associates.

Sproule, S., and N. Archer. 2008. "Measuring Identity Theft in Canada: 2006 Consumer Survey." *McMaster eBusiness Research Centre Working Paper #21.* Hamilton, Ontario: DeGroote School of Business, McMaster University.

Sproule, S., and N. Archer. 2008b. *Measuring Identity Theft in Canada: 2008 Consumer Survey.* McMaster eBusiness Research Centre Working Paper #23. Hamilton, Ontario: DeGroote School of Business, McMaster University.

Wallace, K. 2007 (4 December.) "Passport Applicant Finds Massive Security Breach." *Globe and Mail,* A1, A8.

Chapter 6

Measuring Identity Theft and Fraud

"Nothing great was ever created without enthusiasm."
—Ralph Waldo Emerson

Measuring identity theft and fraud is critically important if society is to make any progress in defending against it. This derives from the old axiom that you can't manage something if you can't measure it. However, there are many problems with determining how identity theft and fraud affects its victims in order to find a basis for measurement. These are discussed in detail, with a number of examples of statistics on reported incidence of fraud, and how this might relate to actual levels, which are often higher. More reliable measures of fraud are then reported from a variety of sources, based on overall measures and the relatively standardized categories of credit card fraud, existing accounts fraud, new accounts fraud, and others. The chapter concludes with a discussion of how to detect identity fraud, and the level of its costs to society.

Problems with Measurement

There are a number of problems associated with getting a measure of how identity theft and fraud are affecting its various stakeholders. The first goes back to the lack of a commonly understood definition. There have been many surveys that ask consumers if they have been victims of identity theft without providing any guidance as to what different kinds of losses, thefts or frauds should be included in this category. If the problem is not clearly defined during the collection of data, the resulting reports are difficult to interpret and impossible to compare.

To illustrate this problem, in a 2006 survey of Canadian consumers, participants were asked if they thought each of a number of different scenarios described a case of identity theft. For example, one scenario described simple credit card fraud and another described cheque fraud involving a close family member. Only 71% and 61% of participants, respectively, regarded these scenarios as cases of identity theft (Sproule and Archer 2008). Had these participants simply been asked if they had been victims of identity theft, the results would have included less than three quarters of the true number of victims of credit card fraud and less than two-thirds of the true number of victims of cheque fraud involving someone close to the victim. Because of the lack of definition, if we want to include these types of frauds, the results of the survey would under report the incidence rate, and if we want to exclude them, the results would over report the incidence rate.

There are also characteristics of the crime itself that hinder data collection and response. First, we can only report and measure crime after it has been detected, and there is often a significant lag between the crime and its detection. Once detected, the theft or fraud must be reported. In the study of criminology, the 'dark figure of crime' refers to the large number of crimes that go unreported. Businesses and other organizations often don't report cases of identity fraud to police, but they may respond to surveys asking about the loss or theft of personal information. In a survey of Australian businesses, researchers found that in total only 9% of identity fraud events were reported to law enforcement (Lacey and Cuganesan 2004).

Statistics Canada conducted a survey of fraud against businesses in 2008.[1] Figure 6.1 shows results for this survey from the retailing and banking sectors. Almost half of the retailers said that they never or seldom report fraud to the police. Reports were

1 Note that these data include all frauds, not just identity fraud.

more common when there were significant losses. In the banking sector, frauds are more likely to be reported, with only 4% of firms stating that they rarely or never call police. Almost all the banks said that they report frauds when there are significant losses, where links to organized crime are suspected and when they want to pursue criminal charges.

Figure 6.1: Percentage of Fraud Incidents Reported to Police

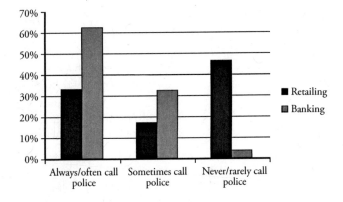

(Adapted from Taylor-Butts and Perreault 2009)

We also know that few individual victims report cases of identity fraud to police. Most victims report the identity fraud to the organization or business involved, but only 25% to 35% of victims report the incident to the police. Police reports are most common in new accounts and other frauds but still reach just over 40% of cases (FTC 2003a; Javelin 2006). Even in US cases where a report was made to the Federal Trade Commission (FTC) central reporting system, less than 40% were also reported to the police. In approximately one fifth of the cases where police were notified, a police report was not taken (Consumer Sentinel 2005).

Some of the barriers to reporting include the belief that police will be unable to locate offenders, or that the available evidence is not sufficient to get a conviction. Both organizations and individuals may not feel that it is worth the time and expense to report the theft or fraud. They may not have suffered any losses, may believe that the losses are insufficient for police to act, and often think that it will be impossible to recover their losses. Organizations may fear the associated publicity, while individuals may be embarrassed that they fell for a scam or were negligent in protecting themselves against the theft or fraud (Smith 2005).

Even when incidents are reported, it is hard to separate reports of identity fraud from frauds in general, and there is usually no consistency in how identity theft is categorized in police logs. Cross-jurisdictional issues also hinder data collection, as investigations often involve many law enforcement agencies in various geographical and geopolitical sectors. Other barriers to police investigation and prosecution include (Gayer 2003; Smith 2002)

- Sophisticated methods of deception
- Translations
- Volume of information
- Encryption of information
- Criminal operations and assets can be moved easily
- Complex evidence to be presented
- Multiple dependents and multiple charges
- Courts let offenders off easy
- Coordination between law enforcement organizations is lacking

All of these problems complicate the job of measuring identity fraud.

Overall Incidence of Identity Fraud

Identity fraud is the use of a false identity to obtain money, goods, services or other benefits, or to avoid obligations. As mentioned in Chapter 4, consumer surveys are the best way to estimate the overall incidence of identity fraud.[2] The following overall incidence results include many types of identity frauds, including credit card fraud, debit card fraud, cheque fraud, other identity frauds on existing accounts, new account frauds and other, non-financial frauds. Each of these types of frauds is discussed in detail in the following sections.

In the United States, we have data from the FTC/Javelin telephone surveys conducted yearly from 2003 to 2008. According to these surveys, between 3.5% and 4.7% of American consumers over eighteen years of age are victims of identity fraud each year. This equates to between eight and ten million victims. In general, the overall incidence rate decreased from 2003 to 2007 but increased slightly (7%) in 2008. This increase is believed to be a result of an increase in debit card fraud in this period (FTC 2003a; Javelin 2005, 2006, 2007, 2008a, 2009). Online surveys tend to produce incidence rates that are about 50% higher than telephone surveys. An online survey, modeled after the FTC/Javelin surveys, was conducted in 2006 by Gartner Research. From this survey Gartner estimates that fifteen million American consumers were victims of identity fraud (IDF) in the previous year (Litan 2007).

A Canadian consumer survey in 2008 was also conducted online, which showed that 6.5% of Canadian consumers over the age of eighteen had been victims of identity fraud in the previous year (March 2007 to February 2008). These percentages are in line with the Gartner results from the United States. This equates to 1.7 million Canadian victims in this timeframe (Sproule and Archer 2008b).

As far as victim demographics are concerned, identity fraud seems to be an 'equal opportunity' crime. Most studies show only minor differences in the likelihood that any particular demographic segment of the population will be victimized. For example, some surveys have found that incidence rates are highest for

---

2 It should be noted, however, that consumer surveys report instances of identity fraud only when the false identity is based on another real person's identity. Cases where the false identity is fictitious or based on the modification of the fraudster's identity are not captured in survey data.

young adults (18–24) (Baum 2006; Javelin 2007) and that young adults are also most likely (twice as likely) to be victimized by people they know (Javelin 2007). In 2009, Javelin first reported that women are more likely to be victims than men (Javelin 2009).

Categories of Identity Fraud

While the previous section reports overall incidence rates, identity frauds can take many forms. To understand the nature and scope of IDF, we need to categorize these frauds so that the particular characteristics of each type can be examined. The original FTC consumer survey reported its results in three categories: existing credit card fraud, frauds involving other existing accounts, and new accounts and other frauds. Many different kinds of fraud can be committed with the personal information obtained in a single case of identity theft. In this schema, each case of IDF is therefore placed in the most serious of these categories. For example, new accounts and other frauds are considered more serious than existing accounts fraud, so if someone opened a new credit card account in the victim's name and also forged a cheque, the case would be counted in both the new accounts and other categories. Similarly, if someone charged telephone calls to the victim's existing telephone account and also used the victim's credit card to make unauthorized purchases, the case would be counted in the existing accounts category.

With some adjustments,[3] some form of these categories has been used in all of the major North American consumer surveys. If new accounts fraud and other frauds are considered to be two different categories, then we can talk about four varieties of IDF. Table 6.1 shows some scenarios that would be included in each category, and in the following sections each category is described in more detail.

---

3 E.g., Javelin surveys include debit card fraud and credit card fraud in one 'existing card' category.

Credit Card Fraud

Credit card fraud involves unauthorized purchases or cash withdrawals on existing credit card accounts. When we look at the results from both US and Canadian consumer surveys, credit card fraud accounts for just over half of all identity frauds. This means that between 2% and 4% of US and Canadian consumers are victims of credit card fraud each year but suffer no more serious types of identity fraud. In 2008, the Canadian Bankers Association reported that over 450,000 accounts were affected by credit card fraud, for losses of $407 million (CBA 2008). High-income individuals are more likely to be victims of credit card fraud, as criminals can identify cards with high credit limits through the numbering systems used for gold and platinum cards. High-income individuals are not more likely to be victims of other frauds (Litan, 2007).

Credit card purchases can be made either in a face-to-face environment, as in a retail store, or through some sort of communication medium. When purchases are made over the telephone, by mail order or through e-commerce, the credit industry labels these transactions as 'card not present' (CNP). Currently, CNP fraud accounts for more than half of the credit card fraud reported in the UK (APACS 2009) and just under half of the credit card fraud in Canada (CBA 2008). In Canada, CNP frauds result in average losses of $610 per account. To accomplish CNP fraud, the perpetrator uses a third party or mail drop as the shipping address on the order. For high-value orders, retailers are now able to check that the shipping address matches the credit card billing address, and if the two do not match they will investigate before processing the order. To reduce CNP fraud, credit card companies also introduced a card verification number—a three- or four-digit number printed on the back of the card. This number is not encoded on the magnetic strip data and thus provides an additional authentication factor that can be matched to the credit card record. Secure payment programs like Verified by

Table 6.1: Examples of ID Fraud (by Fraud Type) and ID Theft

Credit card fraud	Existing account fraud
• Someone steals your wallet and uses your credit card to make purchases at a store. • The credit card company phones to verify a purchase that you have not made or authorized. • You notice unauthorized purchases on your monthly statement.	• Someone takes your chequebook and forges your name on a number of cheques. • Someone obtains your debit/bank card information, including your PIN, and money is withdrawn from your bank account. • You move, but the new resident continues to have telephone and electric utility services billed to your account. • Your roommate uses your computer to list fraudulent items for auction under your name and your eBay account.
New account fraud	**Other fraud**
• Someone opens up a new credit card account in your name and charges purchases on the card for which you are then expected to pay. • Someone takes out a loan and opens a line of credit or takes out a mortgage on your house in your name. • Someone gives your personal information to open a new cellular telephone account and runs up a phone bill in your name.	• You receive a notice from the Canada Revenue Agency that you owe income tax on earnings from a job you never had. • A friend or neighbour gives your name and address as his or her own when he or she is arrested. • Someone applies for car insurance using your personal information. • You find out that someone used your personal information to get a replacement health card and obtain healthcare services under your name.

Visa and MasterCard SecureCode have also been introduced to reduce CNP fraud. In these programs, cardholders register and use a password to verify their identity for any online purchase at participating retailers.

In-store use of stolen or counterfeit cards is more risky than CNP fraud. In Canada, counterfeit cards account for the largest proportion of these frauds, at 35%, with average losses of just over $1,200 per account (CBA 2008). Counterfeiters require special equipment like embossers, laminators and printers, but such equipment is readily available. Lost and stolen cards account for 5% and 11% of credit card fraud respectively, with average losses of approximately $700 per account (CBA 2008).

While merchandise purchased with lost, stolen or counterfeit cards can be fenced, gift card vending is another way to turn stolen credit card information into cash. Gift cards are purchased from a retailer using stolen or counterfeit credit cards and then sold on the black market at a discount from their face value (Abagnale 2001).

In the past, new or replacement credit cards were often intercepted and stolen as they were mailed to cardholders. Credit card companies have now introduced processes that require customers to phone from their home number in order to activate new or replacement cards. Customers may also be offered the option to pick up their cards in person at their bank branch. These measures have reduced the incidence of cards stolen from the mail. The main defense against the use of lost, stolen and counterfeit cards lies in the sophisticated, intelligent systems that credit card companies use to profile their customers' behaviours and identify unusual activities on their accounts. The card company is then able to suspend suspicious transactions until the purchaser is confirmed through additional authentication measures. Once a card has been reported stolen, it is also placed on a hot card list that is accessed as part of the electronic authentication process.

With enough verifying personal information, fraudsters may try to change the billing address on a credit card account, change the cardholder's address to the mail drop address or add another shipping address to the account. Fraudulent address changes or fraudulent authorizations of additional users are known as 'account takeover.' Changing the billing address can extend the time before the fraud is detected, since the victim will not receive mailed statements showing the unauthorized purchases. Surveys indicate that between 8% and 16% of credit card fraud cases involved account takeover attempts (FTC 2003a; Sproule and Archer 2008b). In the United Kingdom, there has been an increase in account takeover losses; the UK Payments Administration (APACS) suspects that this is because economic conditions have made attempts to open new credit card accounts more difficult. When verifying information is available, account takeover may be a more accessible—and therefore more lucrative—fraud than new accounts fraud (APACS, 2009).

The newest weapon in the battle against credit card fraud is the introduction of 'chip-and-PIN' cards. These cards have a microchip instead of a magnetic strip, and a PIN number is used to verify the card owner's identity rather than, or in addition to, a signature. The PIN is encoded on the chip so that the point-of-sale terminal can ensure that the PIN entered on the keypad matches the PIN encoded on the chip. Standards for chip-and-PIN technology were developed first in Europe and are now being introduced around the world. When chip-and-PIN was introduced in the UK in 2004, losses due to credit card fraud dropped. Retailer fraud, where chip-and-PIN technology is used the most, is down 55%, from more than 59% of losses in 1996 to only 16% in 2008.

Existing Account Fraud

The category of existing account fraud includes debit card fraud, cheque fraud and frauds involving existing telephone, utility or online accounts. Data from consumer surveys show that the incidence rate for existing accounts fraud is somewhere between 0.5% and 2.5%.

Canadian survey results show that 75% of existing accounts frauds involved a bank account (Sproule and Archer 2008b). This represents about 488,000 victims a year and the majority of these frauds involved debit cards. In the United States, one quarter of all identity frauds involved debit cards, resulting in an estimated 2.7 million compromises in 2008 (Javelin 2009).

A debit or ATM card may be used to withdraw cash at an automatic teller machine (ATM) or to pay for merchandise at a point-of-sale terminal. A transaction with a debit card requires two types of information: the information from the magnetic strip or chip on the card as it is captured at the terminal, and a PIN number that is entered at the terminal. The identity thief must therefore be able to capture and correlate these two types of information. Methods for doing this with skimming equipment were described in Chapter 5.

Some debit card fraud is accomplished without sophisticated skimming equipment. It results from lost or stolen cards when the PIN number is written down on the card or somewhere in the proximity of the card. A fraudster in possession of the card may also be able to guess the PIN if birthdates or other personal information is used. Debit card fraud can also happen through a combination of shoulder surfing and pick-pocketing, where the thief observes the victim as he or she enters the PIN and subsequently steals the card. Another method for capturing cards and PINs involves a card-trapping device attached to an ATM. The device takes the card, but the machine will not respond. A fraudster then poses as a 'helper' who offers to assist the victim by entering his or her PIN.

Increased use of debit cards and high-volume skimming attacks has resulted in a steep increase in debit card fraud over the last few years. Losses in Canada increased from $60 million in 2004 to more than $100 million in 2007 and 2008. In 2008, 148,000 customer accounts were reimbursed (Interac 2008). Early responses to debit card fraud included provisions for more privacy at terminals, customer education, and the use of closed circuit security cameras (APACS 2009). More recently, institutions have introduced regular inspections of machines, tamper-proofing upgrades to the technology used in the machines and sophisticated response systems similar to those developed to combat credit card fraud. These response systems have been effective in reducing losses, but they result in a great deal of inconvenience for customers, as compromised cards are cancelled and accounts are inaccessible while new cards are issued.

Another common way that fraudsters get access to an existing bank account is through cheque fraud. Cheques can be counterfeited, forged or altered fraudulently. The United Kingdom has seen an increase in cheque fraud over the last few years (APACS 2009). The ability to initiate wire transfers online raises new concerns about existing accounts fraud for the future.

Online accounts like PayPal and eBay are also popular targets for existing accounts fraud. A recent Canadian survey found that online accounts represented about 15% of existing accounts fraud (Sproule and Archer 2008b). With the necessary information, a fraudster can use a victim's PayPal account to purchase merchandise or transfer funds. Existing eBay accounts become targets when the victim has a good reputation as a seller. By taking over the account, the fraudster can post defective or non-existent items for sale and ruin the victim's reputation rating.

New Accounts Fraud

Of financially motivated identity frauds, new accounts fraud is the most serious and costly. While US surveys do not separate new accounts fraud from other fraud, Canadian survey results show that the incidence rate for new accounts fraud is between 0.1 and 0.2%. This equates to about 390,000 victims a year.

About half of new accounts frauds involve applications for new credit cards (FTC 2003b; Sproule and Archer 2008b). These fraudulent accounts often go undetected for months or years, and victims may only find out about these frauds when they apply for credit. At that point, however, their credit rating has been ruined. Losses due to fraudulent applications account for between 1% and 2% of all credit card losses (APACS 2009; CBA 2008).

Wireless telephone accounts are now accounting for a larger proportion of new accounts fraud, reaching almost one third of new account cases in recent consumer surveys (Javelin 2008b). A new wireless telephone account in the victim's name can be used as contact information and is part of the process of developing a credible false identity.

One of the most costly types of new accounts fraud is mortgage fraud. In the broad sense, mortgage fraud can take two forms. One form, which is not identity fraud, involves giving fraudulent information about one's qualifications on a mortgage application. The other is a form of identity fraud and involves someone impersonating the owner of a property and applying for a mortgage on that property. Industry estimates of total annual losses due to mortgage fraud are more than $1 billion in Canada, but we do not know the cost breakdown between these two types of mortgage fraud.

Proceeds of mortgage fraud can be in the hundreds of thousands of dollars, providing ample incentive for criminals. Mortgage frauds are so uncommon that they are generally not captured in consumer surveys; however, because the consequences for victims are so serious, these cases are often reported in newspapers and other mass media. Identity fraud associated with mortgages and property can take several different forms. The fraudster can impersonate the victim and apply for a mortgage on the victim's home (mortgage fraud, as described above). The fraudster can also purchase property in the victim's name and then take out large mortgages. Finally, the identity thief can pose as the victim and sell the victim's property to an accomplice, who then takes out a mortgage on the home. In some jurisdictions, a transfer of title is as easy as a one-page document signed by the alleged owner and a lawyer. In some serious cases of fraudulent land transfers, seller, buyer and lawyer can all be using false identities (Perkins 2009).

Some of the reasons for an increase in mortgage fraud are believed to be higher property values, the easy access to information that is provided by electronic land registry systems, a very competitive lending market and time pressures that limit the due diligence conducted by lawyers and lenders in the real estate market. Until recently, homeowners were responsible for the losses associated with mortgage fraud even if the lender had given the funds to an imposter. In 2006, the province of Ontario changed the law to make mortgage lenders, not homeowners, liable for losses associated with identity fraud.

Other Frauds

Other frauds involve using a false identity to obtain services, benefits or avoid obligations. With other frauds there is not a direct transfer of financial rewards from the impersonated victim to the fraudster. These frauds are often committed because the fraudster is not eligible, or would have to pay a premium, for certain services or benefits. For example, people with poor driving records may use false identities to get vehicle insurance, and illegal residents may use a false identity to access government healthcare services. There may be indirect financial consequences to the IDF victim, as when someone uses a false identity to gain employment, leaving the victim with the income tax bill. Another type of other fraud occurs when a criminal uses a false identity to avoid prosecution or lessen the extent of criminal penalties. These frauds can have very serious consequences for the identity fraud victim.

Canadian survey results show that the incidence rate for other frauds is also between 0.1% and 0.2%, equating to approximately 390,000 victims per year. In US surveys, 0.1% to 0.6% of consumers report that their personal information was used in non-financial ways (FTC 2003a). It is not surprising that the incidence rate for other frauds is higher in the United States. Many types of other frauds require the use of Social Security Numbers as identifiers; the problems associated with SSN security in the United States have been detailed in Chapter 4.

In other frauds, US studies show that false identities were used most often when the fraudster was questioned by police or to obtain identity documents (FTC 2003a). Canadian studies also show cases where the false identity was used to get leases for accommodation, to gain employment, to get vehicle insurance, to harass someone online or to obtain medical services (Sproule and Archer 2008b).

Detecting Identity Fraud

We indicated earlier that individual identity owners can do little to prevent identity fraud as it is a problem of authentication. Individuals can, however, play a large role in minimizing losses due to identity fraud by detecting it early. All costs are smaller when the fraud is discovered quickly (FTC 2003a).

While the online environment is blamed for much of the increase in identity theft and fraud, having online access (including ATM access) to bank and credit accounts is extremely beneficial in terms of consumer ability to monitor accounts and detect fraud as early as possible. When paper statements were used to review accounts, the mean time to fraud detection was 114 days. Electronic review of accounts reduced the time to detection to eighteen days (Javelin 2005). In general, the length of time to detection is longer when the thief is someone close to the victim (Javelin 2005).

Costs of Identity Fraud

Consumer surveys also allow us to estimate the cost of identity fraud to individual consumers. In the US, these surveys tell us that out-of-pocket costs to victims of identity fraud have a mean of between US$ 500 and 700 per case (FTC 2003a; Javelin 2008a). This equates to over US$ 5 billion. In Canada, the mean is estimated to be CA$ 92, which equates to over CA$ 150 million (Sproule and Archer 2008b). The higher incidence of new accounts and other frauds in the United States would contribute to higher victim out-of-pocket costs. It should be noted, however, that in most surveys the median out-of-pocket costs are zero. This is because more than half of all identity frauds are credit card or debit card frauds where there is usually no cost to the victim.

Consumer surveys also attempt to estimate fraud costs by asking victims how much money the fraudster obtained. This is problematic, because credit card and debit card fraud victims usually do not know the amount of the fraud or whether any of the money was recovered. The US surveys estimate, however, that criminal receive between US$ 45 billion and US$ 56 billion from identity fraud each year (FTC 2003a; Javelin 2006, 2008a).

There have been many attempts to measure the larger costs of identity fraud to organizations and national economies. One of the first was by the US Government Accountability Office (GAO). Based on interviews with federal agencies, credit reporting agencies, credit card companies and a set of archetypical victims, its report highlights some of the difficulties in measuring identity theft and fraud and uses a number of 'proxy' indicators like victim reports and prosecutions of associated crimes to determine that the prevalence of identity fraud was increasing. The following are some examples of related data used to reach this conclusion (Government Accountability Office 2007):

- Comparing the last half of 1999 to the last half of 2000, there was a 53% increase in the number of fraud alerts placed by the credit bureaus.
- The number of calls to the FTC fraud reporting centre increased from 445 calls per week in November 1999 to 3,000 calls per week in December 2001.
- SSN misuse in 2001 was five times as prevalent as in 1998.
- FBI bank fraud arrests climbed from 579 in 1998 to 645 in 2000.
- The US Secret Service closed 7,071 identity theft cases in 2000, compared to 8,498 in 1998, but the dollar amount involved in the cases jumped from $73,382 to $217,696.

- US Postal Inspection Services investigations were up 67% from 1999 to 2000.

The report then outlines various estimated costs to the financial services industry, to victims of IDTF and to the criminal justice system.

In 2003, the Australian government commissioned a study to estimate the costs of IDTF (Cuganesan and Lacey 2003). To do this, the authors developed a model that divides costs into two main categories: 'activity-related' costs include costs associated with anticipating and reacting to identity fraud, while 'residual' costs are costs resulting from a fraud, including financial loss, intangible losses and opportunity costs. A sample of 120 organizations was surveyed to collect data associated with all of these costs. In total, the authors estimated the organizational cost of identity fraud in Australia in the period 2001–02 to be $1.1 billion. Activity costs represent 57% of this total, residual costs 38% and opportunity costs 5%. The largest proportion of costs (80%) was borne by identity users, while identity issuers shouldered only 13% of the costs. Considering the interdependence between users and issuers, the study concluded that the financial incentives to reduce identity fraud are far from balanced.

The UK has also been active in trying to estimate costs on a national basis. A 2002 report estimated the minimum cost of identity fraud to the UK economy at £1.3 billion. This was a bottom-up estimate, summing cost estimates from various government departments, the credit card and insurance industries, and CIFAS, the UK's fraud prevention agency (Cabinet Office 2002). Since this report, the UK Home Office established the Identity Fraud Steering Committee (ISFC), and an updated estimate of costs totaling £1.7 billion was issued in February 2006 (Home Office 2006). The IFSC has since changed its methodology, adding costs for identification, prevention and prosecution of IDTF, excluding some money laundering and tax fraud, and excluding credit card fraud unless they involved application fraud (new accounts fraud) or account takeover. With these changes, the IFSC's latest estimate of costs for the period from April 2006 to March 2007, is £1.2 billion.

As these various attempts to quantify costs indicate, there are many different indicators and various sources of information that can be collected—and in compiling this information it is difficult to arrive at a single estimate of cost. The need for an index to track costs and other indicators from various sources is discussed in Chapter 14.

Summary

This chapter has addressed issues related to the measurement of identity fraud, which are extremely important to public policy makers and organizations tasked with suppressing these criminal activities in order to protect a society that has become highly dependent on individual and organizational identities. In particular, the sources of relevant information have been discussed, along with the general nature of identity fraud that can be measured, including more-or-less standard categories that help to compare studies by different organizations and different countries. In addition, the detection of identity fraud and its costs to consumers and the economy in general have also been described.

References

Abagnale, F. W. 2001. *The Art of the Steal: How to Protect Yourself and Your Business from Fraud—America's #1 Crime.* New York: Broadway Books.

APACS. 2009. *Fraud: The Facts 2009.* The UK Payments Association (APACS).

Baum, K. 2006. "Identity Theft, 2004: First Estimates from the National Crime Victimization Survey." In *Bureau of Justice Statistics.* Washington, D.C.: US Department of Justice.

Cabinet Office. 2002. *Identity Fraud: A Study.* London, UK: Cabinet Office. www.statewatch.org/news/2004/may/id-fraud-report.pdf [consulted March 14, 2011].

CBA. 2008. "Credit Card Statistics—Canadian Issued Cards." http://www.cba.ca/contents/files/statistics/stat-creditcardfraud_en.pdf [consulted August 14, 2009].

Consumer Sentinel. 2005. *National and State Trends in Fraud and Identity Theft.* US Federal Trade Commission.

Cuganesan, S., and D. Lacey. 2003. *Identity Fraud in Australia: An Evaluation of its Nature, Cost and Extent.* Sydney: Securities Industry Research Centre of Asia-Pacific (SIRCA).

FTC. 2003a. *Identity Theft Survey Report.* US Federal Trade Commission and Synovate.

FTC. 2003b. *Overview of the Identity Theft Program.* US Federal Trade Commission.

GAO. 2007. *Data Breaches Are Frequent, but Evidence of Resulting Identity Theft Is Limited; However, the Full Extent Is Unknown.* United States Government Accountability Office. GAO-07-737: 1–50.

Gayer, J. 2003. *Policing Privacy: Law Enforcement's Response to Identity Theft.* Los Angeles: CALPIRG Education Fund.

Home Office. 2006. *Updated Estimate of the Cost of Identity Fraud to the UK Economy.* UK Home Office.

Interac. 2008. "Interac 2008 Statistics." http://www.interac.ca/media/stats.php [consulted August 14, 2009].

Javelin. 2005. *2005 Identity Fraud Survey Report (Complimentary Overview).* Pleasanton, CA: Javelin Strategy & Research.

Javelin. 2006. *2006 Identity Fraud Survey Report:* Javelin Strategy and Research, co-released with the Better Business Bureau, sponsored by Visa USA, Wells Fargo Bank and CheckFree Corproation.

Javelin. 2007. *2007 Identity Fraud Survey Report: Identity Fraud Is Dropping, Continued Vigilance is Necessary.* Pleasanton, CA: Javelin Strategy & Research.

Javelin. 2008a. *2008 Identity Fraud Survey Report: Identity Fraud Continues to Decline, But Criminals More Effective at Using All Channels.* Javelin Strategy & Research.

Javelin. 2008b. *Overall Fraud Down 12%, Criminals Trapping Victims over the Phone.* Press Release. Javelin Strategy & Research.

Javelin. 2009. *2009 Identity Fraud Survey Report: Consumer Version.* Javelin Strategy & Research.

Lacey, D., and S. Cuganesan. 2004. "The Role of Organizations in Identity Theft Response: The Organization-Individual Victim Dynamic." *The Journal of Consumer Affairs*, 38: 2: 244–61.

Litan, A. 2007. *The Truth Behind Identity Theft Numbers.* Gartner, Inc.

Perkins, T. 2009. (31 August.) "Feds Probe Mortgage Brokerages." *Globe and Mail.*

Smith, R. G. 2002. *Examining the Legislative and Regulatory Controls on Identity Fraud in Australia.* Paper presented at the Marcus Evans Conferences, Corporate Fraud Strategy: Assessing the Emergence of Identity Fraud, July 25–26, Sydney, Australia.

Smith, R. G. 2005. *Understanding Fraud Reporting as an Effective Risk-Management Tool.* Paper presented at the National Fraud Summit, Sydney, Australia.

Sproule, S., and N. Archer. 2008. "Measuring Identity Theft in Canada: 2006 Consumer Survey." *McMaster eBusiness Research Centre Working Paper #21.* Hamilton, Ontario: DeGroote School of Business, McMaster University.

Sproule, S., and N. Archer. 2008b. *Measuring Identity Theft in Canada: 2008 consumer survey*. McMaster eBusiness Research Centre Working Paper #23. Hamilton, Ontario: DeGroote School of Business, McMaster University.

Sproule, S., and N. Archer. 2010. "Measuring Identity Theft and Identity Fraud." *International Journal of Business Governance and Ethics*, 5: 1/2: 51–63.

Taylor-Butts, A., and S. Perreault. 2009. "Fraud against Businesses in Canada: Results from a National Survey." Ottawa: Statistics Canada, 17. http://www. statcan.gc.ca/pub/85-571-x/2009001/aftertoc-aprestdm1-eng.htm [consulted January 2, 2010].

Chapter 7

Managing the Risks of Data Theft, Identity Theft and Fraud

"Men occasionally stumble over the truth, but most of them pick themselves up and hurry off as if nothing had happened."
—Winston Churchill

The focus of this chapter is on the development of a general model for managing data, identity theft and fraud risks. The purpose of the model is to provide advice in how to contain and counter such risks in an organized manner. The model's concept is similar for organizations and for consumers, although the details of the risks and how to manage them differ substantially between these two classifications. Small businesses also differ from large businesses in the approach they need to take to managing IDTF risks, because they typically cannot afford to employ security specialists to manage these risks, but usually assign this responsibility to an employee as just one among multiple responsibilities. For this reason, the first section of this chapter deals with an organizational model for large organizations, the second section tailors the organizational model to small and medium business, and the third deals with the same conceptual model but adapted specifically for consumers.

Organizational IDTF Risk Management

Identity theft and fraud criminal activities are, or should be, strong motivators for governments and organizations to protect and secure their systems, databases and other assets against intrusion and loss. The continuing increase in the number and cost of data breaches, primarily from external attacks, should be incentive enough to assign a high priority to securing the organization against such attacks. A recent survey of IT security specialists at Canadian organizations (Hejazi and Lefort 2008) studied the costs of data breaches and found that these are growing at a rapid rate, with average annual loss per organization now exceeding $400,000. This figure can provide some guidance in determining suitable resource allocation to manage related issues, subject of course to the size of the organization and those aspects of its operations that involve confidential databases.

Although the focus of this book is on IDTF, this specific risk is only one of multiple risks that need to be addressed in an integrated manner through enterprise risk management (ERM) (Beasley, Clune et al. 2005; Fraser, Schoening-Thiessen et al. 2007; Walker and Shenkir 2008). ERM is emerging as a new paradigm for policy makers interested in mechanisms to improve corporate governance and risk management. Information security and privacy assurance are responsibilities in all organizations, but setting up a comprehensive fully-assured environment is likely to be both technically and financially difficult. Organizations often handle these responsibilities with a 'bottom up,' ad hoc and uncoordinated perspective that deals separately with each type of risk and has no comprehensive plan. In the case of IDTF, this may mean certifying individual systems through ad hoc processes or by focusing on protection from external threats alone. What organizations need is a comprehensive, enterprise-wide risk management approach that is economically practicable and that includes the management of information security and privacy across the organization. The requirements must be addressed through both business processes and the technical infrastructure (Anderson and Rachamadugu 2008), beginning with a knowledge base of both processes and infrastructures that can support strategic planning and prioritized risk-based investment and management.

Based partially on a framework proposed by Jamieson, Smith et al. (2009) for managing IDTF in organizations, we will develop frameworks in this chapter for managing risks from IDTF, first for medium to large organizations, then for small businesses and then for consumers. The organizational perspective differs between medium to large organizations and small organizations due primarily to the resources, organizational units and strategies required. For consumers, the perspectives are again different, since consumer concerns are directed towards protecting themselves as individuals, while organizations need to guard against both internal and external threats to the organization and to its customers. Our model in each instance is based on the three phases of Jamieson et al.'s model (anticipatory, reactionary and remediation) for managing identity fraud in organizations, with a significant adaptation of the model for consumer management of identity theft.

Managing IDTF Risks

In this section, we develop a general framework for organizations and individuals to manage and mitigate IDTF threats. The framework includes three phases in a process that can deal with different aspects: a) understand the threats, b) mitigate the threats where this can be done cost-effectively, c) react to IDTF attacks that occur, d) use the results from such events as feedback to the management process and reduce the likelihood of recurrence, and e) improve the management and control of such events in the future. The three-phase process includes

- An Anticipatory Phase, where actions are taken to protect the organization against IDTF perpetrators. We include within this phase IDTF policy development, risk assessment, risk avoidance, elimination or mitigation, deterrence and prevention activities.
- A Reactionary Phase, in which steps are taken to manage IDTF attacks that occur, including detection, analysis, mitigation and review.

- A Remediation Phase, which manages the process after an attack has occurred, including recovery, policy and deterrence adjustment, and investigation and prosecution of the guilty party or parties.

These phases are spelled out in more detail below, with several specific examples. Many of the fraudulent activities discussed do not necessarily stem from identity theft, but they may be planned for and handled in the same manner since fraud can arise from many different sources. Actions taken against IDTF will also impact on the management of a wide variety of activities, including the control of computer viruses, software updates, employee authentication and sign-on. It should also be abundantly clear from the description of these phases that an increase in the time and effort put into the anticipatory phase will reduce time and resources spent and losses incurred in recovery mode during the Reactionary and Remediation phases, if and when threats materialize into actual attacks. Figure 7.1 depicts the relationships among the three phases, including feedback from the Reactionary and Remediation phases to the Anticipatory Phase so that appropriate adjustments to policies, risk avoidance or mitigation, and prevention can be made when experience has been gained due to an IDTF attack that is occurring or has occurred.

Business Management of IDTF Risks

Anticipatory Phase

Formulating policy and developing an IDTF approach requires defining organizational threats and planning how to manage them. Since IDTF is not the only risk that an organization faces, organizations should engage in a holistic approach to develop a written governance policy for *enterprise risk assessment and management* within an evolving business environment, where IDTF risks are just one component. For example, firms buy fire, casualty and theft insurance to help manage certain physical risks. Although

Figure 7.1: Framework for Managing IDTF Risks

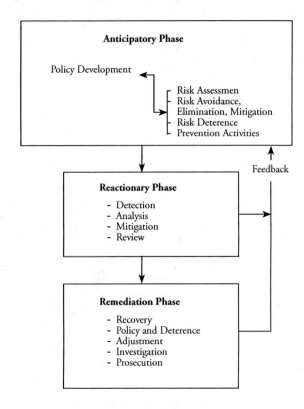

IDTF can involve physical theft, it can also involve attacks on virtual systems, requiring a change in mindset to understand and evaluate virtual risks like online IDTF in a manner that dovetails with managing physical risks. All employees with responsibilities for information content must be made aware of the organization's risk management and governance document and should sign off on its contents, their responsibilities for maintaining adherence to it and any actions that should be taken to enforce its provisions. Enterprise risk assessment and management may involve a number of technologies, including records management, document management, web content management, workflow, business process management, enterprise and digital rights management, identity management, content authentication, online record posting and contextual information filtering (Frappaolo 2006). Using a combination of these technologies to develop a dynamic information access solution requires the development of enterprise policies, procedures and disciplines. These should be adopted by management and explicitly followed, along with a plan of action for when, not just if, a data breach and/or fraud occurs.

Application of business rules provides intelligent assistance to help employees manage content, so employees can be informed of corrective actions to safely create, use, distribute, modify or destroy business content. Regulatory bodies may require particular compliance policies, but it is important to ensure that the technical interpretation of these regulatory rules agrees with the organization's legal interpretation.

Canada has a federal privacy commissioner who regulates privacy issues covered under the Personal Information Protection and Electronic Documents Act (PIPEDA). The federal privacy commissioner's website at http://www.privcom.gc.ca/information/guide_e.cfm gives considerable information on PIPEDA coverage and how to conform to the Act. In addition, British Columbia, Alberta, Ontario and Quebec have their own privacy commissioners and their own privacy acts that govern privacy in these jurisdictions. Organizations that are subject to provincial legislation deemed substantially similar to the federal PIPEDA legislation are exempt from PIPEDA with respect to the collection, use or disclosure of personal information occurring within the respective province. For example, Alberta has a Personal Information Protection Act (PIPA). More details about PIPA are available at the Alberta privacy commissioner's website at http://pipa.alberta.ca/.

Since 2008, US financial institutions and creditors have been required to develop and implement documented programs to detect, prevent and mitigate instances of identity theft. This extensive program is known as the Red Flags Rules (Federal Trade

Commission 2008) and it is part of the US Fair and Accurate Credit Transactions Act (FACTA) of 2003. It is basically a directed program that financial institutions and creditors must implement to identify and mitigate IDTF risks, to detect and report violations when they occur (i.e., Red Flags) and to take corrective action when needed to update the program. Red Flags Rules programs may include, for example, monitoring for unusual account activity, fraud alerts on a consumer report or attempted use of suspicious account application documents. The program also covers medical practices that are typically creditors for patients who receive medical services, in an attempt to address the growing issues related to medical IDTF (see Chapter 10 for a detailed discussion of medical IDTF). Red Flags programs must be managed by a board of directors or senior employees of the financial institution or creditor. They must include appropriate staff training and oversight of any service providers. Red Flags is a template that should be of value to any company that is building a program to deal with IDTF.

IDTF risk assessment involves evaluating all of the potential threats to the organization, including their likelihood of occurring and their impact if they do occur. This includes not just the direct losses from not being able to access potentially valuable identity information but additional losses due to a decline in trust in the company (a major reason why companies are reluctant to admit to database breaches) and potential lawsuits from disgruntled customers, fines from government agencies or lawsuits from other companies affected by stolen identity data. Data breaches of major databases containing confidential records of thousands of consumers and customers are becoming more commonplace. An example (already mentioned briefly in Chapter 5) that illustrates these problems was the theft of personal data in 2004 by Nigerian fraudsters. This data breach affected a database containing the records of more than 163,000 consumers at ChoicePoint, a major US data broker. The theft was made public in February 2005 due to a California state statute stipulating that, if corporate computer systems are breached and the information is unencrypted, companies must notify all individuals affected. ChoicePoint acknowledged that it had focused entirely on preventing hackers from gaining access to its computers and had overlooked operations processes for screening business partners. This allowed fraudsters to become business partners by exploiting ChoicePoint's business practices, where they were able to gain access to consumer identity information in the company's database. That kind of vulnerability can best be uncovered by using risk assessments conducted by the operations team as part of an overall enterprise risk management approach (Minsky 2006). The US Federal Trade Commission assessed ChoicePoint a $10 million fine for security and record-handling procedures that violated the rights of consumers. In another large and more recent (2008) breach of online transactions at Heartland, a major US debit and credit card processor, it was necessary for the card issuers to cancel and reissue a large number of payment cards. Heartland was liable for paying the card issuers for the related costs (Vijayan 2009), in addition to customer and business lawsuits they were likely to face.

As employees and organizations continue to increase telecommuting activities due to the wider availability of broadband connections, the security of remote connectivity to corporate and government networks becomes increasingly important to overall network security (Kuhn, Tracy et al. 2002). Linking secure organizational networks to home networks requires the consideration of many different applications, protocols and architectures. Home broadband architectures (e.g., home wireless) are easier to attack than dial-up connections because of the faster, always-on qualities of broadband and the lack of a consistently high awareness of the risks posed by these systems and the need to guard against unauthorized access. Increasingly, criminals target telecommuter and corporate wireless networks (typically Wi-Fi) and external connections to gain access to related government and corporate networks. For example, what is claimed by the US Department of Justice to be the single largest and most complex hacking and identity theft crime ever prosecuted was announced in August 2008 (USDOJ 2008). After a three-year investigation, eleven men were charged with numerous crimes that involved alleged 'war driving,' during which they hacked into the wireless networks of nine companies (including the TJX corporation) to steal more than forty million consumer credit and debit card numbers. The TJX data breach was alleged to have occurred because of weak WEP encryption[1] at two of its Marshalls stores in Miami, allowing the personal and financial details of their customers to be stolen.

This incident is a warning to both consumers and companies that use or provide wireless network access to systems. Consumers and employees currently use in excess of one billion personal computers and even more mobile phones to send and receive personal data, transact business and share information. Companies that carry and store such information for both consumers and telecommuters have a duty of care to keep it safe from unauthorized access, both during transmission and in storage.

The examples described above involve external threats to the company. While these can be substantial, there are also internal threats from employees, possibly in collusion with outside criminals. Insider attacks are the most difficult to prevent because these are legitimate users using legitimate access for inappropriate purposes. Insiders aren't the most common security problem, but they can be among the most costly and the most damaging to a company's reputation (Greenemeier 2006). Insiders are those who have access to information, and they know where the valuable information is. Trusted insiders may present significant risks to the organization. They possess elevated privileges when compared to external users, have knowledge about technical and non-technical control

[1] Wired Equivalent Privacy (WEP) is an IEEE standard security protocol for wireless 802.11 (Wi-Fi) networks. Introduced in 1997, WEP was found to be inadequate and was superseded by WPA, WPA2 and 802.11i. Its authentication method was extremely weak and even helped an attacker decipher the secret encryption key. As a result, WEP authentication was dropped from the Wi-Fi specification. http://www.pcmag.com/encyclopedia_term/0,2542,t=WEP&i=54412,00.asp (accessed February 19 2009).

measures and potentially can bypass security measures designed to prevent, detect or react to unauthorized access. Best practices are available for preventing, detecting and mitigating insider attacks, including applications of risk management principles specific to insider threats (Brown 2009; Mills, Peterson et al. 2009). These threats must also be considered in the risk assessment process; a recent survey indicated that internal threats are responsible for about the same amount of damage as external threats (CSO Magazine 2007). From this same survey, techniques being used by insiders were found to include social engineering, i.e., manipulation of a person or persons who can permit or facilitate access to a system or data (45%), using compromised accounts (39%), copying secure information to mobile devices like USB drives (36%) and using their own accounts (36%). Another more recent survey (King 2008) indicated that 40% of workers worried about job security might steal sensitive corporate data. These figures show that multiple techniques are used by some employees. Over 70% admitted they would steal sensitive data if they were fired suddenly and would take the data to their next employer or use it as a negotiating tool with their current employers. Even workers content in their jobs sometimes access material not intended for their eyes.

Risk Reduction. When the organization's IDTF policy is in place and a complete assessment of both external and internal IDTF risks is available, steps should be taken to mitigate the relevant risks, beginning with those that are potentially the most serious threats to the organization. Continuing education, empowerment and enforcement are probably the most critical ways to create a climate of security for administrators and users, utilizing and reinforcing the message that everyone has a responsibility for information security. This can play a key role in risk mitigation, and the development of a comprehensive and continuing educational program for employees is essential. Gaining the trust, support and cooperation of management and employees through education concerning IDTF risks and how to manage them is likely to have as much impact as behind the scenes technological solutions.

There are various online listings of precautions that businesses should take to reduce or eliminate IDTF (e.g., IPC/Ontario 2007). As an example, Brown (2009) gives several logical steps that can be used to reduce, deter or prevent potential IDTF risks, as shown in Table 7.1.

Table 7.1: Reducing, Deterring and Preventing IDTF

- Ensure that the histories of all new hires, including permanent and temporary employees, consultants, agency and outsourced functions (including cleaning and security staff) are fully investigated for previous fraud or falsified curriculum vitae (CVs) and references.
- Regularly encourage employees to highlight areas of security concerns that will help reduce threats from both internal and external sources, perhaps through confidential surveys.
- Segregate duties, such as controlling expenditures and how they are accounted for. If this is not possible, another approach is to reassign responsibilities to different members of the team. Strongly encouraging employees to take their holidays and vacations will also result in early discovery of internal fraud activities.
- Encourage an open working environment where people are more willing to contribute to the well-being of the organization, resulting in more satisfied employees who are less likely to engage in fraudulent activities.
- Use proper procurement procedures such as regular tendering and independent review of procurement decisions. Examine how suppliers are linked to system accounts and how inactive accounts are closed out.
- Track suspense accounts and reconciliations to ensure that cash is not disappearing in the accounting process (e.g., losses due to rounding that may be drained off into a fraudulent account set up for that purpose).
- Do not neglect business processes in subsidiaries and branches that may run more or less independently with little head office oversight.
- If some business or accounting process does not seem to be logical, should follow it up until an explanation is forthcoming.

- Use surprise such as unexpected visits and questions to keep potential fraudsters off balance and help to prevent fraud from either starting or continuing.

(adapted from Brown 2009)

Governments are moving to address increased risks due to security breaches of institutional and corporate databases by updating laws and increasing the penalties for such criminal activities (Warren 2007). Risk mitigation may also involve a review of the impact of such risks on privacy. One way to help protect against theft of private information about both customers and employees is to follow the guidelines specified by the privacy commissioner(s) that have jurisdiction over the region(s) where the company operates. This should include a well-documented process that lays out how the company is complying with the legislated requirements, putting the company in a good position to defend the business against any allegations that might be brought against it. At the same time, this would also help a business to resist any attacks on confidential databases by hackers and others intending to do the company harm.

The improvement of data protection legislation and codes of practice for privacy also force organizations to review their operations and systems designs through Privacy Impact Assessments (PIAs). PIAs have been a privacy analysis tool used in Canada and New Zealand and are being considered by the United Kingdom (Warren 2007). PIAs, for example, must be considered when any personal information is being collected, used or disclosed for any work done within or for the Canadian government. The intent is to ensure that new technologies, information systems and initiatives or proposed programs and policies meet basic privacy requirements, thus addressing the potential for loss of privacy. A PIA also assists government organizations to anticipate the public's reaction to any privacy implications of a proposal and, as a result, can prevent costly program, service or process redesign.

In particular, PIAs could assist in assessing privacy risks resulting from the expansion and/or merger of government databases (Warren 2007). Such activities are often associated with the implementation of e-government systems, used to reduce costs and improve citizen online interaction with government services. Common privacy risks that may be identified through privacy impact assessments (TreasuryBoard 2002) include data profiling or data matching; transaction monitoring; identification of individuals; physical observation of individuals; publishing or re-distribution of public databases containing personal information; and lack of or doubtful legal authority.

Reactionary Phase

Once a policy for IDTF management is in place, monitoring for attacks must be a continuous process to detect, analyze, remedy and review any such attacks that occur.

Events that are appearing more frequently in current news are data breaches, closely related to privacy breaches. A privacy breach occurs when there is unauthorized access to or collection, use or disclosure of personal information. Such activity is 'unauthorized' if it occurs in contravention of applicable privacy legislation, such as the Health Insurance Portability and Accountability Act (HIPAA) in the United States, PIPEDA in Canada, or similar state or provincial privacy legislation. Some of the most common privacy breaches happen when personal information of customers, patients, clients or employees is stolen, lost or mistakenly disclosed (e.g., a computer containing personal information is stolen or personal information is mistakenly e-mailed to the wrong people). A privacy breach may also be a consequence of faulty business procedures or operational breakdowns (Privacy Commissioner of Canada 2007). Note that, although there is a relatively stiff law that regulates identity theft and fraud in the United States, there is no US law that provides a guarantee of privacy for citizen records that might be accessed through the

Internet. As a consequence, data brokers can gather and sell private information with no fear of prosecution, as long as it is not obtained or used fraudulently.

Most US states have adopted legislation requiring public disclosure of database breaches of non-encrypted identity information. The US Federal Trade Commission, in fact, provides guidance on how to go about notifying those affected by such occurrences (FTC 2004). Canadian legislation is beginning to appear that will govern data breach notification. Consideration is being given to modifying PIPEDA rules, which apply wherever individual provinces do not have their own privacy acts. The federal privacy commissioner has published guidelines relating to data breaches but they are voluntary and not enforceable until included in a modified PIPEDA. However, the provinces of Alberta and Ontario have mandatory data breach notification regulations.

A large part of information systems (IS) security research is technical in nature with limited consideration of people and organizational issues. Given the fact that the majority of security violations are 'inside jobs,' the organizational and people aspects of security deserve much more consideration. For example, one study (Dhillon and Torkzadeh 2006) adopted a broader perspective of IS security in terms of the values of people from an organizational perspective. This survey used a value-focused approach to identify the fundamental objectives for IS security and the means of achieving them in an organization. Data were collected through in-depth interviews with 103 managers about their values in managing IS security. The findings from this study go well beyond technical considerations and adopt organizationally grounded principles and values.

Monitoring internal staff for harmful activities is as important as managing potential external attacks. If prevention is not sufficient, organizations must be able to detect malicious insider activities and respond expeditiously to analyze, remedy and review the nature of the attacks to assist in future prevention. Preferably, the detection system will be able to detect any illegal activity immediately, but it must have the ability to detect genuinely suspicious activities while ignoring legitimate operations (Mills, Peterson et al. 2009). However, if an insider is highly skilled at evading detection, it may be difficult to distinguish between normal authorized and illegal activities. The primary difficulty in dealing with insider threats is that by definition insiders are trusted, so they possess elevated privileges and insider knowledge when compared to external users. While there are common motivational factors, such as greed and revenge, people who have been caught performing malicious acts do not fit a standard profile (Mills, Peterson et al. 2009). There are a large number of potential observables that could be tracked in order to monitor potentially illegal insider activity (Brackney and Anderson 2004). These include calling patterns, e-mail patterns, travel/vacation, trouble tickets, system logs, network intrusion detection system logs, maintenance schedules, keyboard logs and file system logs. These can be monitored with commercial software on digital systems but are virtually impossible to track on paper-based systems. There is a significant amount of recent literature that discusses what to monitor and how to monitor it efficiently and successfully (e.g., Fry and Nystrom 2009).

In times of economic decline, employee layoffs are endemic. Most employees will resign themselves to the bad news, but a small fraction may react with aggression, either through physical means or by sabotaging data and information systems. Supervisors and managers of employees can provide input on employees who may not handle the news well. While great efforts need to be taken to preserve worker dignity during layoff procedures, steps should be taken to immediately terminate access to information systems, and problematic employees need to be watched closely for potential physical reactions such as copying or destroying sensitive data files.

Remediation Phase

Disaster recovery planning and ensuring business continuity are essential to every firm. However, IDTF is not just more complex than other threats; in addition, it poses a significant threat to the firm's data, which is its lifeblood. The American Data Recovery Association estimates that US small businesses lose over $10 billion per year due to data breaches, and Gartner Corporation claims that 40% of small businesses will go out of business if they cannot get to their data in the first twenty-four hours after a crisis (Serenity Systems 2008). An even more serious situation applies if the data breach involves the theft of private client data. A data breach, whether discovered or suspected, must be taken seriously, and the organization must move quickly to investigate, as follows (Privacy Commissioner of Canada 2007): 1) breach containment and preliminary assessment; 2) evaluation of risks associated with the breach; 3) notification; and 4) prevention.

1) *Breach containment and preliminary assessment.* This step involves immediately containing the suspected breach; designating an individual with responsibility to lead an investigation of the breach; determining who should be informed internally and possibly externally; notifying the police if theft or other criminal activity is involved; and taking care not to destroy evidence that could be useful to remedy the problem or to find and prosecute the criminal.

2) *Evaluation of risks associated with the breach.* If personal information has been accessed, it is important to determine its sensitivity and context, with combinations of personal information being particularly sensitive; if the information is adequately encrypted or anonymized to reduce its accessibility, this greatly reduces the risk; if the information can be used to commit fraud, the risk is higher; if it is lost rather than stolen, the risk may be less. The cause and extent of the breach are used to determine whether it is an isolated incident or systemic problem; how many outsiders or employees are affected by the breach; the foreseeable harm and types of harm from the breach, as determined by the reasonable expectations of the individuals involved; who the recipients are

and what if any are their relationships to the individuals; and the harm to the organization or the public as a result of the breach.

3) *Notification*. Considering all legal or contractual obligations and the risk of harm to individuals (including IDTF, physical harm or humiliation) and the ability of individuals to avoid possible harm, notification may be essential. Notification should occur as soon as reasonably possible, but with the advice of law enforcement authorities. It is preferable to notify the affected individuals directly. If there is a direct relationship with the individuals affected, then the organization should notify them. However, a third party like a credit card issuer might be appropriate to notify all the individuals concerned. There are commercial firms that can assist in the notification process (e.g., Voisin 2008). Privacy commissioners and other regulatory agencies should also be notified, so they can respond to public enquiries about the breach.

4) *Prevention*. It is essential to investigate the cause of a breach and to consider whether to revise the IDTF prevention plan, especially if it is a systemic breach. This may include an audit of physical and technical security; policies and procedures to include any lessons learned; employee training practices; and service delivery partners (e.g., dealers, retailers, etc.). The revised plan may also include a final audit to ensure that the prevention plan has been implemented adequately.

Even with the best controlled environment, fraud can still happen. When internal fraud occurs, the organization must act quickly and decisively, and, if the allegation is proved, prosecution of the individuals involved sends a clear message to all employees that they should not take the risk of being caught in fraudulent activities (Brown 2009). External fraud is more difficult to prosecute, but the authorities should be notified and given full cooperation to ensure that the culprits are tracked down and prosecuted. Websites like Safe Canada,[2] Canadian Credit Report[3] and the US branch of Interpol[4] provide links to the appropriate agencies for both consumer and business identity theft and fraud complaints. Unfortunately, much external IDTF involves overseas criminals, but more is being done to develop links with agencies like Interpol that can reach across boundaries to bring fraudsters to justice. In addition, customers and others affected by data breaches must be notified. While this is not required as yet in any Canadian provinces other than Alberta, the majority of US states have legislation that requires notification of data breaches. Along with the US Red Flags Rules (Federal Trade Commission 2008), this forces organizations to commit resources to formal enterprise risk management processes and procedures, tending to reduce IDTF across the board.

Schreft (2007) suggests that the private sector cannot by itself protect online payment systems, beyond adopting security standards. The main reason is that there must be monitoring of compliance and penalties imposed on companies that do not comply. In the United States, this function for interstate commerce is managed by the Federal Trade Commission, which can impose stiff penalties on non-compliant firms. In Canada, the creation of new laws and the policing of these laws to enforce organizational compliance in the protection of identity information and privacy has lagged technology. At the same time, technological advances have changed the functions for which people use computers and have allowed legal and illegal markets in personal identity information to grow exponentially. The open market itself does not provide protection against IDTF, requiring government intervention to protect the integrity and efficiency of the payment system. Current government efforts to control identity theft almost exclusively take the form of consumer protections, law enforcement initiatives and regulatory oversight of banks and their affiliates,

---

2 http://www.safecanada.ca/identitytheft_e.asp.

3 http://canadian-creditreport.com/identitytheft.htm.

4 http://www.usdoj.gov/usncb/.

but do not adequately address the market failures associated with asymmetric information, externalities and the provision of public goods (Schreft 2007).

It is unlikely that Canadian organizations will commit voluntarily to notifying customers in the case of data breaches, since it might give their competitors an unfair advantage in the case of a breach. For this reason, legislation covering data breach notification is the responsibility of the Canadian and provincial governments if there is to be a level playing field for all organizations, and to help combat the likely migration of criminal IDTF activities across the border to Canada where IDTF criminals may be less likely to be prosecuted.

Small and Medium Business Framework for Managing and Controlling IDTF Risks

Small and medium enterprises (SMEs) typically do not have the resources to develop full-scale plans and major undertakings for IDTF prevention. However, commonsense applications of simple principles can go a long way toward mitigating typical small business risks from IDTF. In this section, we briefly outline suggested adaptations of the general framework for SMEs. It also includes activities under the three phases: Anticipatory, Reactionary and Remediation. As before, the framework involves understanding the threats, mitigating the threats where this can be done reasonably, reacting to IDTF attacks that occur and using the results from such events to reduce the likelihood of recurrence to improve the management and control of such risks in the future.

Anticipatory Phase

Developing and implementing a company policy that is compliant with privacy regulations relevant to the jurisdiction(s) in which the SME operates is the best way to protect the business against IDTF. This both reduces the probability of such an event and protects the organization against the aftermath that could result from such an event. Note that privacy commissioners in Canada don't automatically dish out fines for not following regulations. They are more likely to rely on persuasion to encourage organizational compliance with regulations. If they receive a complaint from a citizen or business that an organization is alleged to have violated privacy legislation, they do have the power to investigate the organization and to get a court order if necessary to shut down the offending operation until it is brought into compliance. The complaining citizen(s) or organization can also bring a civil or class action against the organization if they are so inclined, although to be successful the complainant needs to show causation between the violation and harm to the complainant. To handle technological details, SMEs often do not have the resources to employ full-time technical support staff. It may be necessary to outsource the necessary support to a reputable firm, while at the same time assigning full responsibility to an employee charged with managing company security to work with the supplier firm.

A good source of information on protecting SME personal information databases has been published by the Alberta government agency Access, Privacy and Security, Service Alberta to help prepare for compliance under that province's Personal Information Protection Act (PIPA) (APSS Alberta 2008). A related Alberta government document on the process to implement a compliant company policy has also been published (Private Sector Privacy 2008).

Risk mitigation activities include those outlined in the corresponding subsection for larger corporations, as outlined above. However, particular attention should be paid to risk mitigation activities such as those outlined in Table 7.2.

Table 7.2: Risk Mitigation in Small to Medium Organizations

- Follow processes recommended by the relevant privacy commissioner or other official agency to develop, document and implement a privacy policy to ensure the company is in compliance with the privacy regulations. This will reduce the likelihood of such a breach while at the same time helping to protect the company against liability in the case of a data breach.
- Be constantly on the lookout for corporate identity theft activities that include stealing the identity of a company and fraudulently trading under that name (often through a website) without the knowledge of the company's legitimate owners. It may be necessary to employ a monitoring company to ensure fraudsters have not compromised your business identity.
- Guard against the theft of employee and client identities by taking due care in discarding sensitive employee and customer information, including home addresses, phone numbers and photocopies of passports.
- Check to make sure your customers are genuine before entering into business transactions with them.
- Dispose of sensitive material in a secure way (usually through shredding).
- If private data such as medical records are being stored for either employees or customers, be sure to obtain individual consent to collect, store and analyze that data.
- Keep production and test databases separate.
- Do not allow any employee other than the person designated with security responsibilities to access the production database.
- Log all accesses to confidential data files, so when files are accessed a record is retained of who accessed them and when. Check these logs regularly to spot and take action on any irregularities that might appear.
- Encrypt confidential data.
- Do not allow anyone to download unencrypted confidential data, since it may be stored on unprotected computers (laptop or office computers) and be easily stolen. Such thefts have caused major scandals in Canada and elsewhere, and have done irreparable harm to the companies and institutions involved. Web viewers that do

not allow files to be downloaded from the company database are preferable to allow authorized users to access data as required.

- Canadian companies should not store databases physically in the United States, since US authorities may access any such databases under any implied need for information through the US PATRIOT Act, with little legal redress by the business affected (PATRIOT Act 2006).
- Consider moving production databases offsite to a reputable and well-protected server farm. This will support fail-over and regular backups, strong firewall protection, strong physical protection and continuous operation in the event of a disastrous event at the company site plant (fire, explosion, theft, power outage, etc.).

Reactionary Phase

In the reactionary phase, steps are taken to manage IDTF attacks that occur. This includes reporting IDTF incidents to authorities, including banks, credit agencies and police. These and other priorities appear in online listings of precautions needed to protect the identity and privacy of employees and customers (e.g., IPC/Ontario 2007).

Remediation Phase

Activities in this phase are similar to those discussed above for larger organizations. Management should always consider taking legal action where necessary to protect the firm from perceived external and internal threats. There is no Canada-wide legislation requiring the company, should someone hack into a database containing personal information, to advertise that a database breach has occurred, but such legislation is likely to be adopted in the future. Most American states have such requirements in place, so, in the event of a breach of a database containing information on citizens of that state, everyone whose information is stored in the compromised database must be informed that their information may have been accessed by unauthorized users. Such an incident would clearly have a negative public relations impact on a business.

Consumer Framework for Combating IDTF Risks

The framework for consumers also includes three phases: Anticipatory, Reactionary and Remediation. As before, the framework involves understanding the threats, mitigating the threats where this can be done reasonably, reacting to IDTF attacks that occur and using the results from such events to reduce the likelihood of recurrence in order to improve the management and control of such risks in the future. Some of the suggestions for larger firms in the previous section are also relevant, and those areas of particular focus for SMEs are also very useful.

Anticipatory Phase

In this phase, actions are taken to protect against identity theft and fraud perpetrators. Included in this phase are commonsense planning; risk assessment; risk avoidance, elimination or mitigation; deterrence; and prevention activities. There are many online sources of information on identifying and mitigating potential sources of consumer IDTF (e.g., Milne, Rohm et al. 2004; CMC 2008; Rutgers 2008). Many of these contain useful checklists for assessing individual knowledge and activities that will help consumers avoid many of the obvious pitfalls.

Table 7.3 is a composite checklist, assembled from several sources, suggesting ways in which consumers can guard against physical identity theft.

Table 7.3: Consumer Tips on Guarding against Identity Theft

- Never give personal information by phone, Internet or mail, unless you initiate the contact yourself.
- Be careful about sharing personal information, and don't give out more than you really need to.
- Shield your PIN when using it, and never lend credit, debit or other identification cards.
- Don't write your PIN down where it might be accessed by a stranger.

- Carry only the ID that you need.
- Put other ID documents (SIN or SSN, birth certificate, passport) in a safe place.
- Your SIN or SSN should only be used for employment and tax reporting.
- Dispose of sensitive material in a secure way (usually through shredding).
- Ask about security of your information at work and with businesses and charities.
- Save credit card receipts and check them against creditor statements. Don't leave them in shopping bags where they might be stolen.
- Use a post office box or locked mailbox for incoming mail.
- Place outgoing mail in a secured collection box or post office.
- Have mail held while away or picked up by a trusted friend, neighbour or family member.
- Do not leave personal information where it might be accessible to someone when you are not there.
- Delete credit card and bank account numbers on receipts submitted for travel expenses.
- Place postcards with sensitive information in mailing envelopes.
- Do not leave purse or wallet unattended; zip purse shut; button back wallet pocket; use house lights on timers when away.
- Keep confidential information and valuable documents in a safety deposit box.
- Keep lists of credit card numbers and contact information to report loss quickly.

Table 7.4 is a list of tips on how to guard a computer and its information against identity theft.

Table 7.4 Consumer Tips to Guard Against Computer Identity Theft

- Do not complete Internet 'profiles' for rebates and contests, listings, etc.
- Select complex passwords composed of letters, numbers and symbols.
- Install firewall, anti-virus, anti-spyware and security software, and update frequently.

- Don't try, don't buy and don't reply to spam or e-mails asking for banking or other account information.
- For online transactions, look for https://, a closed lock or an unbroken key icon.
- When disposing of hard drives, use overwrite software or destroy the drive.

A 2008 survey of Canadian consumers showed that media reporting and other educational efforts have had an effect on some consumer behaviours (Sproule and Archer 2008). In terms of physical threats to personal information, 79% of consumers shred documents with sensitive information, 59% use a locked mailbox and 57% keep sensitive documents in a secure location. Half of the respondents had reduced the number of identity documents they carry with them and 30% had stopped or reduced the use of mailed statements and converted to online monitoring of bank and utility accounts.

In terms of social threats, 92% of Canadian consumers reported that they rarely or never give information over the phone for surveys or promotions, and 88% are careful that no one is watching at ATMs or point-of-sale debit terminals. Thirty-five percent say they have stopped or reduced giving their credit cards to waiters and gas station attendants where the card will leave their sight. Hard-to-break passwords are used by 75% of consumers and 50% use different passwords for different applications. Most change their passwords every two to five years, but fully 30% have never changed their passwords.

A further statistical analysis of data from this survey (Gilbert and Archer, 2011) modeled the relationship between past experience of consumers and their levels of concern, and derived the principal components that make up consumer behaviours. The principal components found were physical prevention measures, account monitoring, agency monitoring, password security and risky behaviour avoidance. These components were found to be almost orthogonal, implying that consumers tend to 'buy into' a particular type of behaviour. This indicates that consumers use all the behaviours in one component without regard to other components, potentially leaving 'holes' in their defences against IDTF. Consumer education on IDTF should therefore stress that consumers need to employ all behaviours that can minimize risk and loss.

There are two distinct approaches that individuals must consider. The first focuses on education and publicity about preventive measures to reduce risk proactively (both likelihood and loss if a theft occurs), encouraging citizens to alter aspects of their regular routines to reduce their risk of victimization. This addresses citizens whose daily routines, home environment, consumption patterns and sense of self are modified through education and awareness to reduce the risk of identity theft while living in a society of strangers (Whitson and Haggerty 2008). The second is focused on the reaction to an actual identity theft and/or fraud occurrence. Whereas most crime victims are expected to do little more than contact the police, identity theft victims are in a position such that they are the most responsible for rectifying their situation. This typically involves a program of self-documentation and communication that works towards re-establishing trust with the institutional identity issuer, checker or protector (see Chapter 3) with which the victim is dealing (Whitson and Haggerty 2008).

High-quality, inexpensive computers, colour printers and small office/home office software have been very helpful in making modern business efficient. Perhaps ironically, however, the production of large quantities of counterfeited credentials is a direct consequence of these same computing appliances and productivity applications. Two of the most egregious and worrisome applications of counterfeited credentials have been the development of false IDs for terrorists, who may use them to cross borders, and the counterfeiting of law enforcement IDs by posers for home/office invasion (Berghel 2006). These problems continue to get worse as technology advances, and every step by identity issuers and identity checkers (see Chapter 3) to introduce countermeasures by improving the quality of individual identity credentials and their authentication is matched eventually by criminal counteraction. This results in an unending cycle of security maintenance at levels high enough to counteract the upward spiral of risk from criminal activities. In order to upgrade ID countermeasures, it is necessary to update credentials on a regular basis. For example, passports are renewed every five or ten years (Canada and the United States, respectively) and credit cards are typically replaced every three or four years.

Kim et al. (2008) found that educating consumers about the security and privacy dangers of the Web, as well as the role of assurance seals on websites, does increase their awareness about and the perceived importance of these seals. Despite this increased awareness, however, there is little association between assurance seals and concerns about privacy and perceived information quality, although the assurance seals were significantly related to security concerns after an educational intervention.

Reactionary Phase

In the Reactionary Phase, steps are taken to detect and manage IDTF attacks. This includes reporting IDTF incidents to relevant agencies, including banks, credit agencies, police, etc. These incidents may involve the theft or illegal use of personal identification like credit cards, driver's licenses, health cards and telephone accounts.

As discussed in Chapter 6, early detection is key to minimizing the costs associated with identity fraud. It is recommended that consumers monitor all of their financial accounts on a regular basis. Online access to bank and credit accounts has greatly facilitated the consumer's ability to do this, and 85% of Canadian consumers report having access to at least one bank account and that they monitor it regularly (Sproule and Archer 2008). It is also recommended that consumers check their credit reports at least annually at the major credit bureaus (Equifax, Experian and TransUnion). Almost one half of Canadian consumers have never done this (Sproule and Archer 2008).

Table 7.5 outlines some signs that identity theft may have occurred.

Table 7.5: Signs of Identity Theft (CMC 2008)

- Purchases not made by you appear on monthly statements.
- Bills arrive on accounts you don't own.
- Collection agencies call about unknown debts.
- Credit card or bank statements don't arrive when expected.
- Credit report shows mystery debts.

If any of these signs occur, or if credit or debits cards are lost, consumers must immediately contact their bank, credit card company and police, as necessary. If police are contacted, they may also refer victims to centralized reporting agencies like the Federal Trade Commision (FTC), in the United States, or the Canadian Anti-Fraud Centre (formerly PhoneBusters), in Canada.

Remediation Phase

Remediation manages the process after an attack has occurred. For consumers, this phase can be financially and psychologically damaging. At least, it involves replacing stolen credit cards, health cards, driver's licenses and other stolen identity cards. If the theft occurs when the individual is on a business trip or vacation, recovery may mean contacting a consulate in the country being visited for assistance. Stolen property and identity scams are reported to the police. The likelihood of stolen property recovery is relatively small, particularly if the criminal is a stranger or is otherwise unknown to the victim. If the crime was perpetrated against a bank account, telephone account or other utility account, or real estate owned by the individual, it may be necessary to prove to the service provider and the police that a criminal, not the victim, was involved in an illegal activity. In some cases, the consumer may need to initiate legal action to recover property or money appropriated by a criminal who was using stolen identity information.

In the United States, the Identity Theft Resource Centre (www. idtheftcentre.org) is a not-for-profit organization that provides assistance to victims throughout the remediation phase. Designed around the same model, the Canadian Identity Theft Support Centre (CITSC) at www.idtheftsupportcentre.org began operations in March 2012.

Summary

A general model was developed in this chapter for managing data, identity theft and fraud risks and was applied in specific ways to manage these risks for large organizations and small and medium businesses and individual consumers. The model includes three phases: Anticipatory (where actions are taken to protect against threats from identity theft and fraud perpetrators); Reactionary (involving the management of IDTF attacks as they occur); and Remediation (managing the process after an attack, including changes in policies and operations, and investigation and prosecution of guilty parties).

For large organizations, the Anticipatory Phase includes formulating policies, developing approaches that define organizational threats and planning how to manage these threats. The Reactionary Phase includes monitoring for external attacks in order to detect, analyze, remedy and review any such attacks that occur. The Remediation Phase includes breach containment and preliminary assessment, evaluation of risks associated with the breach, notification of those affected by the breach both internally and externally, and actions toward prevention of a similar, future breach.

For smaller organizations like SMEs, the actions taken during the three phases are similar to those taken by larger organizations, except that the systems involved are far less complex, and the organization does not have at its disposal the resources of a larger organization to ensure that threats can be planned against, managed when they occur and remediated in the same way. Generally speaking, smaller organizations must assign the responsibility for IDTF risk management to one individual and give that individual the time and resources to ensure that the appropriate level of security is in place and that employees are educated in the nature of such events and the harm that can result from them.

In the Anticipatory Phase, individuals must also develop approaches that help to address IDTF risks, usually in a fairly commonsense manner (e.g., locking sensitive documents in a safety deposit box). To manage the Reactionary Phase, individuals must continually be on guard for the occurrence of such negative events, so they can be detected quickly and managed before they get out of control. For example, bank balances should be monitored regularly to ensure no unauthorized activities have occurred. Finally, individuals must take action quickly if negative IDTF events occur, notifying credit card companies, banks or government agencies immediately if credit cards or other documentation are stolen.

References

Anderson, J. A., and V. Rachamadugu. 2008. *Managing Security and Privacy Integration across Enterprise Business Process and Infrastructure.* 2008 IEEE International Conference on Services Computing, IEEE.

APSS Alberta. 2008. "Personal Information Protection Policy for Small and Medium-size Businesses." Edmonton, Alberta: Access, Privacy and Security, Service Alberta. http://pipa.alberta.ca/index.cfm?page=resources/PerInfoPolicy.html [consulted July 13, 2009].

Beasley, M. S., R. Clune, et al. 2005. "Enterprise Risk Management: An Empirical Analysis of Factors Associated with the Extent of Implementation." *Journal of Accounting and Public Policy*, 24: 521–31.

Berghel, H. 2006. "Fungible Credentials and Next-Generation Fraud." *Communications of the ACM*, 49: 12: 15–19.

Brackney, R., and R. Anderson. 2004. *Understanding the Insider Threat.* CF-196. Santa Monica, CA, RAND Corporation.

Bradbury, D. 2010. "Alberta Becomes First Province to Enact Data Breach Notification Law." *SC Magazine.* http://www.scmagazineus.com/alberta-becomes-first-province-to-enact-data-breach-notification-law/article/169944/# [consulted March 19, 2011].

Brown, A. 2009. "Why Fraud Happens and What to Do about It." *Accountancy Ireland*, 41: 30–31.

CMC. 2008. "Consumer Identity Theft Checklist." Ottawa: Consumer Measures Committee. http://cmcweb.ca/eic/site/cmc-cmc.nsf/eng/fe00088.html [consulted July 10, 2009].

CSO Magazine. 2007. "Over-confidence Is Pervasive Amongst Security Professionals: 2007 E-Crime Watch Survey." *CSO Magazine*. http://www.cert. org/archive/pdf/ecrimesummary07.pdf [consulted April 11, 2009].

Dhillon, G., and G. Torkzadeh. 2006. "Value-Focused Assessment of Information System Security in Organizations." *Information Systems Journal*, 16: 293–314.

Federal Trade Commission. 2008. "FTC Will Grant Six-Month Delay of Enforcement of 'Red Flags' Rule Requiring Creditors and Financial Institutions to Have Identity Theft Prevention Programs." Washington, D.C.: Federal Trade Commission. http://www.ftc.gov/opa/2008/10/redflags.shtm [consulted July 8, 2009].

Frappaolo, C. 2006. "Does Your Content Management Strategy Put You at Risk?" *KMWorld, Information Today*, 14: 12–16.

Fraser, J. R. S., K. Schoening-Thiessen, et al. 2007. "Who Reads What Most Often? A Survey of Enterprise Risk Management Literature Read by Risk Executives." *Journal of Applied Corporate Finance*, 19: 4: 75–81.

Fry, C., and M. Nystrom. 2009. *Security Monitoring*. Sebastopol, CA: O'Reilly Media Inc.

FTC. 2004. "Information Compromise and the Risk of Identity Theft: Guidance for Your Business." Washington, D.C., Federal Trade Commission. http://www. ftc.gov/bcp/edu/pubs/business/idtheft/bus59.pdf [consulted April 11, 2009].

Gilbert, J. and N. Archer 2012 "Consumer Identity Theft and Identity Fraud Detection Behaviours", *Journal of Financial Crime* 19(1) 20–36.

Greenemeier, L. 2006. "How to Spot Insider-Attack Risks in the IT Department." *InformationWeek*, December.

Hejazi, W., and A. Lefort. 2008. "2008 Rotman-Telus Joint Study on Canadian IT Security Practices." Toronto: Rotman School of Management. http://telus.com/ securitystudy [accessed July 9, 2009].

IPC/Ontario. 2007. "Identity Theft: Business Take Note: Steps to Protect Customer Personal Information." Toronto: Information and Privacy Commissioner/Ontario.

Jamieson, R., S. Smith, et al. 2009. "An Approach to Managing Identity Fraud." *Cyber Security and Global Information Assurance: Threat Analysis and Response Solutions*. Hershey, PA: K. J. Knapp, pp. 233–48.

Kim, D. J., C. Steinfield, et al. 2008. "Revisiting the Role of Web Assurance Seals in Business-to-Consumer Electronic Commerce." *Decision Support Systems*, 44: 1000–15.

King, L. 2008 (2 December). "Workers Worried about Job Security Might Steal Corporate Data." *Computerworld UK* http://www.computerworld.com/action/ article.do?command=viewArticleBasic&articleId=9122098 [consulted April 2, 2009].

Kuhn, D. R., M. C. Tracy, et al. 2002. "Security for Telecommuting and Broadband Communications." Washington, D.C.: National Institute of Standards and Technology: 63. http://csrc.nist.gov/publications/nistpubs/800-46/sp800-46. pdf [consulted February 1, 2009].

Mills, R. F., G. L. Peterson, et al. 2009. "Insider Threat Prevention, Detection, and Mitigation." *Cyber Security and Global Information Assurance: Threat Analysis and Response Solutions*. Hershey, PA: K. J. Knapp.

Milne, G. R., A. J. Rohm, et al. 2004. "Consumers' Protection of Online Privacy and Identity." *The Journal of Consumer Affairs*, 38: 2: 217.

Minsky, S. 2006. "Information Security and Enterprise Risk Management." http://www.ebizq.net/blogs/chief_risk_officer/2006/11/information_security_and_entep_1.php [consulted April 11, 2009].

PATRIOT Act. 2006. "Avoiding the Pitfalls: Application of Extraterritorial US Laws to Canadian Businesses." http://www.blakes.com/english/view_disc.asp?ID=223 [consulted March 19, 2011].

Privacy Commissioner of Canada. 2007. "Key Steps for Organizations in Responding to Privacy Breaches." Ottawa: Office of the Privacy Commissioner of Canada. http://www.privcom.gc.ca/information/guide/2007/gl_070801_02_e.asp [consulted April 14, 2009].

Private Sector Privacy. 2008. "Ten Steps to Implement PIPA." Edmonton, Alberta: Government of Alberta. http://pipa.alberta.ca/index.cfm?page=resources/ImplementPIPA.html [consulted July 13, 2009].

Rutgers. 2008. "Identity Theft Risk Assessment Quiz." Rutgers University. http://njaes.rutgers.edu/money/identitytheft/ [consulted April 11, 2009].

Schreft, S. L. 2007. "Risks of Identity Theft: Can the Market Protect the Payment System?" *Economic Review*, 92: 4: 5–40.

Serenity Systems. 2008. "Setting Up Your Infrastructure: Disaster Recovery & Business Continuity Best Practices." Serenity Systems. http://www.serenity-systems.com/Mar%20eNews%20Disaster%20Recovery%20and%20Bus%20Continuity%20Best%20Practices.pdf [consulted April 14, 2009].

Sproule, S., and N. Archer. 2008b. *Measuring Identity Theft in Canada: 2008 Consumer Survey*. McMaster eBusiness Research Centre Working Paper #23. Hamilton, Ontario: DeGroote School of Business, McMaster University.

Treasury Board. 2002. *Privacy Impact Assessment Guidelines: A Framework to Manage Privacy Risks*. Ottawa: C. I. O. Branch, Treasury Board of Canada Secretariat. http://www.tbs-sct.gc.ca/pubs_pol/ciopubs/pia-pefr/paipg-pefrld2-eng.asp [consulted February 3, 2009].

USDOJ. 2008. *Retail Hacking Ring Charged for Stealing and Distribution of Credit and Debit Card Numbers From Major US Retailers*. Boston, MA: United States Department of Justice. http://www.usdoj.gov/opa/pr/2008/August/08-ag-689.html [consulted February 19, 2009].

Vijayan, J. 2009. "Heartland Data Breach Could Be Bigger than TJX's." Nymity.com. http://www.nymity.com/Free_Privacy_Resources/Previews/ReferencePreview.aspx?guid=8424e66e-ac1b-4edc-8c13-1240021c0d6f [consulted April 11, 2009].

Voisin, K. 2008. "Data Breach Disaster Recovery: Protect your Organization by Having a Proactive Plan." Europe Assistance USA. www.worldwideassistance.com/pages/services/identity_theft/documents/DataBreachDisasterRecoveryArticle.pdf [consulted April 14, 2009].

Walker, P. L., and W. G. Shenkir. 2008. "Implementing Enterprise Risk Management: A Checklist." *Journal of Accountancy*, 205: 3: 31.

Warren, A. 2007. "Stolen Identity: Regulating the Illegal Trade in Personal Data in the 'Data-Based Society.'" *International Review of Law, Computers & Technology*, 21: 2: 177–90.

Whitson, J. R., and K. D. Haggerty. 2008. "Identity Theft and the Care of the Virtual Self." *Economy and Society*, 37: 4: 572–94.

Chapter 8

A Lifecycle Approach to Identity Asset Protection

"The excitement of learning separates youth from old age. As long as you're learning, you're not old."

—Rosalyn Yalow

In Chapter 7, a general three-phase model (Anticipatory, Reactionary and Remediation) was developed for managing data, identity theft and fraud risks, and it was applied in specific ways to manage these risks for larger organizations, small businesses and individual consumers. This model is *entity oriented* and focuses on how individual organizations or consumers *alone* can better manage IDTF risks. The IDTF issues, however, involve multiple parties that must work together to combat theft and fraud as shown in Chapter 2 (Wang, Yuan and Archer 2006). In this chapter, we further examine IDTF risks by taking a *process-oriented* perspective. More specifically, the purpose of this chapter is to build on what is known about IDTF prevention to design a lifecycle approach that reduces the risk in issuing and managing identity assets. The proposed lifecycle involves three stages: issuance, usage and maintenance. Use of the model is illustrated through the management of risk through the lifecycles of two major and important applications: passport management and credit card management.

Risk Management

Risk management is a structured approach to managing uncertainty through risk assessment, developing strategies to manage it and mitigating risk using managerial resources. Risk management has been applied in many areas, such as insurance, the financial industry and information systems. Risk management in general includes three phases: identification, assessment and mitigation/response (Merna and Al-Thani 2005; Smith, McKeen and Staples 2001). In the project management literature, risk management is viewed as a process that consists of the following: risk management planning, risk identification, risk analysis (qualitative and quantitative), risk response, risk monitoring and controlling (PMI 2000). In the context of information systems security, a similar albeit more granular classification of risk management activities includes six steps: identify, analyze, plan, implement, monitor and control (Alberts and Dorofee 2001).

One approach to risk identification is to break down risk into three components: asset, vulnerability and threat (hereinafter referred as the 'AVT' approach). This approach is mostly used in information security management (see for example Alberts, Behrens, Pethia and Wilson 1999; Alberts and Dorofee 2001; ISO/IEC 2004; Stoneburner, Goguen and Feringa, 2001). Similarly, identity theft risk can also be decomposed into these three components (Wang et al. 2006). More specifically, *assets* are obviously the identities (either in physical or electronic data formats), which are worth securing because they can be used to gain a privilege to access valuable services (Wang et al. 2006). *Vulnerabilities* are weaknesses of identity management that may be exploited by identity thieves. *Threats* refer to the activities and methods that can be used by identity thieves to exploit those weaknesses. The vulnerabilities of and threats to the identity may vary depending on how identity is created and used.

For example, as a consequence of these threats and vulnerabilities, credit card companies apply extensive resources to cope with theft or loss of credit cards, so in some cases they are aware of the theft before the card owner is. Unlike the first years of extensive use of credit cards in the 1950s, when customers were liable for the entire amount when credit cards were stolen, customers in the United States are now only liable for the first $50 of the stolen amount. In Canada, provided that the credit card company is notified as soon as a credit card is lost or stolen, customers are not liable for losses due to criminal activity.

To apply AVT to the special case of identity risk analysis, we need to address a number of issues: First, the AVT approach, such as Carnegie Mellon Software Engineering Institute's OCTAVE framework, is 'context-driven' (Alberts and Dorofee 2001: 49). In other words, the application of the approach should be situated in a specific organization. The management of identity, however, involves multiple stakeholders, such as the issuers, owners and checkers (Wang et al. 2006). As such, there is no single owner of the 'risk' or single party who is fully responsible for the risk. Second, identity information is widely circulated and there are many different scenarios of how identities are created, stored and used. We need to consider this complexity when applying the AVT approach. Combating identity theft involves many technical, managerial and legal issues that should be addressed in an integrated and systematic manner rather than through isolated and uncoordinated efforts.

In order to overcome these difficulties, we propose a risk management framework based on the identity management lifecycle (Figure 8.1). Here we define the identity management lifecycle (IDLC) as a continuous management loop in which an identity is created, used and maintained. For each stage in the lifecycle, we can identify the objectives, the functions to reach the objectives and the methods to perform these functions. By investigating current practices in the lifecycle, we can discover vulnerabilities and threats and propose possible countermeasures. In the next section, we give a detailed description of the lifecycle.

Identity Management Lifecycle

An identity management lifecycle in general consists of three stages:

1. The *issuance stage*, in which identity certificates are issued to an eligible person;
2. The *usage stage*, in which the correct service is provided to the eligible person; and
3. The *maintenance stage*, in which the integrity of identity information is maintained (Figure 8.1).

In each stage of the identity management lifecycle, we can analyze the tasks, objectives and functions that need to be performed in order to reach the objectives.

The identity management lifecycle involves multiple stakeholders: identity owners, issuers, checkers and protectors (Wang et al. 2006). An identity owner is an individual who is the subject of the identity and who has the legal right to own and use it. An identity issuer is a trusted organization that issues identity certificates to authorize certain social or financial rights to the identity owner. An identity checker is a service provider that verifies the authenticity and eligibility of an identity owner. An identity protector is an individual or organization that works to protect identity owners, issuers and checkers from identity theft (Wang et al. 2006).

Stage 1: Identity Issuance

In the issuance (enrolment) stage, identity certificates are issued to eligible persons. The issuance of an identity encompasses the following tasks as shown in Table 8.1:

Applicant authentication. The issuer checks and authenticates the information and documents provided by identity applicants to make sure that the applicants are indeed who they claim to be. The functions of this process can include 1) self-reporting of personal information by the applicants; 2) verifying cross-reference identity documents; 3) checking references; and 4) interviewing applicants in person.

Figure 8.1: Identity Management Lifecycle (IDLC)

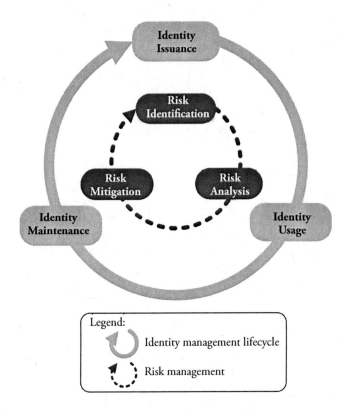

Eligibility check. The issuer may also need to check whether the applicants are eligible for the identity certificates they have applied for. To achieve this objective, the issuer needs to 1) establish criteria of eligibility; 2) collect and verify data related to eligibility criteria; 3) check applicant qualification against the criteria; and 4) approve the application according to internal approval procedures.

Record creation and storage. When the applications are approved, the issuer then needs to properly create and securely store identity records. To achieve this objective, the issuer must 1) determine the appropriate data content and structure; 2) create, collect and store identity and authentication data; and 3) implement encryption and access control to electronic data.

Creation of identity certificates. This process involves the actual production of identity certificates. Depending on the level of security required, the certificates may use different technologies to ensure that they cannot be easily forged. More specifically, the issuer needs to

1. determine appropriate certificate forms;
2. determine authentication methods associated with the certificate;
3. determine anti-counterfeit methods; and
4. generate identity certificates under security control.

Delivery. This process involves the actual delivery of the identity certificate to its designated owner, the applicant. The functions required to achieve this objective are as follows:

1. The issuer selects appropriate delivery channels;
2. The issuer secures and verifies receipt of the certificate by the true owner; and
3. The owner activates the identity certificate.

Stage 2: Identity Usage

In this stage, identity owners present themselves with identity certificates or provide identity information to a service provider (ID checker), who will then offer or deny pertinent privileges or services to the owners. There are a number of activities/procedures in the usage stage, as shown in Table 8.2:

Requirement of ID submission. This is the first process in which the service provider decides what kind of ID certificates would be required for its services and the related eligibility criteria.

Table 8.1: Lifecycle—Issuance Stage

Tasks	Objectives	Functions
Applicant authentication	To check the true identity of the applicant	Self-report of personal information Cross-reference identity document verification Reference check Personal interview
Eligibility check	To check the eligibility of the applicant for service	Establish eligibility criteria Collect and verify data about eligibility criteria Check the qualification against criteria Approval authorization procedure
Record creation and storage	To properly create and securely store identity records	Determine appropriate data content and structure Identity and authentication of data creation, collection and storage Encryption and access control
Identity certificate creation	To create a secure and verifiable identity certificate	Determine appropriate form of certificate Determine authentication method associated with the certificate Determine anti-counterfeit method Generate identity certificates under security control
Delivery of ID certificate	To deliver the ID certificate to the true owner	Select appropriate delivery channel Secure and verify delivery to the true owner Activate ID certificate

Service authentication. Before identity owners request any services, they should verify the legitimacy and authenticity of the service providers. For example, when they shop online, consumers need to make sure the website is what they intended to visit and shop from.

Submission channel selection. The service provider and the ID owner need to agree on the channel of ID submission, which includes the type of ID and the submission method. It can be in-person, online, offline or another mutually agreeable method.

User authentication. Before they provide any services or authorize certain privileges, service providers or authorities need to check and verify that 1) those individuals who request services or privileges are indeed who they claim to be; and 2) they are the true owners of the valid identities they present.

User's service eligibility check. Based on the ID(s) submitted by the owner, the service provider can then check if the owner is eligible for the service according to the eligibility criteria established previously.

Transaction record creation, storage and delivery. Upon the completion of services, the service provider may need to record the transactions for auditing or other legal and management purposes. The recording and storage may be in either paper or electronic formats. Often not only the transaction data but also the identity information of individuals is recorded. As the last process in the usage stage, the service provider may need to produce and deliver to the identity owner certain proof documents such as credit card receipts.

Step 3: Identity Maintenance

In the maintenance stage, the integrity of identity information is maintained. The maintenance stage involves the processes shown

Table 8.2: Lifecycle—Usage Stage

Tasks	Objectives	Functions
Requirement of ID submission	To verify requirement for ID submission	Establish the requirement of ID submission (service or reference)
Service authentication	To verify the legitimacy of service provider	Check the legitimacy and true identity of the service provider
Submission channel selection	To select the channel for ID submission	Select method of submission Submission security control
User authentication	To provide reliable certificate check and user authentication	Certification validation Authentication of the true ID owner
User's service eligibility check	To check eligibility for receiving the service	Check owner's eligibility against established criteria Detect and prevent possible fraud
Transaction record creation, storage, delivery	To establish minimal and secure ID recording, storage and/or disposal	Establish ID recording and storage policy Accurate ID recording and secure storage ID related document delivery and security control

in Table 8.3:

Safeguard of ID certificate and ID information. Each stakeholder (owner, issuer and checker) should take necessary measures to safeguard ID certificates and ID information from being lost or stolen. The latter may include information stored in computer database systems and copies of owners' ID certificates.

Normal updating, renewal and termination process. Any change to a person's identity information needs to be updated with the pertinent identity issuer. Most identity certificates have expiry dates and need to be renewed accordingly. An identity may be terminated under certain situations.

Handling lost and stolen ID. Identity owners need to report any lost or stolen identity certificates to their issuers immediately, who will then put an alert in the identity owners' files and prevent further circulation of the stolen identity. The issuers may issue new or replacement certificates to the ID owners, following certain established procedures.

ID theft and fraud detection. This is performed not only in the maintenance stage but also other stages throughout the whole management lifecycle. This process may involve monitoring the use of identity, detecting irregular activities, creating and sharing a watch list, and so on.

Fraud reporting and damage control. Fraud should be reported to related parties and to law enforcement agencies, if necessary. This will lead to damage control, criminal investigation and victim reputation recovery.

In the following, we use passport management and credit card management as two examples to illustrate how risk analysis can be conducted, based on the identity management lifecycle framework we have described.

Table 8.3: Lifecycle—Maintenance Stage

Tasks	Objectives	Functions
Safeguard ID certificate and ID information	To keep ID safe from theft at each site (owner, issuer and checker)	Set and enforce sufficient security policies on ID information Implement security control on ID information Keep ID certificate in safe place
Normal updating, renewal and termination process	To keep information updated To renew ID certificates to valid eligible owners To terminate invalid or expired ID certificates	Set up updating policies and procedures Updating request authentication and authorization Follow the same standard of issuing a new certificate Destroy expired or terminated ID certificates and disable their circulation
Lost and stolen ID handling	To prevent illegal use of lost or stolen ID and minimize possible damage	Reporting and verification request Cancel lost certificates and disable circulation Issue a temporal or replacement certificate Retrieve or reset forgotten passwords
ID theft, fraud detection and investigation	To detect possible ID-related frauds	Fraud monitoring and detection Watch list creation and sharing
Fraud reporting, damage recovery	To limit the magnitude of damage	Fraud reporting Suspend the ID certificate in question Criminal investigation and law enforcement Damage recovery Rescue of victim's reputation

Risk Analysis in a Passport Management Lifecycle

A passport is a document issued by a government to identify the bearer as a citizen of the issuing country. Passports allow people to travel abroad and return. It serves as a major identity certificate in foreign countries (e.g., for boarding airplanes or staying in hotels), and it is widely used as a fundamental certificate when applying for other identity certificates such as those needed for immigration, study or work visas and opening a bank account in a destination country. The mutual recognition of passports between countries is arranged by government diplomatic contact between the issuing country and the destination country.

As an example, Canadian citizens who apply for a passport need to fill out an application form (http://www.ppt.gc.ca/index.aspx?lang=eng) and provide proof of citizenship (e.g., birth certificate, citizenship card), proof by photo ID (e.g., driver's license) and recent photos signed by an eligible guarantor. Passport Canada (the issuer) will check the eligibility of applications by taking measures such as selectively contacting guarantors for reference checks and checking against criminal watch-lists (OAG 2007). If an application is approved, a passport with certain user authentication and security features will be issued.

Step 1: Risk Analysis at the Passport Issuance Stage (summarized in Table 8.4)

Insufficient Applicant Authentication. Generally speaking, insufficient authentication is one of the major vulnerabilities in the identity management lifecycle. Offenders can exploit this vulnerability in obtaining passports by using fake names, other people's true names or even dead people's names, as in a case in Britain, where passport fraudsters stole the identities of dead children (Bennetto 2002). In Canada, a guarantor is required to verify the true picture of the applicant, but the eligibility of guarantors is not always checked and the guarantors are not always contacted to check the truth of their guaranty. A possible countermeasure is to maintain a database of eligible guarantors and implement a standardized sampling method to check selected cases.

Reference Document Easy to Counterfeit but Difficult to Verify. Some supporting documents such as birth certificates do not have sufficient security features and are easy to counterfeit. This makes it difficult to verify their authenticity.

Inadequate Watch-List Check. In the United States, a report suggested that insufficient oversight by the State Department allows criminals, illegal immigrants and suspected terrorists to fraudulently obtain US passports far too easily (Lipton 2005). According to the report, passport applications were not routinely checked against comprehensive lists of wanted criminals and suspected terrorists. For example, one of the sixty-seven suspects included in a test managed to get a passport seventeen months after he was first placed on the FBI wanted list. To mitigate these risks, the issuer should coordinate with other federal and provincial/state agencies to share relevant data like criminal records and birth records.

Violation of Internal Control. Passport officers may not follow the regulations. For example, a case was reported where a passport examination officer issued eleven Canadian passports to illegitimate applicants who used counterfeit Canadian citizenship certificates with altered names and dates of birth (Seymour and Jaimet 2007). To mitigate such risks, the issuer must have a strong policy for employee security clearance in addition to other internal control measures (OAG 2007).

Passport Counterfeiting. Since it is a paper document, a passport can be counterfeited or modified. Insiders or criminals can access authentic blank passports if the latter have not been safeguarded properly (Shishkin 2001). Stolen passports may be modified and forged passports produced by using high-quality copy and printing technology and then sold on the black market by organized criminals (Anonymous 2008a). To mitigate counterfeiting risk, laser images and encryption, such as machine-readable 'ghost photos,' have been used, and electronic chip-based passports have been proposed.

Delivery Risk. Passports are exposed to delivery risk if they are mailed to the owners, since the mail may be stolen or lost. Cases have been reported where passports were delivered to wrong addresses (Anonymous 2008b) and where poor postal security caused losses of passports (Branigan 2003). To lessen this risk, registered mail requiring the receiver's signature should be used as the only delivery method, other than physical pick-up by the owner.

Step 2: Risks at the Passport Usage Stage (summarized in Table 8.5)

Passports are always required for foreign travel. Visas may also be needed, depending on agreements between the passport holder's home country and the destination countries. At ports of entry, customs officials use various methods to check traveler identities. Typical methods include token authentication (checking whether a passport is authentic), attribute authentication (checking whether information on a passport matches the holder's physical characteristics), commonsense knowledge checking and behavioural checking. Entry records are created on forms such as printed visas, passport photos, paperless visas (e.g., Australian Electronic Travel Authority), stamped/handwritten records on passports and electronic records in computer systems.

Inadequate Owner Authentication. Since many different countries issue passports, customs officials may lack knowledge about the security features of foreign passports and may therefore not be able to identify fakes. It is also difficult to determine if criminals have modified personal information recorded on a passport, without online checking of original records stored in the issuer's office.

Table 8.4: Passport Issuance Stage

Tasks	Current Practice in Canada	Vulnerabilities/Threats
Applicant authentication	Proof of citizenship (birth certificate, citizenship card) Proof of photo identity (driver's license, etc) Non-photo identity with signature.	Supporting identity documents easy to counterfeit and difficult to verify Guarantors must be Canadian passport holders, but are not always contacted and verified
Eligibility check	Watch-list of ineligible persons (e.g., criminals)	Watch-list not updated against other federal and provincial databases
Record creation and storage	Access control	Unauthorized access Backdoor creation of certificate
Identity certificate creation	Photo (printed on passport) Photo (printed in encrypted format on passport, or 'ghost photo')	Unauthorized access to physical blank certificate Counterfeit passport Unauthorized personnel may trigger unauthorized issuance of passports Forgery of stamps Photo manipulation
Delivery of ID certificate	Mail Pick-up in person	Unreliable delivery method (e.g., mails can get lost, stolen or forwarded to wrong addresses)

Manual checks of passport pictures often fail to provide accurate identification of the passport holder. A possible solution—although expensive and difficult to implement, since it requires international cooperation among national immigration and customs agencies—is to provide online checking across nations similar to the online international verification of credit cards. In this way, customs officials could simply check online data from the passport issuer against the characteristics of a passport holder or other information (in the form of answers) provided by the holder.

Data Security Risk (Transaction Records). Entry records on the physical passports are often handwritten or in the form of stamps. Due to their low-tech nature, handwritten and stamped records may be forged or modified by offenders. While there is no silver bullet for this kind of risk, matching records on passports with records in computer systems can help detect fraud.

Step 3: Risks at the Passport Maintenance Stage (Summarized in Table 8.6)

At the maintenance stage, tasks include safeguarding passport and related information, renewals, handling of lost/stolen passports, and handling fraud. Holders are responsible for the physical security of their passports, while the issuer needs to protect the information in databases at its site. Different countries may have different practices for renewing passports. One practice is to put a note (e.g., a stamp) on the passport to indicate that its expiry date has been extended. The other practice is to treat the renewal process as a new application, in which the old passport is invalidated and a new one is issued. In Canada, the renewal process is simpler than a new application. In case a passport is lost or stolen, the holder is required to report the loss to police.

Physical Security Risk. Physical passports can be stolen or damaged if not properly managed and safeguarded. For example, a

Table 8.5: Passport Usage Stage

Tasks	Current Practice	Vulnerabilities/Threats
Requirement of ID submission	Hotels and airlines may require travelers to present passports Banks may request passports for new accounts (foreigners)	Passport or copy of passport may be lost or stolen
Service authentication	n/a (usually submitted at port in person)	n/a
Submission channel selection	Visa application: Mail, online application for visa At port of entry: in-person submission of 'physical' ID	Unreliable mail delivery
User authentication	At port of entry: Token authentication (i.e., whether the passport is an authentic one) Attribute authentication Commonsense knowledge checking Behavioural checking	Checkers lack knowledge about security features of foreign passports Personal reference data only on the passport Human errors
User's service eligibility check	Attribute authentication (i.e., verify true nationality of passport holder)	No online check
Transaction record creation, storage and delivery	Printed visa paper Printed visa paper with photo Paperless visa (e.g., Australian Electronic Travel Authority) Entry records on passport Entry record in computer system Paper customs form	Forged records on passport (e.g., stamps, entry dates)

case has been reported where passports were stolen at a passport office (Anonymous 2006). It is not uncommon for passports to be lost or stolen when they are used by their owners. In the United Kingdom alone, more than 290,000 passports were reported lost or stolen in 2006 (UK IPS 2007).

Owner Authentication Risk (Updating and Renewal). This risk typically exists in the normal updating and renewal process. This is not a big problem if the process requires the owner to submit the old passport, which itself is a proof of identity, provided it has not been stolen, or if the holder is required to appear at the passport issuing office.

Risks Related to Handling Lost and Stolen Passports. Holders are required to report lost and stolen passports to the issuers and government agencies when appropriate. There are two risks related to handling lost and stolen passports. First, consulates abroad may not have the necessary tools and training to issue passports (OAG 2007). They may not be able to implement the authentication and security policies that are implemented at local passport authorities in the owner's home country. The second risk is that temporary travel documents issued by consulates abroad are often easy to counterfeit. To mitigate this risk, passport issuers may consider building an online database of temporary travel documents to be accessed only when needed by immigration and customs officials in the home country.

Handling Fraud Risk. The risk associated with fraud detection and handling is more salient for credit cards than for passports. In the latter case, illegal use of passports is usually investigated by police through international agencies like Interpol. However, fraudulent use of a passport (whether or not it has been stolen or forged) will involve the actual identity owner in a criminal investigation.

Table 8.6: Risks—Maintenance Stage

Task	Current Practice	Vulnerabilities/Threats
Safeguard of ID certificate and ID information	Access control Security measures such as firewalls, encryption	Unauthorized access to critical data and systems
Normal updating, renewal and termination process	Stamps on passport for renewal Simplified process (in Canada, without submitting documentary evidence of citizenship, supplementary identification and a guarantor declaration) Same as new application	Expired ID not deactivated Data modification on passport
Handling lost and stolen ID	Holder required to report to local police and the ID issuer Investigation to be conducted before replacement passport issued Statutory declaration concerning a lost, stolen, damaged, destroyed or inaccessible Canadian passport Information on stolen and lost passports is forwarded to a centralized database maintained by police	Consulates abroad don't have necessary tools and training to issue passports. Temporary travel documents are thus easy to counterfeit
ID theft and fraud detection and investigation	Maintaining watch list of ineligible persons Suspension, confiscation or revocation of passports held by criminals Other legal actions (e.g., extradition of illegal immigrants at port of entry)	No electronic system to track use of passports Illegal use of passport often investigated in other 'main' criminal activities
Fraud reporting and damage recovery	Legal actions	

Risk Analysis in a Credit Card
Management Lifecycle

As with passports, credit cards play an important role for consumers, albeit for different purposes. Credit cards provide a convenient way to make purchases or to get short-term financing. Normally, participants in a credit card network include consumers, issuers, merchants, acquirers and network operators (Chakravorti 2003). Issuers are financial, retail or wholesale institutions, which issue credit cards to consumers; acquirers are the merchants' financial institutions; network operators are credit card companies like MasterCard and Visa. Based on the identity theft contextual framework discussed in Chapter 2 (Wang et al. 2006), merchants, acquirers and network operators may all play identity checker roles.

There are some differences between the credit card lifecycle and the passport lifecycle. In the issuance stage, credit card companies often send out "pre-approved" applications based on personal information they have collected from various sources. Applications are often processed without authentication of applicants' true identities. Credit card issuers tend to focus on the 'creditability' of applicants in terms of credit rating, income, employment status, etc. Once an application is approved, a credit card is mailed to the applicant by regular mail. A plastic card with a magnetic strip and verification code on the back is the common form factor, or the newer cards that use chip-and-PIN verification. Some issuers provide photo cards (e.g., Citi PhotoCards, www.citicards.com). Upon receipt of the card, the owner activates it by contacting the issuer by phone.

There are five types of plastic card (credit and debit) fraud (Devos and Pipan 2009): card not present (e.g., telephone or Internet transactions); counterfeit; lost or stolen; mail non-receipt; and identity theft. It is instructive to consider how these types of fraud have been addressed in the United Kingdom, where the amount lost to such frauds continued to grow until 2005. These losses were mainly due to organized criminal activities in advance of the adoption of chip-and-PIN security for plastic cards. The UK payments industry, comprised of approximately thirty companies, has established the APACS[1] trade association, which says it invests approximately £5 million each year in initiatives to combat fraud. In the five-year period prior to 2008, for example, it rolled out the chip-and-PIN initiative (also recently introduced in Canada) and has seen credit card fraud decline as a result. It also established the Dedicated Cheque and Plastic Crime Unit (DCPCU), a special police unit that specifically tackles plastic card and cheque fraud, and promoted retailer take-up of the Industry Hot Card File (IHCF). This is an electronic database that enables retailers to check for fraudulent use of a card at the time of purchase, and over 335,000 cases of attempted fraud were prevented by this system in 2006. However, criminals are still copying magnetic strip data from UK cards to create counterfeit magnetic strip cards to be used in countries that haven't upgraded to chip-and-PIN. Unfortunately, fraud in card-not-present transactions (purchases over the Internet, telephone, mail order and international) has continued to increase, accounting in 2007 for just under 50% of all card fraud losses. Other measures that can help to reduce card-not-present and online fraud are being introduced, including automated cardholder address verification and card security code systems, like *MasterCard's SecureCode*[2] and Visa's *Verified by Visa.*[3]

At the usage stage, in addition to their main purpose of providing a convenient form of payment, credit cards may be used for credit checking and as a guarantee of future payments. Before actually submitting credit cards, holders may need to verify the service provider's status, which is especially important in an online environment. Credit cards may be used in two ways: 'card present' and 'card not present.' In case of 'card present,' cardholders show their physical cards in order to make purchases. In some

---

1 Association for Payment Clearing Services: http://www.apacs.org.uk/index. html.

2 www.mastercard.com/uk/securecode.

3 www.visaeurope.com/verified.

situations, they may need to sign the 'retailer copy' of the receipt. In case of 'card not present,' the credit card number and other information, such as the three- or four-digit verification code or the holder's billing address, is submitted through various media like fax, telephone or the Internet. In most transactions, the true identities of cardholders are not verified. Transactions are normally approved if the cards are valid and the transaction is within the allowed credit limits. Different types of records are created for transactions: printed receipts (retailer copy and customer copy) and electronic data in computer systems. Statements of transactions are usually mailed to cardholders monthly.

The maintenance stage of the credit card lifecycle has processes that are similar to other identity certificates. However, there are some major differences. Credit cards are often automatically renewed, albeit with new expiry dates (typically every two years) and verification codes on the back. Change of address is done by phone, with the caller's identity being verified by question-and-answer challenge. Card issuers usually implement information systems to identify suspicious transactions and detect credit card frauds. Finally, cardholders usually bear no or little liability for fraudulent transactions they did not initiate themselves.

Using the lifecycle framework, we identify the major risks of credit card theft as shown in Tables 8.7, 8.8 and 8.9. Credit cards have a number of risks that are similar to passports. Examples of these risks include 1) information systems security risk (e.g., unauthorized access may result in data theft, unapproved internal creation and issuance of identity certificates to ineligible persons); 2) identity certificate risk (e.g., counterfeit, theft of authentic blank certificates, data on the magnetic strip being copied by criminals); and 3) delivery risk (e.g., lost and stolen mail). Numerous cases in which offenders have exploited this type of vulnerability have been reported. The following are just a few of them: 1) stolen and forged credit cards and other ID cards (Anonymous 2008a) and 2) in a recent police investigation, police seized credit cards, driver's licenses, debit terminals, card readers, card embossers and other materials that were used to make phony cards, including piles of plastic blanks and magnetic strips (Young 2008). In this section, rather than explaining the risks one by one, we will focus on those risks that are unique to credit cards.

Step 1: Risks at the Credit Card Issuance Stage

Authentication Risk. A typical credit card application requires only a minimum of personal information and financial status, such as the applicant's annual income. Because the true identity of an applicant is not verified against proof of identity documents such as those for passport applications, credit card applications may be made by someone in another person's name. A possible countermeasure to this problem is to require credit card applicants to provide photo identity proof and verification of applicant identities through in-person application.

Generally speaking, inadequate authentication procedures are one of the major vulnerabilities in the credit card identity management lifecycle. Offenders can exploit this vulnerability to obtain credit cards by using fake names, real names of other people or even the names of dead people. The number and type of possible credit card frauds is virtually endless. In the United States, more than 240,000 complaints of credit card fraud were filed each year from 2005 to 2007 (FTC 2008). More than 14% of these cases were 'new-account' frauds (new accounts opened under other people's names).

Reference Document Risk. Reference document risks exist in both the applicant authentication process and eligibility checking process. Because issuers usually focus on applicant financial status and do not verify their true identities, fraudulent applications may be approved if they are submitted by offenders in the names of other persons who have good financial status such as credit ratings. To reduce this type of risk, the verification of applicants' true identities should be implemented.

Table 8.7: Credit Card—Issuance Stage

Tasks	Current Practices	Vulnerabilities/Threats
Applicant authentication	Submit personal information without authentication of true identity	Applications may be made by someone in another person's name
Eligibility check	Credit report Self-reported employment information Tax status and qualifications (without Social Security Number)	Fraudulent applications in the name of someone with good credit rating
Record creation and storage	Access control	Unauthorized access Backdoor creation of credit card through insider access
Identity certificate creation	Verification code Electronic data in magnetic strip Electronic data in chip Photo on cards	Card can be counterfeited Insider fraud
Delivery of ID certificate	Mail Activation by home phone	Unreliable delivery method Activation may be done by family members or others with access to applicant's mail

Step 2: Risks at the Credit Card Usage Stage

Service Authentication Risk. Service authentication risk is especially acute in online environments where credit card ID numbers are entered to make purchases. Criminals may pose as legitimate online businesses and try to cheat consumers of their credit card numbers, bank accounts, passwords and other personal information. Indeed, this 'phishing' problem is a huge obstacle to the growth of electronic commerce. To reduce this risk, businesses may consider implementing digital certificates, as well as mutual authentication (see Chapter 11 for more details on authentication processes).

Delivery (Submission) Risk. As we discussed earlier, there is a delivery risk at the issuance stage, when issuers mail identity certificates (passports or credit cards) to applicants. This risk also occurs at the usage stage, when owners submit identity certificates or identity information to prospective checkers. Credit card information can also be stolen by fraudsters during this stage using various technologies. For example, software installed at cash registers can be used to steal information from credit and debit cards (Sidel 2006). Identity information may be stolen in 'card-not-present' situations. Faxes and mailed letters with credit card information can be lost or stolen; and the online submission of credit information may be insecure. To reduce these risks, checkers or issuers should encrypt online communications or require the use of passwords (or PINs) to authorize transactions (e.g., Verified by Visa).

Owner Authentication Risk. Owner authentication is not always required by service providers, allowing fraudulent transactions with stolen or fake credit cards. Very often, businesses rely on 'card authentication,' e.g., assuming that the physical card is valid and that the requested purchase is not beyond the card's limit. In situations such as taxi fare payments, where card authentication cannot be done in real time, offenders may be able to get free rides with fake credit cards. Many US credit cards lack preventive measures, like verification codes for purchases (Mangla 2007). To alleviate these credit card risks, businesses may require customers to show photo identity proof, although this may cause some inconvenience. Advanced technologies like biometrics (e.g., iris scans) may also be used. Another increasingly common solution in Europe and Canada is password security (e.g., PINs to authorize transactions).

Data Security Risk (Transaction Records). Credit cards have different data security risks than passports because transaction records are often stored in databases or printed on receipts. Data in both electronic and paper forms can be stolen or lost, although the magnitude of losses from database breaches can be far more significant. Another problem is that credit card owners may not be able to detect suspicious transactions until they receive monthly statements. There have been many reported cases of data breaches, where large amounts of credit transaction information have been lost. In 2005, for example, a security breach at CardSystems, a credit card network transaction processor, exposed about forty million credit card accounts to theft (Evers 2005). Some possible measures to reduce data security risks are as follows:

1. Businesses should not store customer credit card information.
2. Historic transaction data involving credit card information should be purged regularly according to relevant laws and regulations.
3. Complete credit card information should not be printed on receipts.
4. Cardholders should be notified immediately about any transactions against their accounts via e-mail or cell phone SMS.

Table 8.8: Comparison of Credit Card Risks—Usage Stage

Tasks	Current Practices	Vulnerabilities/Threats
Requirement of ID submission	Used for credit checking Used as guarantee of payment	n/a
Service authentication	Used in physical stores Used for online websites	Personal information may be sent to fake service providers
Submission channel selection	Card not present (telephone, Internet, mail, fax): submit information only Card present: in person, e.g., at gas station Offline processing (e.g., use of credit card for taxi fare payment)	Insecure online submission Unreliable delivery Stolen card information may be used in card-not-present transactions
User authentication	User authentication is not always performed, often through card authentication only (i.e., whether the card is valid)	Rely on "certificate authenticate" only Human errors Card authentication done in real time
User's service eligibility check	Credit balance check online	n/a
Transaction record creation, storage and delivery	Mass storage of transaction data Outsource of data processing Monthly statement for cardholders	Data lost or stolen Credit card number printed on receipts Cardholders able to detect frauds only on monthly statements

Step 3: Risks at the Credit Card Maintenance Stage

Owner Authentication Risk (Updating and Renewal). This risk typi-cally exists in the normal updating and renewal process. For credit cards, this risk is not a trivial one. Updating and renewal may be triggered without proper authentication of the owner's identity. First, a mailing address may be changed by offenders so that mail is forwarded to another address. For example, a case was reported where a fraudster had changed a person's mailing address and sub-sequent mails were stolen (Crawford, 2006). This is far from a unique situation, one that can happen if the credit card issuer does not have a strict authentication procedure. Second, mail may be forwarded illegally to offenders if the post office does not verify the identity of the person who requests mail forwarding. Last but not least, mailing address records may be changed by a cardhold-er's unethical acquaintances.

To reduce this type of risk, card issuers may consider imple-menting password security, i.e., requiring card owners to use PINs to authorize changes. The issuers may also enforce a policy that only allows changes to be made in person and requires proof by photo identity. Last, the post office may stop forwarding mails that are related to credit cards. This solution, however, requires cooperation between credit card issuers and post offices. Most credit cards have expiry dates several years from the date of issue. When the expiry day approaches, the issuer issues a new card with a new expiry date. This type of renewal does not prevent credit card fraud, as the new expiry date can easily be guessed even if identity thieves have stolen expired cards.

Handling Fraud Risk. In the case of credit card fraud, it is difficult for holders to detect information lost until fraudulent transactions show up on their monthly statements, although many check their online status more frequently. A major problem is that issuers are reluctant to use stricter authentication methods for fear of losing customers. Last but not least, data mining implemented by card

Table 8.9: Comparison of Credit Card Risks—Maintenance Stage

Tasks	Current Practices	Vulnerabilities/Threats
Safeguard of ID certificate and ID information	Access control Security measures like firewall, encryption	Unauthorized access Difficult to protect credit card information
Normal updating, renewal and termination process	Automatic renewal Set criteria for renewal Change address by phone (caller identity authenticated by question-and-answer challenges)	Mailing address may be changed by others Mail forwarded to other addresses by ID thieves
ID lost and stolen during handling	Cardholder required to report lost and stolen cards	Holders may not know of information lost until fraudulent transactions show on statement
IDTF detection and investigation	Checking suspicious activities Analysis of selected transactions Electronic system–based Data mining	Holders may not detect information lost for a long time Data mining may not detect all fraudulent transactions Phishing (fraudulent security measures)
Fraud reporting and damage recovery	Zero or limited consumer liability Handling of payment default (e.g., legal actions) Fraud treated as cost of doing business by credit card issuers	Issuers have no incentives to use stricter authentication methods Loss of some profit to the firm would be preferable to bad publicity

issuers may not be able to detect all fraudulent transactions. To reduce this type of risk, the following countermeasures may be used:

1. Use advanced technologies to analyze and verify all transactions.
2. Empower cardholders to detect frauds by notifying and alerting cardholders when card transactions occur via e-mail or SMS.
3. Share fraud knowledge among card issuers.
4. Encourage cardholders to check their credit card statements online frequently.

Summary

In general, the lifecycle framework we have suggested appears to be effective and comprehensive for analyzing identity theft risks. The analysis shows that in each stage of the lifecycle there are vulnerabilities that can be exploited by identity thieves. There is no shortage of reported cases that have resulted from these vulnerabilities.

The analysis revealed some differences in the risk of fraud between passports and credit cards. For passports, the physical booklet is the main medium that carries the owner's identity information, serving as the reference point when the passport is used to verify the owner's true identity. It lacks an online system for identity verification purpose. If identity thieves have the technologies to make fake passports with the same security features as those authentic passports have, identity checkers would not be able to detect fraud. For credit cards, on the other hand, issuers usually have online systems for card verification purposes. Thus, even if identity thieves have the necessary technologies to make fake credit cards, they would not be able to use them if credit card information does not match that stored in the online systems.

A major problem with credit cards is that card checkers seem to focus on the correct identification of an *account* and whether the account has exceeded its credit limit, rather than on the *true identity* of the cardholder. This only identifies "which account to charge this purchase to" and "does the person who owns the account have the ability to pay." Furthermore, although our analysis indicated that significant risks exist in each of the three stages—issuance, usage and maintenance—credit card issuers seem to focus only on detecting frauds in the latter two stages. Preventive measures, like strict applicant authentication, are minimal if not lacking, or absent altogether.

Another major credit card risk exists due to the circulation of credit card information like credit card number, expiry date and verification code. While credit card issuers advise consumers to keep their cards safe and not to disclose credit card information to other people, at the same time they supply this information to credit reporting agencies, whose business activities inadvertently help to spread consumer credit information to other parties, including criminals. Furthermore, in order to complete transactions, cardholders have to submit all related information, especially in card-not-present situations. This process is open to online theft by criminals monitoring these transactions.

Finally, the identity management lifecycle risk analysis provides the following findings:

1. Organizations rather than individual identity owners are most vulnerable to identity theft. There is not much that individuals can do to reduce the risk other than safeguarding identity tokens such as passports and credit cards. Our analysis confirms that the 'tips to consumers' approach does not significantly minimize the risks and effects of identity theft (Cavoukian 2005). Organizations, as sites of identity use (Lacey and Cuganesan 2004) are better positioned to prevent and detect identity theft.

2. Because risks are inherent to all identity systems, risk management is a viable approach to combating identity theft. Most organizations' current practices assume the risk by taking identity theft costs as a 'cost of doing business' (Hemphill 2001) and

simply writing it off. A better approach would be to lower the risk of loss by acknowledging vulnerabilities and researching controls to correct them (Stoneburner et al. 2001). This approach would also help reduce the identity theft risk of a transaction system as a whole.

3. Another possible approach to risk reduction by individual identity owners is risk transference, i.e., transferring risk by using other options such as insurance (Stoneburner et al. 2001).

4. The limitation of the lifecycle approach is that it does not address how to prioritize vulnerabilities and threats. This can be done by surveying consumers and agencies or organizations that use or issue identity tokens.

References

Alberts, C. J., S.G. Behrens, R. D. Pethia and W. R. Wilson. 1999. *Operationally Critical Threat, Asset, and Vulnerability Valuation (OCTAVE) Framework.* Pittsburgh: Software Engineering Institute, Carnegie Mellon University.

Alberts, C. J., and A. J. Dorofee. 2001. *OCTAVE Criteria, Version 2.0.* Pittsburgh: Software Engineering Institute, Carnegie Mellon University.

Anonymous. 2006 (18 May). "Home Office Loses 1,500 Passports." http://www.politics.co.uk/news/domestic-policy/immigration/home-office-loses-1500-passports-$440216.htm [consulted March 14, 2008].

Anonymous. 2008a (8 February). "Alberta Police Arrest Two on Card, Identity Theft Charges." *CardLine,* p. 9.

Anonymous. 2008b (25 January). "Looks Nothing Like Me." *Globe and Mail,* A16.

Bennetto, J. (2002, 9 October). "Passport Fraudsters Stole Identities of Dead Children." http://www.independent.co.uk/news/uk/crime/passport-fraudsters-stole-identities-of-dead-children-613549.html [consulted March 10, 2008].

Branigan, T. 2003 (26 May). "Poor Postal Security Lets Criminals Grab Passports." http://www.guardian.co.uk/uk/2003/may/26/ukcrime.post [consulted March 9, 2008].

Cavoukian, A. 2005. *Identity Theft Revisited: Security Is Not Enough.* Toronto: Information and Privacy Commissioner/Ontario.

Chakravorti, S. 2003. "Theory of Credit Card Networks: A Survey of the Literature." *Review of Network Economics,* 2: 2: 50–68.

Crawford, S. 2006 (25 March). "How Safe Is Your ID?" *Globe and Mail,* F8.

Devos, J., and I. Pipan. 2009. "The Role of IT/IS in Combating Fraud in the Payment Card Industry." *Journal of Internet Banking and Commerce,* 14: 3.

Evers, J. 2005. "Credit Card Breach Exposes 40 Million Accounts." http://news.com.com/Credit+card+breach+exposes+40+million+accounts/2100-1029_3-5751886.html [consulted December 2, 2006].

FTC. 2008. *Consumer Fraud and Identity Theft Complaint Data: January–December 2007*. US Federal Trade Commission.

Hemphill, T. A. 2001. "Identity Theft: A Cost of Business?" *Business and Society Review*, 106: 1: 51–63.

ISO/IEC. 2004. *Information Technology—Security Techniques—Management of Information and Communication Technology Security—Part 1: Concepts and Models for Information Technology Security Management*. Switzerland: International Organization for Standardization.

Lacey, D., and S. Cuganesan. 2004. "The Role of Organizations in Identity Theft Response: The Organization-Individual Victim Dynamic." *The Journal of Consumer Affairs*, 38: 2: 244–61.

Lipton, E. 2005 (30 June). "US Passport Fraud Is Going Unseen, Auditor Says." *International Herald Tribune*.

Mangla, I. S. 2007 (November). "The Safest Credit Cards." *Money*, 36: 22.

Merna, T., and F. F. Al-Thani. 2005. *Corporate Risk Management: An Organisational Perspective*. West Sussex, England: John Wiley & Sons.

OAG. 2007. *A Status Report of the Auditor General of Canada to the House of Commons*. Ottawa: Office of the Auditor General of Canada.

PMI. 2000. *A Guide to Project Management Body of Knowledge (PMBOK Guide)*. Newton Square, PA: Project Management Institute.

Seymour, A., and K. Jaimet. 2007 (17 May). "Passport Officer Admits to Document Scam." *Ottawa Citizen*.

Shishkin, P. 2001 (8 October). "Officials Find Forged Passports Are Big Business." *Wall Street Journal*, A14.

Sidel, R. 2006 (17 March). "Visa Warns of Data-Theft Risk for Customers." *Wall Steet Journal*, A2.

Smith, H. A., J. D. McKeen and D. S. Staples. 2001. "Risk Management in Information Systems: Problems and Potential." *Communications of Association for Information Systems*, 7: 12.

Stoneburner, G., A. Goguen, and A. Feringa. 2001. *Risk Management Guide for Information Technology Systems*. United States National Institute of Standard and Technology.

UK IPS. 2007. "Passport Warning for Winter Wanders." https://ips.gov.uk/identity/press-2007-01-26.asp [consulted March 20, 2008].

Wang, W., Y. Yuan, and N. Archer. 2006. "A Contextual Framework for Combating Identity Theft." *IEEE Security & Privacy*, 4: 2: 30–38.

Young, L. 2008 (29 February). "RCMP Smash Massive Identity-Theft Ring." *Globe and Mail*, S1.

Chapter 9

Employee Responsibility
for Risks to Identity Assets

"Hard work never killed anyone but why take a chance?"
—Edgar Bergen

Are employees responsible for identity theft risks? Organizations are the sites of identity information collection, use and storage, and employees are involved in all the stages of the identity management lifecycle. How they deal with information at hand will have a major impact on information security and ultimately identity theft. To answer the above question, we examine in this chapter the role of employees in identity theft problems. We identify and analyze those factors that could influence employee mishandling of information. Finally, we make some recommendations that organizations may implement to prevent employees from mishandling critical identity information.

Employee Mishandling of Identity Information

As discussed in Chapter 2, combating identity theft involves multiple stakeholders, including identity owners, identity issuers, identity checkers and identity protectors (Wang, Yuan et al. 2006). In Chapter 8, we examined the risk of theft at each stage of the identity management lifecycle and recommended some countermeasures that each stakeholder may implement to prevent and detect identity theft. The holistic analysis presented an overall picture of identity theft risks.

In this chapter, we turn to organizational stakeholders and focus specifically on the role of their internal employees. 'Organizations,' in this context, refers to identity issuers and checkers defined by Wang et al. (2006). Organizations are the sites of identity use (and misuse) and are central to the detection of identity theft (Lacey and Cuganesan 2004). Identity thefts happen when identity issuers issue identities to the wrong people or identity checkers fail to detect false identities. Indeed, identity theft problems are "in the hands of organizations" (Cavoukian 2005) and the primary institutional responsibility for identity theft prevention rests in organizations (Hemphill 2001).

Organizations may contribute to identity theft risks at all stages of the ID management lifecycle described in detail in Chapter 8: issuance, usage and maintenance. At each of the stages, internal employees play an important role in protecting identity information. After all, it is employees who handle these processes in an identity management lifecycle. Employee mishandling of identity information will therefore have an impact on identity theft.

At the *issuance* stage, where identities are established or issued to identity owners, employees may fail to authenticate properly and check the eligibility of individuals who apply for an identity. Such failures will ultimately result in the possession by identity thieves of valid identities, such as credit cards being issued to identity thieves under victim names.

At the *usage* stage, where the right service should be provided to the right and eligible person (identity owner), organizations are identity checkers that verify a person's identity before providing any services. The key factor that contributes to the identity theft problem at this stage is that organizations (and thus their employees) often do not put sufficient effort into verifying customer identities and detecting possible fraud. For example, businesses rarely verify whether a customer is the true owner of the credit card with which she or he makes a purchase. Only a handful of businesses, like Best Buy, require customers to show a photo ID, and only when the purchases are over a certain amount.

At the *maintenance* stage, the integrity of identity information is maintained. The responsibility for safeguarding identity information rests largely with organizations, including identity issuers and identity checkers. Poor information management practice by organizations is arguably the single largest cause of identity theft (Cavoukian 2005). Organizations should enforce policies and implement proper internal control to secure identity information. However, organizations often fail either to implement or to enforce these controls. As a result, there has been an outbreak of high-profile security breaches that have exposed the personal information of millions of individuals (discussed in detail in Chapter 5). According to the Identity Theft Resource Center (ITRC), a not-for-profit identity theft tracking website in the United States, in 2010 there were 662 reported security breaches that exposed more than sixteen million records (Identity Theft Resource Center 2010). Many of the breaches can be traced to internal employees where, for example, laptops are lost that hold large volumes of unencrypted personal information, where there are failures to safeguard passwords and where insider theft occurs, among other threats.

We classify employee behaviours causing identity theft into three categories: intentional theft and abuse, unintentional error and non-malicious mishandling.

Intentional theft and abuse. This category of behaviour refers to the outright theft of identity information by internal employees, with either malicious intent to cause damage or to make illegal gains. Employees have direct access to sensitive data and have the greatest opportunity for this type of abuse. According to the ITRC report mentioned above, a substantial number of data security breaches can be attributed to theft by insiders. Stolen identity information can be sold to other criminals or criminal groups. A particular type of intentional theft/abuse is the backdoor issuance of identity certificates by internal employees to their friends or other people who are not qualified to access the privileges or services in question.

There have been many reported cases of insider theft and abuse. For example, in a review of 517 cases that were closed by the US Secret Service, one third were committed by insiders (Anonymous 2007); in another example, insurance fund employees were found to have pilfered office files and used stolen identities to obtain goods (New York State Attorney General 2001). Other evidence of insider threats was previously discussed in Chapter 5.

Unintentional error. This category of behaviour refers to mistakes made by employees that may cause damage to information security. In this case, employees may not have malicious intent such as theft. Human error has been found to be one of the major causes of information security breaches (Im and Baskerville 2005). For example, employees may make mistakes or act carelessly when they need to verify a person's identity by comparing signatures or comparing photos with the person (Kemp, Towell et al. 1997). One example of an infamous unintentional error was a continuing stream of faxes that sent confidential customer information to a company that was not the intended receiver (Anonymous 2004). Still another example was a father who pretended to be his daughter in a phone call to change a password, where the employee did not question that his voice was to be matched to a woman's name.

Non-malicious mishandling. This type of behaviour refers to actions by employees who violate or bypass organizational information systems security or ID handling policies in order to carry out normal tasks. The key difference between mishandling and intentional theft is that the former does not exhibit malicious intent. Instead, employees may simply intend to save time or make it easier to do their job, although they may be aware that this could put sensitive identity information at risk. Most employee mishandling behaviours have one thing in common: employees may simply ignore or violate security policies if the organization has such policies in place. These behaviours can take on a variety of forms. For example, many reported data breaches have been the result of stolen laptops or of hackers who stole passwords. However, the root causes of such breaches may be employee mishandling of information. Employees who handle data may have copied sensitive information to laptops for convenience (e.g., in order to work at home); they may throw copies of documents containing customer IDs (like passports) into wastebaskets rather than shredding them as required by company policy; or other similar breaches.

In many reported cases, identity theft may be traced to employee mishandling of ID information. For example, according to instances compiled by the Privacy Rights Clearing House (http://www.privacyrights.org/identity.htm), merchants accepted fraudulent cheques without verifying misspelled names on the cheques; a police officer accepted a stolen driver's license without carefully comparing the ID photo with the imposter while issuing a traffic violation ticket. In another case (Levitz and Hechinger 2006), a laptop that contained the names and account numbers of 158,000 clients of Amerprise, a financial and insurance company, was stolen. The employee in this case did not encrypt the data as required by company policy.

Why Employees Mishandle Information

Why do employees intentionally mishandle information? The factors (as shown in Figure 9.1) that influence (either prevent or cause) employee ID mishandling behaviour may be classified as either organizational or individual factors.

Organizational Factors

Organizational security culture and climate. Organizational security culture and climate refers to the general principles, assumptions and practices that concern how organizations manage information security. This provides a broad context for employees when behavioural decisions are needed for managing security issues. If security is not a priority for an organization, it will not be a priority for its employees, either. Prior research has suggested that there is a positive relationship between employee perceptions of the information security climate and their behaviour related to security (Chan, Woon et al. 2005).

What are the sources from which employees infer security culture and climate? One of the key factors is top management's practice and support (Chan, Woon et al. 2005; Knapp, Marshall et al. 2006). The influence of top management is critical in two ways. First, it provides critical support for the IS department, which is normally responsible for implementing and enforcing security policy. Second, it leads by example, demonstrating good security behaviour for employees. Another factor is workgroup norm, which refers to the approval or disapproval of information mishandling behaviour by an employee's supervisor and co-workers (Guo et al., 2011).

Figure 9.1 Factors Influencing Employee Mishandling of Information

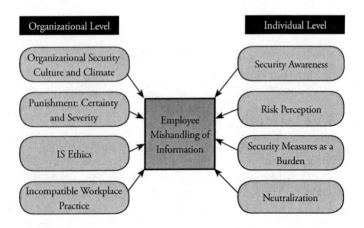

Accountability (or punishment). Punishment (also referred to as sanction or deterrence) is a security control measure based on general deterrence theory, which builds on the assumption that people are rational and they pursue their self-interest by minimizing cost or pain and maximizing benefit or happiness (Beccaria 1986). Wrongdoers should be punished so that the punishment can serve as an example to deter others from doing likewise (Beccaria 1986). In practice, the theory serves as the guiding principle for various security management standards (Theoharidou, Kokolakis et al. 2005), which include the British Standard BS7799 and its successor ISO17799 (ISO/IEC 2000).

In the IS security research literature, general deterrence theory has been applied to investigate the effect of organizational deterrent measures on computer abuses by employees. For example, the security impact model (Straub 1990) suggests that deterrent measures can reduce computer abuse by potential offenders if the risk of punishment is high (certainty) and penalties for violations are severe (severity). Although findings in the literature are mixed on this subject, the effectiveness of deterrence measures has been generally confirmed (e.g., Kankanhalli, Teo et al. 2003; D'Arcy, Hovav et al. 2009).

Information systems ethics. Some studies have investigated user security behaviours from an ethics perspective. IS ethics, which refers to the ethical content of informal norms and behaviour, may help deal with those situations where there are no formal rules or policies (Dhillon and Backhouse 2000). Harrington (1996) investigated the effect of codes of ethics on computer abuse judgment and intention. It was found that codes of ethics (those specifically written for IS management) have an impact on certain abuses, such as sabotage.

Incompatible workplace practice. Another factor that may lead to employee circumvention of security procedures is incompatible workplace practices (Adams, Sasse et al. 1997; Adams and Sasse 1999). One example of such incompatibility involves the use of individual passwords for group work or the use of group passwords for individual work. If they perceive that security mechanisms are incompatible with their work, employees will likely ignore them.

Individual Factors

Security awareness. Security awareness refers to employees' general understanding of information security issues. Such awareness includes but is not limited to 1) general appreciation of the importance of information security to the organization; 2) general knowledge about security risks; and 3) awareness of common countermeasures for reducing security risks and preventing security breaches. Without a certain level of awareness, employees may not fully appreciate and be supportive of security measures that organizations try to implement. As a result, they may sacrifice security for convenience.

There are two factors that are related to security awareness:

1. Security education, training, and awareness (SETA) programs. Prior research has found that SETA programs will increase awareness of the certainty and severity of punishment perceived by employees (D'Arcy, Hovav et al. 2009).

2. Employee security self-efficacy. Based on the more general concept of self-efficacy (Bandura 1977), security self-efficacy refers to employee beliefs in their ability to perform security-related tasks. Prior research has suggested that self-efficacy in information security is expected to influence security-compliant behaviour: the higher the level of security self-efficacy, the more willing an employee will be to follow security policies (Chan, Woon et al. 2005; Workman, Bommer et al. 2008).

Risk perceptions. Risk is an important factor in influencing human behaviour. When future negative consequences of some actions are expected, people will likely refrain from engaging in those actions or take measures to reduce the related risks. In the context of information security, employees will be more likely to take precautions and follow the organizational security policy if they perceive a higher risk of security breaches, such as data loss. On the other hand, if they perceive a lower risk, they will likely be less alert and more likely to ignore security policies.

Among the security breaches compiled by ITRC (2008), many were caused by stolen laptops. Storing and carrying sensitive information on mobile devices is known to be risky. Why do employees continue to do this? One likely reason is that they may believe the risk of losing their laptops is low, or that, even if there is such a risk, it will not happen to them. A related factor is threat appraisal or assessment, which refers to employee perceptions of threat severity and vulnerability (Pahnila, Siponen et al. 2007; Workman, Bommer et al. 2008). This concept is essentially the same as risk. The notion is that, if employees recognize there are threats to IS security and the organization's IS is vulnerable, they will comply with security policies and refrain from mishandling information.

Security as an extra burden. Security measures require employees to do something extra in addition to normal business tasks. In general, employees often perceive security measures as 'interference' with their job responsibilities (Post and Kagan 2007). For example, employees may be required to change passwords at a certain frequency specified by the IS department. Some may find it difficult to memorize new passwords. Some may have a hard time creating new passwords that are not only difficult for other people to recognize but also easy to remember. Some security measures may cause inconvenience from an employee's standpoint. For example, prohibition of the use of USB keys for transferring and storing data sacrifices the benefits of mobile devices and causes inconvenience for employees. Employees may also violate security policies for the sake of improving their job performance (Guo et al. 2011).

Because of the extra burden and inconvenience, employees may circumvent security policies and thus unintentionally put sensitive identity information at risk. For example, they may write down passwords somewhere on a piece of paper or on devices like mobile phones, just in case they forget the passwords. Despite a ban on USB keys, they may ignore the policy and use them anyway for convenience. A particular issue in this regard is how employees manage their passwords. Lost passwords have caused several large-scale data breaches. Organizations tend to address security issues by enforcing more restrictive authentication policies (Adams, Sasse et al. 1997), such as more frequent changes of password, longer and more complex passwords and lockout of user accounts upon maximum unsuccessful logons. However, the effectiveness of such policies is questionable. Users have been found to circumvent these policies by writing passwords down or choosing easy-to-guess ones (Zviran and Haga 1999).

Neutralization. Siponen and Vance (2009) proposed a neutralization model to investigate the problem of employee IS security policy violations. Based on neutralization theory in the criminology literature, the model suggests that employees rationalize their violations of security policies by a number of neutralization techniques: 1) defense of necessity; 2) appeal to higher loyalties (justifying by appealing to organizational values or hierarchies); 3) condemning the condemners (justifying by blaming the target of action, e.g., IS security policy); 4) metaphor of the ledger (justifying bad behaviours with prior good behaviours); 5) denial of injury (justifying by minimizing harms); and 6) denial of responsibility (justifying by beyond-control excuses). The study found that neutralization had significant effects on employee intentions to violate security policies. Because of the neutralization techniques used, the effects of formal sanctions and informal sanctions can become insignificant.

Perceived identity match. Perceived identity match (Guo et al. 2011) refers to how end users perceive dealing with security issues and following security policies that relate to their identity as business professionals. Perceived identity match plays a role in influencing employee security-related behaviours. If employees believe that strictly following organizational security policies does not improve their identities as business professionals, or that doing otherwise (i.e., violating security policies) will not necessarily hurt their professional identities, they are more likely to ignore organizational security policies.

Recommendations for Organizations

What can organizations do to prevent employees from mishandling sensitive identity information? We make the following recommendations (Table 9.1) to address organizational- and individual-level factors: 1) top management leading by example; 2) enforcement of accountability; 3) security education, training and awareness programs; 4) security behaviour as a part of employee performance evaluation; and 5) involving users in security policy design.

Top Management Leading by Example

Top management is the key player in building a positive organizational culture in general and security culture in particular. In order to nurture a good security culture, top management has to lead by example and demonstrate that identity information security and privacy is indeed very important to the organization's overall business operations and to the accomplishment of organizational goals. The leadership of top management in information security will demonstrate that there is no excuse for violation of identity security policies. This will help discourage employees from violating security policies by 'neutralization' tactics.

Based on the indicators of top management practice and support (Knapp, Marshall et al. 2006), the actions that organizations may take include 1) consider information security an important organizational priority; 2) demonstrate interest in security issues;

3) take security issues into account when planning corporate strategies; 4) communicate security as a priority through words and actions; 5) visibly support security goals; and 6) give strong and consistent support to the security program.

Table 9.1: Recommendations for Security Management

Recommendations	Factors Addressed
Top management leading by example	Security culture and climate Neutralization
Security education, training and awareness (SETA) programs	Security awareness Risk perception
Enforcement of accountability	Punishment certainty and severity IS ethics
Security behaviours as part of employee performance evaluation	Security as an extra burden Perceived identity match
Involving employees in security policy design	Security as an extra burden Incompatible workplace practice

Security Education, Training and Awareness (SETA) Programs

Because non-IS employees often lack the knowledge and skills to deal with information security issues, it is imperative for organizations to provide proper training and education. This will help raise employee awareness of security issues and help them to understand the importance of security. SETA should also have programs to help disseminate security policies within the organization and help employees to understand what actions should (or should not) be taken under what circumstances, and where they can get help if needed. Until this type of policy is implemented, organizations should not expect employees to embrace security policies fully.

Education and training also help employees to develop a better understanding of external threats to organizational information systems. This helps them to evaluate properly the possible risks involved in using computers. Very often employees may underestimate (or lack the knowledge to estimate) the risk level, and as a result they may act in a way that can cause security breaches.

Based on the indicators of SETA programs (D'Arcy, Hovav et al. 2009), some of the actions that organizations may take include (but are not limited to) the following: 1) providing training to help employees improve their awareness of security issues; 2) briefing employees on the consequences of modifying data in an unauthorized way; 3) educating employees on their computer security responsibilities; and 4) briefing employees on the consequences of accessing computer systems that they are not authorized to use.

Enforcement of Accountability

Punishment (in terms of severity and certainty) as a part of accountability can work only when security policies are enforced and employees who violate the policies are truly held accountable. Certain factors may contribute to the failure of organizations to enforce security policies. One possible factor is that security policies may be viewed as an extra by some organizations. They may take policies as a necessary additional step to meet security management standards or to satisfy external regulatory requirements. In this case, organizations may fall short of enforcing adequate security policies. Another possible factor is a lack of IS department power to enforce security policies. The enforcement of accountability must begin at the top of the management hierarchy. As mentioned earlier, top management support and leadership is the key not only to nurturing a positive security culture but also the enforcement of security policies. To accomplish this effectively, the IS department should be truly empowered to discourage or prevent employees from violating security policies.

Security Behaviour as Part of Employee Performance Evaluation

To provide the extra effort required to address the issue of employee ignorance of security measures, organizations may treat security as a routine end-user business task and include security behaviour as a criterion for employee performance evaluation. With such measures in place, employees will be motivated to take security issues more seriously. Instead of viewing security as an extra burden or impediment that can prevent them from accomplishing their tasks, employees will become more likely to regard security as one of their objectives. This will encourage employees to engage in the two types of 'beneficial' behaviours: 'awareness assurance' and 'basic hygiene' (Stanton, Stam et al. 2005). To implement this measure, organizations need to balance properly the trade-off between business objectives and security objectives. From a strategic standpoint, security practices must be aligned with an organization's overall business strategy.

Involvement of Users in Security Policy Design

To address the issue of incompatible workplace practices and to facilitate a 'dual objectives' strategy (business objectives and security objectives), organizations should involve end-users in the security policy design process (Post and Kagan 2007). This will help to ensure that workplace practices and user requirements are properly taken into consideration and incorporated in security policies. Another benefit of user involvement in the design process is that it helps to simplify security policies and makes them easier for end-users to follow. This will also give end-users an incentive to take partial 'ownership' of security policies and thus facilitate their acceptance and adoption.

Summary

Organizations are major sites of identity information collection, use and storage. The databases that hold such identity information will continue to grow in size. Any security breaches that lead to data leaks could be potentially disastrous to customers, employees and the organization itself, due to the magnitude of such exposure. Thus, it is critical for organizations to secure the information and prevent identity theft and any related fraud.

In this chapter, we examined the role of organizations, and particularly their employees in potential identity theft problems, from an information security perspective. Employees are involved in all the stages of the identity management lifecycle. How they deal with information at hand will have a great impact on information security and ultimately on identity theft. Indeed, many reported security breaches may be partially attributed to employee mishandling of information. We have identified different forms of actions by employees that could cause security breaches. Employee mishandling of identity information can be caused by factors at both the organizational and individual levels. Organizational-level factors include organizational security culture/climate, punishment (certainty and severity), IS ethics and incompatible workplace practices. Individual-level factors include security awareness, risk perceptions, burden of security measures and neutralization.

To prevent employees from mishandling critical identity information, organizations should consider implementing a number of measures, including 1) top management leading by example; 2) enforcement of accountability; 3) security education, training and awareness programs; 4) security behaviour as part of employee performance evaluation; and 5) involving users in security policy design.

References

Adams, A., and M. A. Sasse. 1999. "Users Are Not the Enemy." *Communications of the ACM*, 42: 12: 41–46.

Adams, A., M. A. Sasse, et al. 1997. "Making Passwords Secure and Usable." *People and Computers XII: Proceedings of HCI '97*. Berlin: Springer, pp. 1–19.

Anonymous. 2004. "The Fax, and Nothing But." *Globe and Mail*, A22.

Anonymous. 2007. "ID Thieves Lurk on and Beyond the Net." *Point for Credit Union Research & Advice*, 10.

Bandura, A. 1977. "Self-Efficacy: Toward a Unifying Theory of Behavioural Change." *Psychological Review*, 84: 2: 191–215.

Beccaria, C. 1986. *On Crime and Punishments*. Indianapolis: Hackett Publishing.

Cavoukian, A. 2005. *Identity Theft Revisited: Security Is Not Enough*. Toronto: Information and Privacy Commissioner/Ontario.

Chan, M., I. Woon, et al. 2005. "Perceptions of Information Security at the Workplace: Linking Information Security Climate to Compliant Behaviour." *Journal of Information Privacy and Security* 1: 3: 18–41.

D'Arcy, J., A. Hovav, et al. 2009. "User Awareness of Security Countermeasures and Its Impact on Information Systems Misuse: A Deterrence Approach." *Information Systems Research*, 20: 1.

Dhillon, G., and J. Backhouse. 2000. "Information Systems Security Management in the New Millennium." *Communications of the ACM*, 43: 7: 125–8.

Guo, K. H, Y. Yuan, N. P. Archer, and C. E. Connelly. 2011. "Understanding Nonmalicious Security Violations in the Workplace: A Composite Behaviour Model", *Journal of Management Information Systems* 28(2) 205–238.

Harrington, S. J. 1996. "The Effects of Codes of Ethics and Personal Denial of Responsibility on Computer Abuse Judgments and Intentions." *MIS Quarterly*, 20: 3: 257–78.

Hemphill, T. A. 2001. "Identity Theft: A Cost of Business?" *Business and Society Review*, 106: 1: 51–63.

Identity Theft Resource Center. 2010. "2010 Data Breach Statistics." http://www.idtheftcenter.org/ITRC%20Breach%20Stats%20Report%202010.pdf [consulted May 1, 2011].

Im, G. P., and R. L. Baskerville. 2005. "A Longitudinal Study of Information System Threat Categories: The Enduring Problem of Human Error." *The DATA BASE for Advances in Information Systems*, 36: 4: 68–79.

ISO/IEC. 2000. *Information Technology—Code of Practice for Information Security Management (ISO/IEC 17799)*. Geneva, Switzerland: International Organization for Standardization.

Kankanhalli, A., H. H. Teo, et al. 2003. "An Integrative Study of Information Systems Security Effectiveness." *International Journal of Information Management*, 23: 139–54.

Kemp, R., N. Towell, et al. 1997. "When Seeing Should Not Be Believing: Photographs, Credit Cards and Fraud." *Applied Cognitive Psychology*, 11: 3: 211–22.

Knapp, K. J., T. E. Marshall, et al. 2006. "Information Security: Management's Effect on Culture and Policy." *Information Management & Computer Security*, 14: 1: 24–36.

Lacey, D., and S. Cuganesan. 2004. "The Role of Organizations in Identity Theft Response: The Organization-Individual Victim Dynamic." *The Journal of Consumer Affairs*, 38: 2: 244–61.

Levitz, J., and J. Hechinger. 2006. "Laptops Prove Weakest Link in Data Security." *Wall Street Jounal (Eastern Edition)*, B1.

New York State Attorney General. 2001. "State Worker Charged in Massive Identity Theft Scam."

Pahnila, S., M. T. Siponen, et al. 2007. *Employees' behaviour towards IS security policy compliance*. 40th Annual Hawaii International Conference on System Sciences, IEEE.

Post, G. V., and A. Kagan. 2007. "Evaluating Information Security Tradeoff: Restricting Access Can Interfere with User Tasks." *Computer & Security*, 26: 229–37.

Siponen, M. T., and A. Vance. 2009. "Neutralization: New Insight into the Problem of Employee Information Systems Security Policy Violation." *MIS Quarterly* (to appear).

Stanton, J. M., K. R. Stam, et al. 2005. "Analysis of End User Security Behaviours." *Computer & Security* 24: 2: 124–33.

Straub, D. W. 1990. "Effective IS Security: An Empirical Study." *Information Systems Research*, 1: 3: 255–76.

Theoharidou, M., S. Kokolakis, et al. 2005. "The Insider Threat to Information Systems and the Effectiveness of ISO17799." *Computer & Security*, 24: 472–81.

Wang, W., Y. Yuan, et al. 2006. "A Contextual Framework for Combating Identity Theft." *IEEE Security & Privacy*, 4: 2: 30–38.

Workman, M., W. H. Bommer, et al. 2008. "Security Lapses and the Omission of Information Security Measures: A Threat Control Model and Empirical Test." *Computers in Human Behaviour*, 24: 6: 2799–816.

Zviran, M., and W. J. Haga. 1999. "Passwrod Security: An Empirical Study." *Journal of Management Information Systems*, 15: 4: 161–85.

Chapter 10

Consumer and Business Perspectives

"Too bad all the people who know how to run this country are too busy running taxi cabs or cutting hair."

—George Burns

Reducing the risk from identity theft is very much the responsibility of both individuals and organizations, who must also become aware of and take certain steps to protect themselves against identity theft and fraud threats. This chapter deals with several of the specific risks from IDTF that have not been covered elsewhere in this book. For consumers, we first examine perceived risks in shopping that influence customers in their choice of shopping venue. Then mortgage fraud and its ramifications to consumers is reviewed. This is an example of a high-impact but low-probability risk for consumers. Medical identity theft and fraud (MIDTF) is a relatively low-profile crime in Canada, because insurance payments are managed primarily by provincial authorities and incidents are unlikely to be made known to consumers. In the United States, where consumers are more likely to know about or to be billed directly for medical costs, MIDTF is more of a public concern. These issues are reviewed in some detail. IDTF risks to organizations are also covered, including data breaches, organizational costs, organizational responses to security threats, risks through outsourcing and potential risks through the disposal of electronic goods.

Risks to Individuals

Perceived Risks in Shopping

Shopping in a retail store can involve perceived risks due to the high media profile that terrorism, mugging and theft have received in the recent past, which may encourage consumers to stay home and shop online, where perceived risks are different but possibly more acceptable. Feelings of insecurity in any place where large numbers of people congregate, like shopping malls, can encourage people with low physical risk tolerance to go elsewhere or to shop at home (Predmore, Rovenpor et al. 2007). But there are a number of different perceived risks that have been identified in the consumer literature: functional, physical, financial, social, psychological and time (Evans and Berman 2005). One study of consumers (Predmore, Rovenpor et al. 2007) found that physical risks from shopping in retail stores did have an impact on the behaviour of US women consumers. In the United States, more men than women were concerned about financial risks and identity theft from shopping online, but men were less concerned about physical risks from shopping in retail stores. Online shopping also raises expectations of quick product delivery, which would result in time savings, although receiving damaged goods and/or having to return unsatisfactory goods can eliminate any such time savings, thus encouraging shoppers to face the risks of physical shopping. Perceptions of store brand quality and familiarity tended to reduce perceived risks from shopping online. Many shoppers believe that they must inspect products physically before purchasing, especially those that are not commodities or that have standard forms, like books. This is an indication that stores with both an online presence and a physical retail outlet are more likely to be considered safe for online shopping. Online retailers, however, must also focus significant efforts toward reducing perceived financial and identity theft risks to improve their attractiveness to online shoppers.

Consumer surveys show that the threat of identity theft affects consumer behaviour. A 2005 US survey found that nine out of ten Internet users had changed their behaviour because of the threat of identity theft. 25% said that they had stopped shopping online, while 29% said that they had reduced their purchasing frequency (Princeton 2005). In Canada, a 2008 survey found fewer, but still significant, changes, with 5% of consumers saying that they had stopped shopping online altogether and 15% saying that they had reduced the amount of shopping that they did online (Sproule and Archer 2008). These results indicate that the threat of identity theft is having a significant and detrimental effect on business-to-consumer e-commerce. If consumers do not trust electronic markets, then businesses cannot benefit from the productivity and market gains promised by e-commerce.

In response to the increased risk of losses through online payments, the UK payment card industry has tightened retailer compliance by requiring retailers to encrypt customer names and account details on all card-based transactions. Although a significant additional expense to retailers, they are required to install firewalls and intrusion detection and prevention systems to protect their networks against unauthorized access (Knight 2008). To confirm compliance, audits of their systems may be required, and retailers need to formalize and document their information security arrangements. This is very similar in concept to the Privacy Impact Assessment (PIA) audits required of government agencies in Canada (see Chapter 7).

Mortgage Fraud

Mortgage fraud is the deliberate use of misstatements, misrepresentations or omissions in funding, purchasing or securing a loan; any scheme designed to obtain mortgage financing under false pretences, such as using fraudulent or stolen identification or falsifying income statements, falls into this category. The risk of mortgage fraud tends to increase when there is strong competition between financial lending institutions during boom periods, resulting in rapid mortgage approvals that are needed to satisfy individuals searching for the best mortgage rates. In such an environment, financial institutions may bypass the due diligence that is necessary to ensure that all the relevant information about purchaser, vendor and property is accurate (CISC 2007). A particular problem raised in the United States is the practice of 'robo-signing,' or "the use of highly-automated processes by some large services to generate affidavits in the foreclosure process without the affiant having reviewed facts contained in the affidavit or having the affiant's signature witnessed in accordance with State laws" (Bair 2010). Criminal gangs and others in Canada, taking advantage of advanced communication techniques and counterfeited documents and signatures, annually cause mortgage fraud losses in the hundreds of millions of dollars (CISC 2007).

Some of the more egregious identity frauds are mortgages and property takeovers obtained illegally through property title forgeries and/or fraudulent mortgage applications. Organized crime groups are often involved, using fabricated information about the prospective buyer or property through the use of false appraisals and employment records (CISC 2008). Criminal groups may also recruit nominees, which can include family members, close associates or other ineligible buyers, to submit fraudulent mortgage applications. The movement toward remote application processes (whereby in-person applications may not be required) is also facilitating anonymity for those engaged in mortgage fraud.

There are many possible types and variations of mortgage fraud schemes in terms of sophistication and complexity. Common features include misrepresentations of the borrower's income and/or identity and manipulation of the property's age, size and value. Often borrowers fraudulently overstate their income and use false names on documents, and/or the property in question is fraudulently described as being more valuable than it really is. One highly egregious form of mortgage fraud is title fraud, involving the fraudulent transfer of property (CISC 2007). Homeowners who rent out their homes or who have no existing mortgages on high-value properties are more vulnerable to being targeted in title-fraud schemes, since large mortgages can be secured with their properties. The perpetrator assumes the legitimate owner's identity to sell or refinance the property fraudulently, based on the actual owner's credit rating and property. The individual then absconds with the stolen funds. In another twist to this type of scam, the criminal may illicitly sell the property to a straw buyer who intends to default while the criminal seller steals the mortgage funds. The legitimate homeowner is left with unwanted refinancing, an illicitly obtained new mortgage, or a property that has been sold to someone else. The perpetrator can undertake title theft without the existing homeowner's knowledge by using false identification and forged documents that take advantage of automated financial and real estate records systems. If the property is sold to an unsuspecting buyer, both the original homeowner and new buyer each believe they have clear title to the property. Title theft victims in Canada have paid extensive legal fees and spent considerable time to restore title to their properties (CISC 2007).

Until recently in Canada, the rightful owners of the property were left to fend for themselves in cases of mortgage scams. While the fault was often with the mortgage firm that did not perform its due diligence, the real owners (sometimes now the new owners) were left having to pay off an illegally obtained mortgage with nothing to show for their payments. This is an example of a low-probability, high-impact event (see Figure 3.1 in Chapter 3), which often leads to bankruptcy of the affected consumer(s) through no fault of their own. One remedy is to place the onus on the mortgage firm and the land titles office to manage the related risks by undertaking due diligence that would reduce the likelihood of this type of fraud. In addition, property owners should buy title insurance to cover the risk of such an event. At the same time, the penalties for this type of crime can be increased to keep the perpetrators off the streets once they have been apprehended. The Province of Ontario indeed took such steps in December

2006 (Sheppard 2010), introducing Bill 152 in response to several widely publicized cases of mortgage fraud. The revisions to legislation are now in the Ontario statutes. The maximum penalties for such an offense have been increased to two years in jail and a fine of $50,000. The federal government has also been urged to classify mortgage fraud as a separate criminal offense in order to increase penalties for criminals when they have been brought to justice. Regrettably, homeowners in the four Western Canadian provinces still must take lenders to court in order to deal with antiquated laws that allow lenders to abdicate responsibility for title fraud due to fraudulently obtained mortgage loans. For example, in the 2009 BC mortgage fraud case Gill v. Bucholtz (Clark 2009), the BC Court of Appeal ruled in favour of the original and rightful owner of the property, with the result that the lender lost the money advanced to the fraudster, who had vanished with the proceeds of the fraudulently obtained mortgage. The Court of Appeal suggested that the province should come up with stricter laws that force lenders to do a better job of vetting mortgage applicants and to ensure they aren't securing property that has been stolen.

Medical Identity Theft and Fraud

Medical identity theft and fraud (MIDTF) is a type of IDTF that can cause physical and financial harm to its victims. A false entry made to a consumer's medical history as a result of identity theft can lead to a range of negative consequences. MIDTF is challenging to detect, and consumers often discover only accidentally that they have been victimized by this crime. Not only have consumers and insurers been left to pay for medical charges incurred by others masquerading in their place, but physical harm can come to patients who have the medical records of imposters mixed in with theirs. For example, in one case a person who was hospitalized for an operation was mistakenly thought to have diabetes, which was suffered by an imposter who had fraudulently assumed the person's identity in order to pay for the amputation of a foot

(Anonymous 2007). Threats can also come from internal sources, such as healthcare workers or others with access to institutional databases or physician files, who falsify claims for procedures or treatments to the government agency that reimburses such claims. Illegal access to patient information has been used to blackmail patients, deny insurance benefits, etc. Such uses are privacy violations, and all Canadian provinces have laws to protect patients and prosecute violators when patient privacy has been violated. These violations must first be detected, however, and this requires vigilance on the part of healthcare institutions, which must have the appropriate safeguards in place to minimize their occurrence (Orbuch, O'Brien et al. 2004). The Ontario Health Insurance Plan (OHIP), for example, audits physician billing activities. Among techniques that are used is to send letters to random samples of patients requesting responses on whether they had appointments with their physicians on particular days.

In the United States, the new Red Flags program mentioned in Chapter 7 covers many healthcare providers and should help to reduce the growing problem of MIDTF. Figure 10.1 shows a simplified graphic of consumer health, identifying flows in a provincial healthcare system as reimbursement is sought by practitioners and institutions from either the provincial authority or another insurer for healthcare services provided to a citizen. The fraction of services not covered by insurance (e.g., some prescriptions and physiotherapy services) are billed by the provider and paid directly by the citizen. A US study claims that MIDTF accounts for 3% of identity theft crimes (AHIMA 2008). This is a lucrative form of identity theft, as stolen medical identity information has a US street value of about $50, as compared to stolen Social Security Numbers, which are valued at $1. MIDTF is also among the most difficult identity theft crimes to detect and correct. In Canada, for example, with its single-payer system (provincial health authorities), consumers are often not responsible for and rarely see medical bills. It is only when a consumer requires medical treatment that fraudulent medical records that have been added to their files might be detected and exposed as incorrect. However, it is when such errors are *not* detected that physical harm to the patient might occur. For example, based on a medication given to an impostor as indicated in the fraudulent record, a similar medication might be prescribed to the genuine patient to which he or she might be allergic. Another instance occurred where a fraudulently obtained limb amputation was discovered only when the genuine patient was being prepared for a different operation.

Medical record access abuse is a constant security concern for healthcare practitioners and institutions and requires a zero-tolerance approach to access and privacy breaches. Dealing with MIDTF requires a proactive approach, as suggested by the American Health Information Management Association (AHIMA 2008), including the following:

- Establishing department/position access passwords, authority levels and protocols
- Restricting system functionality to prevent unauthorized copies or transfers
- Communicating policies and requirements for ethical conduct by users
- Creating whistleblower protection when reporting access abuse
- Defining and enforcing employee disciplinary actions
- Defending against external access violations and attacks
- Guarding against the growing threat of identity theft, ranging from commandeering employee identity and access to stealing confidential patient information

An additional concern surfaced recently due to the increased use of social networking sites, which are intended for interpersonal communication but which may be abused when used for patient-doctor communications. Because of recent incidents that violated the privacy of patient-doctor communications and the need to maintain arm's-length relationships, the British Medical Defence

Union has warned doctors against using Facebook or other social communication networks for communications among medical workers and/or patients (BBC News 2009). These sites do not offer the privacy of point-to-point communications and are not recommended when private information or information potentially damaging between medical practitioners and patients is involved. The same caution applies to the growing use of e-mail messages for patient-doctor communication. Unless these messages are enciphered, they are prone to hacking, resulting in the risk of blackmail and other offences against the patient.

Consumers have shown an increasing concern about the security of medical records. A British survey (Dunstone 2007) of consumer perceptions of personal data theft found that 46% of all respondents were most concerned about protecting their medical records, in comparison with financial, online shopping and other Internet activities. Moreover, the concern about medical records was highest among the over-forty-five age group. A report by the World Privacy Forum estimates that up to a half million Americans have been victims of this crime (Dixon 2006). The Canadian Health Care Anti-Fraud Association[1] (CHCAA) holds annual conferences to discuss prevention, monitoring and investigation of MIDTF. This association claims that from 2% to 10% of every healthcare dollar in North America is lost to fraud. In Canada, over $120 billion is spent annually on healthcare, which suggests that the cost of healthcare fraud could surpass $12 billion each year. Unfortunately, the proportion estimated lost through MIDTF was not specified in the survey.

Although Americans and Canadians look forward to the benefits of national networks that will support interconnection of multiple sources of medical records within their respective countries, there is a great deal of concern about the possibility that these networks may facilitate MIDTF. In Canada, very little information has been made known publicly about MIDTF, but provincial health authorities have been moving toward better authentication

1 http://www.chcaa.org/blog/.

of consumers. Free healthcare in Canada is a tempting prize for uninsured foreigners. Many cannot afford medical insurance and may enter Canada seeking to use a borrowed health card to obtain healthcare fraudulently. The fraudulent use of health cards in these circumstances can result in two negative effects: a) fraudulent use of public funds; and b) mixing medical records from two different individuals in one file. The latter effect will be felt much more in Canada when provincial health authorities move toward linking sources of health records within and between their provinces. When these systems gather records that are ostensibly associated with particular individuals from across the province and the nation, this may lead to confusion and potentially deadly errors by healthcare practitioners.

The Province of Ontario began introducing photo ID health cards in 1995 in order to reduce healthcare fraud, but many of the old, embossed, red-and-white health cards are still in circulation. The newer photo ID cards must be renewed every five years, while the old cards are permanent, even though they are far less reliable for authentication purposes. According to the Ontario Auditor

Figure 10.1: Patient Information Flows

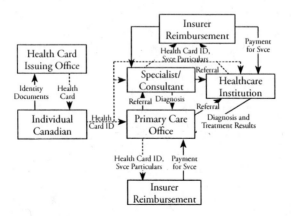

General, at the current rate of replacement of the old cards, it will be 2020 before they are completely replaced (Ontario Auditor General 2006). Meanwhile, there are 300,000 more health cards in circulation in the province than the entire provincial population. Very little was being done to measure, identify and investigate fraudulent use of health cards (Ontario Auditor General 2006), but in response to the Auditor General's report, Ontario has begun to improve health card usage auditing. Apart from fraudulently obtaining social benefits and potentially causing physical harm to the victim, an inaccurate health record resulting from such criminal activities can impact a victim's future insurability and employability, and these errors can be extremely difficult to find and correct.

A model for ensuring secure knowledge management in healthcare has been proposed by Mundy and Chadwick (2005). The model addresses the five major relevant components of secure knowledge management: authentication, authorization, data security (supporting privacy), data integrity and policies relating to information security. These components are essential and mutually supportive. Authentication without authorization would mean that, although only valid users could gain access, they could execute any operations within the system. Authorization without authentication could allow anyone falsely to use a valid user's access rights. A suitable security policy provides risk management, controls, recovery processes and auditing procedures. This supports secure practices and ensures that security is implemented in an integrated and appropriate manner. Finally, a system without privacy and integrity would be untrustworthy, so that practitioners would quickly abandon its use. In a worst-case scenario, details about clinical procedures might be modified erroneously without being detected, with potentially disastrous consequences for patients.

Risks to Organizations

As the risk of IDTF continues to increase, one would expect a growing awareness of the need to combat these threats. Yet, according to a 2006 study commissioned by the UK Department of Trade and Industry (DTI), three-fifths of UK businesses were still without a security policy and just 44% of companies had conducted security risk assessments in the previous year (Warren 2007). Also, as more and more customers and suppliers are being granted direct access to corporate systems, 30% of transactional websites were not encrypting the transactions that pass over the Internet. The wave of database breaches that continues to occur would not be happening if organizations were developing and implementing security policies that guard against unauthorized access. For example, given what is known about potential criminal attacks, the loss of large, confidential databases stored unencrypted in laptop computers is inexcusable when simple precautions would prevent such losses.

Data Breaches

Data breaches were discussed in Chapter 5. But it is not clear just how serious organizations are in responding to these risks. A 2007 report on security commissioned by CMI, a member of the Canadian Advanced Technical Alliance (CATA) (CMI 2007), surveyed one hundred Canadian companies from a range of industries. The survey found that 79% of respondents rated IT security as a critical priority in their organization and that all had multiple security solutions or tools already in place. Almost all who rated IT security as a high priority had at least one unresolved security challenge. Of those who rated IT security as a high priority, 31% planned IT security initiatives in security infrastructure enhancements or security infrastructure management. Thirty-five percent of the respondents identified forty-four upcoming technology initiatives involving security infrastructure strategies.

An empirical study examined the actual response of the two hundred largest US banks to security threats (Sarel and Marmorstein 2006). Its findings indicated that many banks, particularly smaller ones, were not meeting these challenges. Major security breaches continue to be reported, where hackers have stolen the personal information of thousands of individuals from banks, credit bureaus, insurance companies and health maintenance organizations. Stolen data may include such sensitive information as social security and driver's license numbers, financial or medical histories and bank account numbers and balances (Freeman 2006).

Banks, payment processors, merchants, card associations, security firms and Internet service providers all participate in one or more networks that process non-cash payments. A data breach at any one can result in losses at the others, but individual corporations tend to under-invest in data security because each only receives part of the benefit from it; the rest of the benefit accrues to other network members and their customers. For example, telecommunications companies are major providers of Internet services in Canada, and these companies spend significant amounts on network security to defend their networks and customers against the current huge growth in malicious data traffic. This traffic can originate both from within their own customer ranks or externally from other networks. If each network supplier does not carry a fair share of the responsibility and cost of guarding against such traffic, customers in all the networks will suffer. So, a network's security is only as effective as the security of its weakest link—the participant most likely to experience a data breach. As Schreft (2007) has pointed out, networks can adopt policies that impose minimum security practices or contractually assign liability for data breaches to improve investment in security within the network; but a network's security will still be too lax from a global perspective if the network's own breaches can impose losses on entities outside the network.

Understanding the potential financial and reputational harm that can result from publicly revealing security and privacy breaches should be enough to persuade businesses to take preventative measures against such incidents. If such events occur, however, businesses should take necessary steps to reduce the associated risks and potential losses. Issues that may come to light include the following (Foster 2005):

- Will consumers form a class-action suit?
- Will banks and credit card companies demand compensation for the costs to reissue consumer credit cards?
- Will directors and officers be sued by stakeholders alleging that lax internal controls led to fraud, direct financial losses, brand damage and a drop in the company's stock price?
- Will a company's network and IT infrastructure be able to recover quickly and provide functions that will support business applications and customers?
- Will an extortionist threaten to post the confidential information on the Internet for all to see unless paid an exorbitant sum of money?
- Will the company be able to restore consumer confidence?

Recent US court judgments have tended to reduce the risks of likely class-action suits in that country. In 2009, for example, a federal court in Missouri threw out a consumer class-action lawsuit against pharmacy benefits company Express Scripts over a 2008 data breach (Vijayan 2009). In dismissing the suit, the judge took a position taken by a number of judges in the past. Although it was alleged that millions of consumer records had been accessed illegally, unless actual harm could be shown to have been done, no damages could be sought. The plaintiff in the case failed to show exactly how the data breach had caused him any direct injury or put him in danger of injury.

Recent publicity on international data breaches has apparently had a dramatic impact on UK consumers that is relevant to databases in the United Kingdom and outsourced data storage facilities managed abroad. A 2007 survey of more than 1,200 UK consumers (Dunstone 2007) reviewed their concerns about personal data theft. Only 5% of respondents claimed not to be concerned about the security of their personal data. However, 63% were concerned about the ability of data centres to protect their data. The study suggests that the issue of data breaches needs to be addressed on a political level, since 58% of respondents want to see governments and financial institutions take greater responsibility for protecting personal data. The survey also indicated a greater need for improved customer communication, as 82% of the respondents wanted immediate notification of data breaches, which is not currently required of European firms. At the present time, however, companies maintaining personal databases have a disincentive to report data breaches since they will probably be punished, as soon as news of the breach is made known, through loss of customers, damage to reputation, costs of clearing the problem and potential negative impact on share prices.

Businesses should also develop and apply appropriate security measures and protocols for handling payroll records and personnel files. Well designed controls should also be put in place for access to company data, including background checks for employees who work with sensitive information (Anonymous 2008). Not everyone who wants access really needs access, and the internal theft of employee information can be managed by limiting the number of people who have access to employee data. Proper file storage and destruction of employee information is also critical. Standards and procedures must be developed for employee data, just as they are for customer data.

Organizational Costs of Identity Theft and Fraud

The negative effects of identity theft or a breach of information to a business can have long-term and far-reaching ramifications in both financial and intangible costs, including the concerns of customers about the misuse or loss of information. For example, a 2002 US Government Accountability Office study of identity theft estimated the cost of prosecuting such theft (GAO 2002) at

$11,443 for white-collar crimes. The US Secret Service estimated the average cost per financial crime investigation was $15,000, while the FBI estimated it at $20,000.

A logical approach to evaluating return on investment (ROI) for generic network security activities and processes, based on independent research, includes several steps (CISCO 2001):

- Analyzing potential economic consequences
- Determining e-business intensity (for example, it is high-intensity if the majority of the organization's revenue is generated through Web-based or online supply-chain applications)
- Examining the cost of security
- Calculating a generic ROI for security

With careful consideration of the likelihood of negative events, balanced against the cost of these events (see Figure 3.1 in Chapter 3), it is possible to address security issues without over-spending on those areas under less threat, while investing appropriate amounts on those areas that may be under threat but are highly critical to the organization's future.

A Forrester Research data breach study (Kark, Stamp et al. 2007) of US firms revealed that

- Of eighty-three corporate IT managers interviewed, twenty-eight acknowledged having to cope with a data breach.
- The costs of a data breach varied widely, ranging from $90 to $305 per customer record.
- The cost per customer record exposed was estimated to be $50 for discovery, notification and response, in expenses associated with legal counsel, call centres and mail notification.
- Lost employee productivity was estimated to range from $20 to $30 per customer record.

These costs, of course, are negatively related to the costs of securing the organization against IDTF (not included in these estimates). It is clearly impossible to guarantee that there will be no loss of data due to IDTF, no matter how much money is spent on data security. However, each organization should attempt to find the point at which increased spending on security will cost more than the expected reduction in tangible and intangible losses from these criminal activities. Intangible costs, although they are difficult to estimate, can be even more devastating than tangible costs to a company. An excellent reputation and a good public image that has taken years to build can be lost overnight if the public becomes aware of a data breach resulting from a lack of due diligence by the company or its employees. This is especially acute for customers who must take the time and trouble to have identification and accounts revised to avoid losses due to the theft of their personal information, or in the extreme cases when private information is used by criminals for blackmail and direct threats to them or their families.

Organizational Response to Security Threats

There are many examples of public and private corporations that have been less than diligent about preventing identity theft and fraud. For example, Canada's postal system is a conduit for hundreds of thousands of documents containing financial and personal information, including cash, cheques, gifts and documents. Mail thieves can steal identity information from bank and credit card statements, government documents and pre-approved credit applications (W5 Staff 2009). Canada Post has been slow to respond to such threats, measures against which can include making improvements to external security (better locks on mailboxes), ensuring their employees do not have criminal records and prosecuting employees found to have committed identity theft and fraud. Moreover, Canada Post inspectors do not have the power to arrest and charge employees and must rely on police to investigate and prosecute suspected mail fraud crimes. Mail thefts that are investigated and prosecuted by police, although they can cause enormous and continuing problems for individuals and corporations, often result in light sentences for the perpetrators, who are soon back on the street, again plying their criminal activities (W5 Staff 2009). This compares poorly with the United States, where US Mail inspectors have police-like powers to prosecute IDTF and where the laws provide more significant penalties for criminal activities involving the regular mail system.

Outsourcing Information and Computing Technologies

While outsourcing Information and Computing Technologies (ICT) has become popular in recent years, outsourcing of security for these very same systems has become a significant issue due to its organizational, legal and technical aspects. It should therefore be considered in a completely different manner (Karyda, Mitrou et al. 2006). The market growth in outsourced ICT security services makes it essential that additional issues relating to privacy protection are addressed in the contractual arrangements with the outsourcing providers. Meeting privacy protection requirements like liability, protection of intellectual property, security and confidentiality are critical issues for outsourcing because of an organization's constraints within its relevant legal and regulatory framework. An equally important issue is that privacy is also essential to building and maintaining trust relations between organizations and their customers and/or business partners. These issues are mostly addressed through the technical infrastructure. Legal and regulatory frameworks within which organizations operate do restrict outsourcing arrangements, but they also provide guidance on such issues as liability and intellectual property rights in setting up the outsourcing contracts. On the other hand, considerations of legal jurisdiction, in which the organization and the outsourcing provider operate, must guide the contractual arrangements, especially when operating across state or international borders.

Preserving security and confidentiality of information are primary inhibitors for organizations in considering whether to outsource certain functions, and meeting related obligations imposes potential liabilities on organizations (Karyda, Mitrou et al. 2006).

Risks from Disposal of Electronic Goods

Thousands of tons of electronic goods are discarded each year. Many of the discarded items are computers with hard drives or other storage media containing confidential information that should have been destroyed, but which, when it is not, may be used for criminal purposes. There are laws in some countries governing the disposal of computers, and often military and business contracts specify that storage media be wiped clean of information or crushed so the information is no longer accessible. These rules are not always observed, and many discarded computers are shipped in bulk to foreign countries like Ghana, China and India for disposal. A recent documentary from Frontline/World (Klein 2009) recounted how computers were shipped to Ghana, where they were dismantled so certain materials could be recovered. Although the disposal methods had little regard for the health of the people doing the recovery operations, it was also discovered that computer hard drives often contained private, personal information and industrial or military secrets. Since Ghana is also regarded as one of the top sources of cybercrime, it is not hard to believe that this information can find its way into the hands of criminals who will find some way to benefit from its use. It is therefore incumbent upon any business or consumer to ensure that storage media on discarded computers are disposed of properly through a reputable firm.

Summary

In this chapter, we examined a number of consumer and business perspectives relating to IDTF. First, we discussed shopping risks, where consumers must balance the risks and benefits of physically visiting a retail store against the risks of identity theft and fraud that may be experienced while shopping online from the safety of home. We reviewed mortgage fraud, a particularly egregious crime involving identity theft, which can bankrupt individuals exposed to it. The lack of appropriate legal remedies is an example of a legal system that has not been adapted quickly to this type of threat. Medical identity theft and fraud is an ongoing problem that is often not apparent in Canada, where Medicare pays the bills and consumers are rarely made aware of the direct costs to the system. Public awareness of this type of crime is more common in the United States, where consumers learn directly about the cost of medical procedures. This kind of fraud has the possibility of causing serious physical harm to the consumers it victimizes, since it can result in serious errors in permanent medical records.

There are a number of organizational risks from IDTF, several of which were described in detail—including data breaches, the frequency of which continues to increase and have an impact in industrialized nations. Actions taken to publicize these breaches in the United States have resulted in an increased interest in addressing and reducing their likelihood. The organizational costs of IDTF were also examined, along with how to balance the costs of prevention against the benefits from reducing the probability of occurrence. Organizational responses to security threats were discussed, using the particular example of Canada Post, which is particularly vulnerable to physical theft of identity information but which lacks sufficient power to police its operations properly. Finally, the risks of outsourcing security operations and disposing of used electronic equipment containing stored databases were described.

References

AHIMA. 2008. "Mitigating Medical Identity Theft." *Journal of the American Health Information Management Association*, 79: 9: 63–69.

Anonymous. 2007 (8 January). "Diagnosis: Identity Theft." *Business Week*.

Anonymous. 2008 (1 March). "Identity theft: Helping Employees Help Themselves." *Risk Management*, 55.

Bair, Sheila C. 2010. "Statement on Problems in Mortgage Servicing from Modification to Foreclosure." Chairman, FDIC. http://banking.senate.gov/public/index.cfm?FuseAction=Files.View&FileStore_id=318beba2-a775-4a7b-98b8-14aff84c07ab [consulted April 21, 2011].

BBC News. 2009 (2 December). "Doctors Warned about Risk of 'Facebook Flirts.'" http://news.bbc.co.uk/2/hi/health/8389458.stm.

CISC. 2007. "Mortgage Fraud and Organized Crime in Canada." Strategic Intelligence Brief, November 2007. Ottawa: Criminal Intelligence Service Canada—Central Bureau. http://www.cisc.gc.ca/products_services/mortgage_fraud/document/mortgage_e.pdf [consulted April 5, 2009].

CISC. 2008. "2008 Report on Organized Crime." Ottawa: Criminal Intelligence Service Canada—Central Bureau. www.cisc.gc.ca/annual_reports/annual_report_2008/document/report_oc_2008_e.pdf [consulted January 28, 2009].

CISCO. 2001. "The Return on Investment for Network Security." Cisco Systems. http://www.cisco.com/warp/public/cc/so/neso/sqso/roi4_wp.pdf [consulted May 31, 2009].

Clark, B. C. 2009. "A Risky Business for BC Lenders." *Slaw*. http://www.slaw.ca/2009/06/26/a-risky-business-for-bc-lenders/ [consulted March 19, 2011].

CMI. 2007. "Canadian Security Technology Readiness Intelligence Report." Canadian Advanced Technology Alliance: 18. http://www.cata.ca/Media_and_Events/Press_Releases/cata_pr06070701.html [consulted July 3, 2009].

Dixon, P. 2006. *Medical Identity Theft: The Information Crime that Can Kill You.* World Privacy Forum, 56.

Dunstone, E. 2007. "Lack of Consumer Trust in Data Security in the UK." *International Journal of Micrographics and Optical Technology*, 25: 1/2: 4.

Evans, J., and B. Berman. 2005. *Marketing, 9e: Marketing in the 21st Century.* Cincinnati: Atomic Dog.

Foster, P. C. 2005. "Managing E-business Risk to Mitigate Loss." *Financial Executive*, 21: 43–45.

Freeman, E. H. 2006. "Disclosure of Information Theft: The ChoicePoint Security Breach." *Information Systems Security*, 14: 6: 11–15.

GAO. 2002. "Identity Theft, Appendix V: Cost of Identity Theft to the Federal Criminal Justice System." *Identity Theft*. Washington, D.C.: United States Government Accounting Office, 64–67.

Kark, K., P. Stamp, et al. 2007. *Calculating the Cost of a Security Breach*. Forrester Research: 7.

Karyda, M., E. Mitrou, et al. 2006. "A Framework for Outsourcing IS/IR Security Services." *Information Management & Computer Security*, 14: 5: 403–16.

Klein, P. 2009. "Ghana: Digital Dumping Ground." Frontline World. http://www.pbs.org/frontlineworld/stories/ghana804/video/video_index.html [consulted July 15, 2009].

Knight, W. 2008 (17 March). "Legacy Retailers Find Payment Card Security a Tough Standard." *Computer Weekly*. http://www.computerweekly.com/Articles/2008/03/17/229895/legacy-retailers-find-payment-card-security-a-tough.htm [consulted July 17, 2009].

Mundy, D., and D. W. Chadwick. 2005. "Secure Knowledge Management for Healthcare Organizations." *Creating Knowledge-Based Healthcare Organizations*.

Edited by N. Wickramasinghe, J. N. D. Gupta and S. Sharma. Hershey, PA: Idea Group Inc.

Ontario Auditor General. 2006. *Annual Report of the Auditor General of Ontario: Section 3.08 Ontario Health Insurance Plan.* Toronto: Auditor General of Ontario: 188–99.

Orbuch, D., J. O'Brien, et al. 2004. "Identity Theft: A Compliance Officer's Next Generation of Concerns." *Journal of Health Care Compliance,* March–April: 5–7.

Princeton. 2005. "Leap of Faith: Using the Internet Despite the Dangers." Princeton Survey Associates International.

Predmore, C. E., J. Rovenpor, et al. 2007. "Shopping in an Age of Terrorism." *Competitive Review,* 17: 3: 170–80.

Sarel, D., and H. Marmorstein. 2006. "Addressing Consumers' Concerns About Online Security: A Conceptual and Empirical Analysis of Banks' Actions." *Journal of Financial Services Marketing,* 11: 2: 99–115.

Schreft, S. L. 2007. "Risks of Identity Theft: Can the Market Protect the Payment System?" *Economic Review,* 92: 4: 5–40.

Sheppard, S. 2010. "Bill 152: Ontario's Response to Real Estate Fraud." Toronto: MortgageRatesToday. http://mortgageratestoday.ca/bill-152-ontarios-response-to-real-estate-fraud/ [consulted March 19, 2011].

Sproule, S., and N. Archer. 2008b. "Measuring Identity Theft in Canada: 2008 Consumer Survey." *McMaster eBusiness Research Centre Working Paper #23.* Hamilton, Ontario: DeGroote School of Business, McMaster University.

Vijayan, J. 2009 (12 December). "Judge Throws Out Data Breach Lawsuit Saying No Harm Was Done." itBusiness.ca. http://www.itbusiness.ca/it/client/en/home/news.asp?id=55634 [consulted December 12, 2009].

W-5 Staff. 2009. "Stamp Out the Crime: When Your Mail Is the Target of Thieves." CTV News. http://www.ctv.ca/servlet/ArticleNews/story/CTVNews/20090228/wfive_postal_090228/20090228?hub=WFive [consulted March 1, 2009].

Warren, A. 2007. "Stolen Identity: Regulating the Illegal Trade in Personal Data in the 'Data-Based Society.'" *International Review of Law, Computers & Technology,* 21: 2: 177–90.

Chapter 11

Technical Perspectives On Security

"The nice thing about standards is that there are so many to choose from."

—Author unknown

The most important network security issues are those that involve defending against the increasing degree of criminal activity on the Internet. In previous chapters we have discussed risk management (Chapters 7 and 8), employee behavioural issues (Chapter 9) and financial impacts (Chapter 10). In this chapter we address related technical issues. We discuss organizational security first, then identity and access management and the general concepts of network protection when handling external traffic. Finally we include a detailed review of authentication issues for both internal and external users. All of these topics are important to the technical management of risks in the presence of network threats at a time when network dependency continues to increase for both institutions and individuals who rely on it to carry transactions, information and communications.

Organizational Security Issues

Security improvement is often hard to sell to management and to implement effectively because it is an abstract concept that deals with hypothetical events (Allen 2004). Security measures are typically viewed as disaster preventing rather than payoff producing, which is similar to insurance; this makes it difficult to justify investing in security. Installing security safeguards has negative aspects such as added cost, diminished performance and inconvenience. Benefits from security can be seen only in events that do not happen. The key to investing in security is to balance the resulting improved security against reduction in risk. Security is not unlike other areas of the software industry, regarding efforts to improve software quality, conduct proper testing, keep documentation up to date and maintain current configuration and hardware/software inventory records. Another difficulty is persuading organizational management that security is a holistic problem that involves more than technology. It also includes organizational, regulatory, economic and social aspects.

The Internet's security today is worse than it should be, and there is also a lot of room for improvement in evaluating and publishing relevant best practices. Table 11.1 lists the types of computer crimes about which organizations should be concerned, including both internal and external threats, and what aspect of security is involved in defending against these threats.

Because security often does not come to the attention of executive management until a serious breach occurs, it may not be given the attention and support required to meet some specified level. But there are drivers for the adoption of security practices and standards at all levels of the organization, including compliance with government regulations (and potentially compliance with international standards), fear of publicity from required announcements about data breaches and external auditing reports about lax security measures (Phifer and Piscitello 2007). Technical security drivers include concerns about wireless security, spam and anti-virus protection, data protection and web security threats (CMI 2007).

IT operations and security functions should attempt to prevent significant negative events from happening. As discussed in Chapter 7, prevention, detection and remedial measures can be implemented at the three phases of risk management: anticipatory, reactionary and remediation. If organizations can't prevent something from happening, they need to be able to detect it, and if they can't detect it, they need to be able to recover from it and restore service in a timely manner. Organizational change management must be considered, planned and applied in both the prevention and detection activities that are required to get to this level of maturity. Although change management is not a technical issue, it has a strong positive impact on implementing technical changes that affect users, both internal and external to the organization. Effective change management does not slow things down, isn't bureaucratic, doesn't reduce productivity and isn't burdensome. If it is done properly it can actually enable, improve and accelerate business level performance (Allen 2004).

Compliance with regulations and standards like the Health Insurance Portability and Accountability Act (HIPAA), the Gramm-Leach-Bliley Act (GLBA), Sarbanes–Oxley (SOX), Payment Card Industry (PCI) (Dreger 2010) and Canada's Personal Information Protection and Electronic Documents Act (PIPEDA) (OPCC 2010) contribute to overall network security. The financial and legal repercussions of non-compliance have prompted many companies to track and control data access to a far greater degree than any prior imperative. However, laws and regulations are not panaceas and have their limitations. For example, the Canadian PIPEDA legislation lacks enforcement sanctions, making compliance more difficult to encourage in Canada. Organizations in the United States, at least partially due to the penalties that may be enforced if they are found to be non-compliant and/or if confidential databases of consumer or customer data are accessed illegally, tend to be more motivated in undertaking vulnerability assessments that can help to find and fix policy deviations before their databases are attacked or before outside auditors discover the deviations (Phifer and Piscitello 2007).

Working against tighter security are employee attitudes that must be changed in order for secure solutions to be successful (see Chapter 9). Organizations must balance the need for both

Table 11.1: Computer Crimes

Crime	Description	Security Defence
Sabotage	Physical attacks	Safeguarding physical assets
Computer-based physical fraud	Altering input Theft of computer time Software piracy Altering or stealing data files Theft or use of computer output Unauthorized access to computers or networks	Improved identity management Restricted access to and protection of physical assets
Computer-based virtual fraud	Trojan horse (unauthorized software code) Salami techniques (diverting rounded-up financial data to illicit accounts) Trapdoors (bypassing normal computer access controls) Piggybacking (unauthorized signals added to communications messages) Masquerading (unauthorized access using legitimate user ID) Hacking (breaking into a system illegally through a communications link) Eavesdropping (listening to transmissions intended for others) Browsing (searching for password or other access information) Viruses (destructive programs that can damage memory or files)	All employees trained to detect and prevent fraud Identifying risks and introducing measures to reduce risks, such as: passwords, firewalls, connectivity security and cryptography

(Adapted from Haugen and Selin 1999)

security and convenience. As restrictive measures are put in place to improve security, convenience of access is almost certainly reduced. "The sloppy use of many technologies of convenience reduces our privacy, which, in turn, leaves us more vulnerable to such serious threats as stalking, identity theft, intellectual property theft, and even espionage (both industrial and conventional). The problem is not with the technologies themselves but with our unwillingness to take the requisite precautions when using them" (Caloyannides 2004).

It is important to raise the perception that detection is the key to deterrence. This can be accomplished by (Wells 1997)

- employee education,
- proactive fraud policies,
- increased use of analytical reviews,
- surprise audits, and
- adequate reporting programs.

Internal controls should be designed to encourage people to be honest and are the primary defense against fraud. An internal control system should (Haugen and Selin 1999)

- safeguard assets of the firm,
- ensure the accuracy and reliability of accounting records and information,
- promote efficiency in the firm's operations, and
- measure compliance with management's prescribed policies and procedures.

Internal control systems should also detect fraud when it has occurred. However, most internal frauds are detected by accident rather than by a specific examination for fraudulent activities. An organization can emphasize security and protection against fraud by (Thompson 1992)

- providing an environment that does not tolerate fraud against the organization
- prohibiting fraud for the benefit of the organization and
- ensuring that executives, managers and operating personnel are trained to recognize the symptoms of fraud and to expose it when it is detected.

Identity and Access Management

Identity and access management (IAM) policies deal with the difficulties in an organization when one user has multiple user IDs and passwords on separate systems, or granting specific access rights and permissions to such users (Peterson, Smedegaard et al. 2008). Inadequate attention to such policies can greatly increase risk exposure. IAM becomes more difficult as organizational size and complexity increases, so the potential benefit from software-based IAM will be much greater for these organizations. Even smaller organizations, however, can benefit greatly from IAM readiness reviews, which will facilitate compliance and information security improvements. IAM policy and process improvements can include user ID naming, process work instructions, segregation of duties policies and reviews that focus on high-risk systems. There are substantial benefits of IAM to internal control, including centralized monitoring, detecting policy violations and segregation of duties. Tight control over an IAM system use is essential, since this system has ultimate control of system users. Both internal and external auditors need to be involved during the implementation process to certify policies and change management procedures. The IAM system controls should also be integrated into the regular internal controls and change management processes (Peterson, Smedegaard et al. 2008).

The growth of mobile business requires companies to provide context-aware services, to focus on the development of trust relationships between trading partners and to be able easily to reconfigure value chains (Roussos, Peterson et al. 2003). The integration of the Internet, traditional telephony networks and consumer electronics brings mobile business to the point where mobile identity management can play a central role in addressing usability and trust issues in mobile business through the telecommunications infrastructure. Identity management is used in mobile services to identify, acquire, access and pay for services that follow the user from device to device, location to location and context to context. Thus, it is the network component that can meld novel services that use innovative business models. At the same time, considerations of users play a fundamental role when planning and managing both internal and external user identity.

Network Protection

Network protection can involve many complex technical issues. High-quality network security is essential for handling external traffic that can carry malicious software. Serious external Internet threats include vulnerable routing infrastructures, vulnerable name service verification, lax system and network administration, sloppy programming and new application features that trump security. For example, a firm implementing VoIP (Voice over Internet Protocol) may decide to 'add security later,' leaving the network open to threats until the appropriate security level is implemented, providing that it is not forgotten until a security infraction occurs (Phifer and Piscitello 2007). In addition, security from internal threats must also be part of any effective solution.

Perhaps the best way to discuss network security is through a diagram like Figure 11.1, where each component layer contributes to the overall security of the corporate network by handling a certain specific aspect. In the diagram, messages and documents can arrive from the Internet and are filtered by a network firewall that restricts allowable traffic ports and sources; for example, it may block traffic that does not originate from recognized sources. The next layer is a web application firewall that filters HTTP traffic and blocks external application level attacks. Traffic can then enter the corporate web farm, which is a group of computer systems and web server software that collectively provide webpage delivery mechanism to internal users. This may provide both internal and external (Internet) support for the organization. The network security scanner looks internally for unauthorized installations, vulnerabilities and missing software patches, thus providing a monitoring function for the security of the internal network and the web farm. Traffic from the web farm undergoes additional filtering through the inner network firewall before entering the protected private network. External mobile workers and telecommuters access the internal private network through a virtual private network (VPN) concentrator that allows traffic only from pre-authorized users. The central directory controls access across the organization. Workstations all run anti-virus software that continually scans communications traffic and internal files for viruses and other threats. E-mail, file and application servers protect data by encryption and centralized authentication controls. Database network access control is through stored procedures and encryption that protects stored data from unauthorized access.

Cell phone networks are subject to certain security threats such as viruses hidden in application software, although cell phone and PDA operating systems tend to be relatively secure and can warn against installing software that may be contaminated. Bluetooth-enabled cell phones are also vulnerable to attack from other devices that may make use of this technology to access cell phone data and software. Wi-Fi network providers, including home-based PC systems, are at serious risk from system intrusion and disruption due to unauthorized access and security violations by roaming users (Sipior and Ward 2007).

There are additional considerations for security in a wireless LAN environment. In such an environment, it is necessary to have a strict and well-published security policy, to use 128-bit encryption end to end, a firewall between the WLAN and the corporate network, strong authentication of both the device and the user and a virtual private network for wireless transmission (Karygiannis and Owens 2002). A suggested best practice approach to

Figure 11.1: Network Security Functions

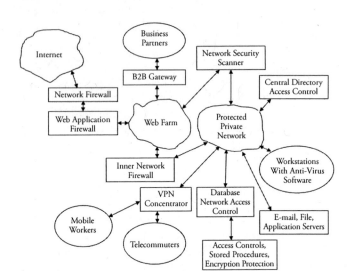

(Adapted from Dyck 2003)

maintaining wireless system security also includes the following (Turner and Hazari 2007):

- Maintain a full topology of all wireless connections and access points.
- Label and maintain an inventory of all wireless devices.
- Create regular backups, with no data being stored permanently on wireless devices.
- Perform regular security tests of network and devices.
- Perform random but regularly timed audits, and ensure that all staff are educated in the proper use of the WLAN and devices.
- Apply patches and security enhancements.
- Monitor the industry for new standards affecting security and new products to enhance security.
- Monitor vigilantly for new threats and vulnerabilities.

Authentication

Online banking, consumer trading, and product and service transaction activity has grown exponentially in recent years. Commercial institutions have increasingly focused their marketing activities on consumers by providing improved online customer convenience and flexibility. At the same time, these institutions (particularly online banks) have been plagued by a rapidly growing number of criminals who continue to employ more advanced scamming techniques like 'phishing,' 'pharming' and 'man-in-the-middle' attacks. (In this section, we delve into the more technical aspects of authentication, which have already been introduced in Chapter 5). *Phishing* is criminal creation and use of e-mails and websites—designed to look like e-mails and websites of well-known, legitimate businesses, financial institutions and government agencies—in order to deceive Internet users into disclosing financial account information or other personal data like usernames and passwords when requested to do so by an authentic-looking e-mail. An authentication process will fail if customers cannot recognize they are on a fake website, no matter how strong the customer authentication. To defeat this problem, site-to-customer authentication can be as important as the standard customer-to-site authentication.

Pharming is similar to phishing, but it accomplishes similar results for multiple rather than individual users by inserting false information into the DNS (the domain name server, which translates domain names into Internet Protocol addresses so they can be accessed on the network by the requesting computer), resulting in misdirection of the user request to a non-legitimate site. *Man-in-the-middle attacks* are a form of active eavesdropping in which a hacker makes independent connections with the victims and relays messages between them so information in the messages can be used for criminal purposes. Among all the related online relationship issues—such as security, privacy, non-repudiation and trust—authentication plays a critical role in determining the effectiveness of the entire interaction process in defeating scamming techniques, because all of these issues depend so extensively on authentication.

Authentication is defined as the process of determining whether someone or something is, in fact, who or what it is declared to be. In the online environment, authentication is a way to ensure users are who they say they are—that the user who attempts to perform functions on a system is in fact the user who is authorized to do so. The most commonly used authentication method for consumers is to use usernames and passwords to gain access to online e-commerce, banking or other services. This is known as single-factor authentication, since it involves only the second one of three normally used factors: 'something you have,' 'something you know' and 'something you are.'

Since the early days of online access, authenticating customers to a website being accessed has been the primary focus of authentication, and the site itself has typically been assumed to be an authentic site provided by a trusted institution. But, as scamming techniques have become so widespread and losses to these scams have continued to grow, institutions have begun to strengthen customer authentication. One example with which North Americans are familiar is the recent wholesale replacement of magnetic strip credit cards with chip-and-PIN credit cards, with the intent of reducing fraudulent activities with stolen credit cards or copied credit card information. This is known as 'two-factor' authentication since it involves both something you have (a bank card) and something you know (the PIN). This has been shown to succeed in reducing fraud (at least in the short term, before criminals find a way to defeat the new methodology) in the UK (Parr 2006). This authentication technique has recently been implemented throughout Canada, and has been in service for several years of online credit card transactions in Europe (MasterCard 2008).

In the United States, financial regulators have recommended strengthened authentication from customers to bank websites (like two-factor authentication, mentioned above) (FFIEC 2005). However, there is a stronger methodology called mutual authentication (see discussion later in this chapter) which, in addition to authenticating customers to the online site, also authenticates the online site to the customer. Technically, this requires clients or users to authenticate themselves to a server and that server authenticating itself to the users in such a way that both parties are assured of the other's identity.

Online Authentication Attacks

The nature of authentication attacks continues to become more active. Previously, passive threats included password guessing or physical password theft, dumpster diving and shoulder surfing. Active attacks include online intrusions to the computers of victims, or lulling victims into giving up their credentials. Active attacks can be classified into two types: offline credential-stealing attacks and online channel-breaking attacks (Hiltgen, Kramp et al. 2006). Offline credential-stealing attacks aim to fraudulently obtain customer credentials, either by using malicious software (e.g., Trojan horses) or by phishing or pharming. Online channel-breaking attacks are also known as 'man-in-the-middle' attacks.

Malicious software. The Trojan horse is an example of this type of software. An attacker installs a Trojan horse, such as a keylogger program, on a customer's computer without his or her knowledge during a customer visit to a particular website. When the user logs into a commercial website, the information keyed in during that session is captured and transmitted to the attacker by the Trojan horse software. Subsequently, the attacker can use the illegally obtained information to make fraudulent transactions on the commercial website that was being accessed by the customer.

Phishing. Phishing is one of the fastest-growing forms of Internet attacks. The growth in the rate of phishing attacks is due in no small part to the fact that criminals interested in phishing expeditions can go online and get all the tools needed to start a phishing campaign for a relatively small investment—usually less than $1,000. This cost includes the software to create the mailing list, the software to send out the e-mail and a list of legitimate e-mail addresses. A typical phishing attack involves sending customers an 'urgent' e-mail to ask them to login to a fake web address that duplicates a legitimate online site. If the user is accustomed to doing business with this organization, and the website appears to be authentic, then he/she can be easily fooled into entering the data. By logging in, the customer provides credentials that can be used to repair an 'urgent' problem. Of course, there is no such problem and the attacker now has the identity information needed to login to the real commercial address and access the customer's account. Phishing can also be combined with pharming, which is a more advanced technology, as it attacks the vulnerability of DNS server software by making the DNS server redirect a website's traffic to a fake site. A customer who succumbs to a phishing or pharming attack, resulting in fraudulent losses and time wasted in clearing up the problem, will lose trust and confidence in that institution, and in online commerce in general.

Thieves also frequent peer-to-peer (P2P) file-sharing networks through which participants share music and movies, searching for files on participant computers containing tax returns, credit reports, Social Security Numbers or Social Insurance Numbers, and bank account information. P2P software, when loaded on a computer, allows others to access the computer to search for shared files. If the software is not installed properly or the computer is compromised by certain viruses, the machine's entire hard drive is accessible to other network users, with the obvious potential of identity theft and the fraud that may result. It is clear that the theft of personal identifiers continues to grow in parallel with the accompanying risk of becoming victimized by identity fraud.

Social networking sites like MySpace and Facebook, as well as online resumes, can provide a host of information for those intent on identity theft. Other sources of identity information include newspaper websites (e.g., birth announcements, with newborn's birth date, city of residence and names of parents, grandparents and siblings). Obituaries and marriage announcements are also a source of information. One study found that a mother's unmarried name can be inferred with alarming certainty through automated searches of public records. From information publicly available from the US Social Security Administration (SSA), an SSN can be matched to the issuing state and date, estimated age range of the recipient and activity status. It also makes it easier for an identity thief to infer other personal information, like place of birth. Combined with access by an identity thief to a LexisNexis account or to the database of a credit reporting agency or data broker, compiling extensive information on a person becomes very simple (Schreft 2007).

Man in the Middle. Man-in-the-middle (MITM) attacks are basically an extended version of pharming. MITM is a form of active eavesdropping in which the attacker makes independent connections with the victims and relays messages between them, making them believe that they are talking directly to one another over a private connection, when in fact the entire conversation is controlled by the attacker. The attacker is able to intercept all messages going between the two victims and inject new or modified ones without either party knowing that the link between them has been compromised. The MITM attack can even work against public-key cryptography. Customers sometimes naively ignore messages about invalid certificates or, even worse, are fooled into trusting fake server certificates generated online from a nested intruder certification authority (CA) (Hiltgen, Kramp et al. 2006).

The above are just three common classes of attacks on Internet transactions, and no doubt more will continue to appear. To combat such attacks, and to minimize their disruption of Internet commerce, effective authentication plays a critical role.

Authentication Approaches

The online banking environment continues to grow rapidly, as financial institutions encourage customers to complete money transfers, pay bills and access critical information online. At the same time, online banking has been plagued by Internet criminals and fraudsters attempting to steal customer information through a variety of attacks such as those described above, enabling fraudsters to obtain information from customers and, thus, access to online banking accounts. Customer authentication is therefore a major concern of financial institutions. There are many options available when implementing enhanced authentication in online banking. A detailed analysis of the many authentication solutions available, as well as a set of guidelines for selecting and implementing enhanced authentication, has been outlined by Williamson (2006).

US regulatory authorities have strengthened authentication requirements in response to heightened threats to online banking (Cocheo 2006). Comodo (2006) discusses the stiffened regulations for US banks and how multi-factor authentication might or might not improve authentication, in addition to how one company has a proposed a solution to the problem, based on Public Key Encryption (PKI). A taxonomy of user authentication processes (Pulkkis, Grahn et al. 2006) is based on how a user identifies himself or herself. This taxonomy has four main branches; three of these represent normally used identification methods, in order of least to most secure:

- 'Something you know': knowledge-based user authentication (such as a password that identifies the user—though this only verifies that someone knows the password),
- 'Something you have': token-based user authentication (such as a digital certificate on the user's computer or a smartcard—but computers and smartcards can be stolen),

- 'Something you are': includes biometric user authentication (such as fingerprints or iris recognition; although these are difficult to forge, it is possible to defeat this form of authentication) and dynamic biometrics (something you do, like a handwritten signature or voice recognition; these can also be fooled by replay attacks) and
- 'Recognition-based user authentication': mutual authentication, where both system and user must authenticate themselves to the other party.

Each of the first three processes, used individually, is known as single-factor authentication. These methods are becoming less secure, however, as criminals become more sophisticated in defeating them. One way to improve authentication security is to use more than one of these processes, or multi-factor authentication (Howie 2006). Schneier has attacked the notion of two-factor authentication (Schneier 2005), pointing out its vulnerability to phishing and Trojan horse attacks. He suggests that two-factor authentication may work well for local logins, and within certain corporate networks, but it won't work for remote authentication over the Internet. Schneier suggests that financial institutions will spend large amounts of money outfitting users with two-factor authentication tokens. This may result in an early drop in fraud, but more sophisticated attacks will ultimately defeat two-factor authentication, with little if any ultimate drop in fraud and identity theft. Sheward (2006) has pointed out how a man-in-the-middle attack has already been used to defeat two-factor authentication at Citibank.

Customer-to-Site Authentication

Customer-to-site authentication is typically dependent on customers providing valid identification data (identifiers) through one or more authentication factors to prove their identities. Identifiers may include a bankcard for ATMs or some form of user

ID for remote access. An authentication factor is information used to verify a person's identity for security purposes. The three factors used are the first three factors in the taxonomy presented above: something you know, something you have or something you are.

Something a customer knows. This factor can be thought of as a shared secret, such as a password or PIN, which are known or shared by both customer and authentication entity. Usually shared secrets include questions of specific knowledge about the customers. For example, "What is the name of the (city, town or place) where you were born?" Such shared secrets are often included during the initial enrolment process as an additional security element. While this factor is the most widely used and lowest cost authentication method, it is also the least secure form of authentication, as it can be easily compromised. Passwords are often easy to guess or steal, and once a password is compromised the thief has the same access rights as the legitimate user. This is especially troublesome if the legitimate user does not even know that his or her password has been compromised, since usually no physical evidence of the compromise exists. In addition, the shared knowledge of questions may be obscure, and, as more and more information is collected from diffuse databases, the reliability of this technique comes into question (FDIC 2005). This is also known as single-factor authentication, commonly thought of as inadequate for online transactions. In the United States, for example, the Federal Financial Institutions Examination Council (FFIEC) required banks to have a plan to implement stronger forms of authentication (two-factor, as opposed to single-factor) by the end of 2006 (FFIEC 2005).

Something a customer has. Something a customer has represents some sort of physical device or CA (Certification Authority) digital certificate that may be used in a multi-factor authentication protocol. There are several types of tokens: USB token devices, grid cards, smart cards and password-generating tokens.

A *USB token device* is a small piece of hardware that plugs into a computer's USB port. It is similar in size and appearance to the memory sticks that are in wide use for transporting files from one computer to another. A USB token usually contains a microprocessor and uses strong encryption to communicate with the various security applications on the user's computer. It does not require the installation of any special hardware on the user's computer (FDIC 2005). When a customer attempts to login to a secure system, the system checks the validity of this device; once the device is recognized, the user is then prompted to enter his or her password (the second authenticating factor) in order to gain access to the computer system. An advantage of this device is its compliance with the standard USB ports on most computers. These devices also have the ability to store digital certificates in their secure flash memory areas to be used in a public key infrastructure (PKI) environment.

Grid cards display a variety of numbers and characters on visible windows and are distributed to persons authorized to access a secured system or resource, like an online bank account. Customers who want to access a secured resource are challenged to prove they have the grid card that was distributed to them by answering questions about the contents of that card. This helps to prove that the persons are who they say they are. The grid authentication method has shown itself to be especially attractive for financial institutions looking to reduce the cost and complexity of securing their applications. A disadvantage to the grid card is ease of duplication.

Smart cards are physically about the size of credit cards. Like a USB token, a smart card contains a microprocessor that enables it to store and process data. To be used, a smart card must be inserted into a compatible reader attached to the user's computer. If the smart card is recognized as valid (the first factor), customers are prompted to enter their password (the second factor) to complete the authentication process. Smart cards are hard to duplicate and are tamper resistant; thus, they are a relatively secure vehicle for storing sensitive data and credentials (FDIC 2005). Smart cards are easy to carry, but they require the installation of a hardware reader and associated software drivers when used on the consumer's home computer. This technology is similar to the technology used for the chip-and-PIN credit cards.

Password-generating tokens are used to produce a one-time password (OTP) each time customers want to login to their accounts. These tokens have a small screen that displays a specially generated password for a short period of time. One-time passwords may be generated using one of three kinds of algorithms: 1) a mathematical algorithm based on the previous password; 2) an algorithm based on time synchronization between the authentication server and the client providing the password; and 3) a mathematical algorithm based on a challenge (e.g., a random number chosen by the authentication server or transaction details) and a counter instead of being based on the previous password. Password-generating tokens are more secure than the other technologies because of the time-sensitive, synchronized nature of the authentication. However, this technology is vulnerable to phishing and both non-time-synchronized and time-synchronized passwords have been attacked by phishers. In 2005, for example, customers of a Swedish bank were tricked into giving up their non-time-synchronized one-time passwords (Anonymous 2005) and in 2006 a similar attack succeeded against customers of Citibank's CitiBusiness service (Krebs 2006).

Something a customer is. 'Something a customer is' usually refers to biometrics. Biometric technologies identify a living person on the basis of physiological characteristics (e.g., fingerprints, iris configuration or facial structure) or physical characteristics (the rate and flow of movements such as the pattern of data entry on a computer keyboard). Biometric authentication provides a strong level of authentication, since each person is assumed to have his or her unique biometric characteristics. It does have drawbacks, however, when used as an authentication method. First, special hardware is required, which increases deployment cost. Second, storing biometric templates for all customers securely and economically is a challenge (Crosbie 2005). Also, customers may believe that this method will compromise their privacy and that it is too intrusive. In addition, this 'strong' method does not resist phishing or other online frauds.

There is a large variety of customer authentication methods and some of the most common have already been discussed. Selecting from among the three authentication factors—what you know, what you have and what you are—any combination of two or more of these can provide two-factor or multi-factor authentication (FFIEC 2005; Beaumier 2006; Furnell and Zekri 2006). At a minimum, two-factor authentication is a key component for secure Internet transactions, but it cannot solve all problems (Schneier 2005). The most obvious gap in the authentication process is that it will fail if customers cannot recognize they are not on legitimate websites no matter how strong the authentication is represented to be—single-, double- or multi-factor. In this case, site-to-customer authentication becomes as important as customer-to-site authentication.

Site-to-Customer Authentication

Currently, most institutions do not authenticate their websites to their customers. One reason phishing attacks are successful is that unsuspecting customers cannot determine whether they are being directed to genuine or fraudulent, spoofed websites during the collection stage of an attack. The spoofed sites may be so well constructed that casual users cannot tell if they are not legitimate. Institutions can aid customers in differentiating legitimate sites from spoofed sites by authenticating their websites to customers (FFIEC 2005). In this section we apply the three authentication factors systematically to site-to-customer authentication.

Something an online site knows. As in customer-to-site authentication, this factor is based on secrets shared among customers and specific websites. Various solutions at this factor level have been proposed by certain banks or developers (Dhamija and Tygar 2005; FFIEC 2005; Bruno-Britz 2006; Sausner 2006). One method is a *shared digital image*, whereby a small image or background picture, previously chosen by a specific customer, can be displayed to the customer when he/she inputs his/her username at the bank website, so that the customer can be convinced that the website is legitimate. A *personalized keypad* (either with characters or images) is an enhanced implementation of the digital image method. The legitimate website will provide a keypad containing all the necessary images to form the customer's password. Because the phishing attacker does not have access to the customer's password character subset, a phishing keypad would not be able to contain the characters necessary to allow the correct password to be entered. The user would normally spot the generic keypad immediately and become suspicious.

The first method (single image or background picture) is equivalent to a static password used by customers to authenticate the website; the second method (personalized keypad) is equivalent to a dynamic password to protect customers from being phished. However, as long as these technologies are acting as passwords, they can be compromised. This technology is also vulnerable to shoulder surfing.

Something an online system has. Secure Sockets Layer (SSL) certificates have been used as a strong technology for authenticating websites. However, some clever phishers have added a new layer of subterfuge called the 'secure phish,' which uses the padlock icon indicating that the customer's browser has established a secure connection to a website to lull the customer into a false sense of security. Phishers have also begun to outfit their counterfeit sites with self-generated SSL certificates. To guard against such activities, customers should carefully scan the security certificate prompt for a reference to either 'a self-issued certificate' or 'an unknown certificate authority.'

Something an online system is. A Uniform Resource Locator (URL) address can be thought of as a company's 'biometric' identity. The safest way for customers to resist phishing is to key in the correct URL address of the company of interest. Customers should always check URL addresses carefully to make sure they are legitimate websites. A logo is one aspect of the brand of a company or economic entity, and the shapes, colours, fonts and images are usually distinct from others in a similar market. Logos may be used to identify organizations or other entities in non-economic contexts. In an online situation, a logo can be used as an authentication factor to show that a website represents the legitimate company. The disadvantage of this method is that logos are easily imitated or duplicated. Because a website is a virtual environment, an illegitimate web site can be masked by a similar or even a copy of the same logo to cheat customers. The eBay toolbar is a dynamic tool that tracks customers and tells them they are on the real eBay and PayPal websites or on a suspected spoof site. A drawback of this technology is that there will always be a period of time between when a spoof goes live and when the toolbar can begin detecting spoofs for customers (Dhamija and Tygar 2005).

Additionally, customer fingerprints or facial structures can be copied or duplicated; a company's website has the same problem. The method that works best (in the absence of further detailed information) is to enter the correct URL manually in order to access the desired website.

Summary of Authentication Measures

Sausner (2006) has presented a realistic conclusion on the site-to-customer authentication: "There was more than a smattering of snickering when Bank of America launched PassMark's SiteKey mutual authentication technology last year; by those who derided the picture-based approach as cutesy and simplistic, and by those who worried that it wasn't a foolproof solution to the phishing problem…. But site-to-user authentication as part of the bank login procedure seems set to become the new standard." Although digital image or personalized keypad solutions seem too simple, they actually represent an advanced solution to authenticating websites to customers to help overcome many of the problems with other authentication technologies. This direction toward reliable authentication appears to represent a better alternative to the multi-attribute approach. The current role of site-to-customer authentication methods is discussed below.

Conceptual Model of Mutual Authentication

Based on the foregoing discussion, a conceptual model for mutual online authentication is demonstrated in Figure 11.2. This model contains three authentication layers. The first is the mutual SSL/TLS authentication channel, which acts as a technological support-ing layer. The second is the website communication layer between customers and company websites, with three types of authentication factors. The third layer is the out-of-band authentication channel, which is communicated by other means than through the website.

The Basic Layer

Secure Sockets Layer (SSL) is the technology most frequently used to encrypt and protect information transmitted over the Web via the HTTP protocol. The standard is for 128-bit encryption, which is relatively impervious to most code-cracking systems within rea-sonable amounts of time. SSL provides a website's users with the assurance of access to a valid, 'non-spoofed' site and prevents data interception or tampering with sensitive information. Support for SSL is built into almost all major operating systems, web applica-tions, and server hardware. SSL certificates protect sensitive data transmitted between servers, consumers and business partners.

Figure 11.2: Conceptual Model of Mutual Authentication

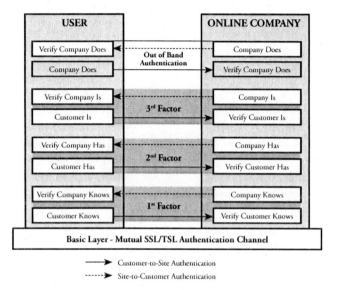

Virtually all Internet browsers have the appropriate signed digital certificate installed and can initiate SSL communications with Internet servers (VeriSign 2005). If a user (client) tries to submit information to an unsecured site (a site without a SSL certificate), the browser will by default show a warning, which can lead the user to question the trustworthiness of this site and to defect if there is any doubt about its authenticity.

SSL, renamed the Transport Security Layer (TSL) in Figure 11.2, includes the cryptographic protocols that provide secure Internet communications for web browsing, e-mail, faxing and other data transfers. The process works as follows: the site typically uses a symmetric encryption technology to secure messages and asymmetric (public/private key) cryptography to authenticate parties. For example, to authenticate that a message came from the sender, the sender encrypts the message using a private key that only the sender knows. The message can be read only by using the sender's public key. Since the message can only be read using the sender's public key, the receiver knows the message came from the expected sender. Mutual SSL provides the same functionality as SSL, with the addition of authentication and non-repudiation of the client, using digital signatures. However, due to issues with complexity, cost, logistics and effectiveness, most web applications are designed so they do not require client-side certificates. This leaves an opening for a man-in-the-middle attack.

The website communication layer. This layer contains communications between customers and websites. Both customer-to-site authentication and site-to-customer authentication are depicted in this layer. Both customers and institutions can have up to three authentication factors: something they know, something they have and something they are. We will shortly focus on the important role of current authentication methods, especially for site-to-customer authentication, which plays such an important role in authentication.

The out-of-band layer. This layer acts as an additional authentication layer when necessary. Out-of-band authentication includes any technique that allows the identity of the individual to be verified through a channel different from the website channel, where other authentication processes are implemented. Out-of-band authentication provides a convenient means of authenticating customers through e-mail, SMS, telephone and other modes of communication. While out-of-band communication is usually a convenient and low-cost channel, it has a high probability of being compromised. For example, e-mails can be made to look as if they are from the institution involved, or the institution's address can actually be forged by a technique called 'domain spoofing' (FDIC 2005). Therefore, customers using out-of-band techniques need to be aware of potential issues and verify the actions taken by the institutions with which they are communicating: e.g., what the institution does. Likewise, institutions need to verify the actions taken by customers: e.g., what the customer does.

Mutual Authentication as a Symmetric Authentication Mechanism

Mutual authentication is an important mechanism for protecting both sides in online authentication. Customer-to-site authentication has always played an important role in online transactions and communications. If everyone were trustworthy and there were no fraudsters to interfere with these communications, then customer authentication would be unnecessary. However, this is not the case in the real world. And it is possible for either simple or sophisticated customer authentication methods to be compromised. Hence, as criminals continue to evolve in their use of ever-more-sophisticated techniques to attack legitimate communications, stronger customer authentication (two-factor or multi-factor) methods are required to resist criminals. Unfortunately, this is an endless battle, since creating a perfect authentication method is virtually impossible.

The case can be made that, no matter how strong customer authentication is, the authentication process will fail if customers cannot recognize when they are on a legitimate website. For this reason, mutual authentication (site-to-customer combined with customer-to-site authentication) must be considered as a solution to this increasingly serious issue, which is resulting primarily from the enormous growth in phishing attacks. As these attacks grow in their complexity, the skill required to defeat them must also increase (Collette and Gentile 2006). Attacks by phishing, pharming, Trojan horse, or man in the middle have been successful primarily because of the absence of site authentication. For example, successful phishing attacks succeed due to the fact (Dhamija and Tygar 2005) that customers

- cannot reliably, correctly determine sender identities in e-mail messages,
- cannot reliably distinguish legitimate e-mail and website content from illegitimate content that has the same 'look and feel,'

- cannot reliably parse domain names,
- cannot reliably distinguish actual hyperlinks from images of hyperlinks,
- and more…

In order to resist phishing successfully, customer attention and awareness must be aroused, both through technology and education. Site-to-customer authentication methods can be classified into two types: active and passive. More and more customers have come to realize that they cannot trust that every online site is a legitimate site and have been educated through negative experience or through media publicity about the possibility of being phished or pharmed. Some surveys have shown that "customers expect stronger authentication in their online banking experience, but they expect the bank to provide it as a standard feature and not as a cost to the customer" (Dhamija and Tygar 2005). Unfortunately, many customers still remain unaware of the dangers represented by online criminals or don't think of them as serious problems. In such situations, mutual authentication methods can help to address the problem. Although current solutions (see below) are relatively simple and need further development, they deserve serious consideration.

Active authentication. Customers who are aware of potential attacks may take an active role during the authentication process. They may check company logos, digital certificates, HTTPS links and other relevant information before they proceed to log in. Basically, these customers are performing manual site authentication (e.g., what the bank has, what the bank is) as their contribution to the mutual authentication process.

Passive authentication. A crude yet realistic comment about customers is, "some just won't learn unless they have to pay." But it would be irresponsible to say, "let them suffer and then they will be aware of it." Institutions must take an active role in implementing site-to-customer authentication in order to overcome customer apathy to the problem, since both institutions and customers suffer when there is a successful attack. That is, the customer may lose funds to fraud (in addition to psychological damage and time lost trying to fix the problem), but the institution also suffers through negative publicity, loss of customer trust and, of course, loss of business.

Two arguments can be made regarding customer responsibilities in guarding against phishing attacks. The first is that customers should learn about taking responsibility for guarding against phishing and associated criminal attacks. Customer education is recommended to encourage more active site-to-customer authentication. An opposing argument is that customers cannot be expected to be knowledgeable about online security; their main purpose in accessing a site is simply to gather information and/or to complete online transactions, and they should not be expected to spend a lot of time and effort that does not directly help them to complete their tasks. The amount of time required to accomplish mutual authentication would be more than justified, however, by customer satisfaction in the knowledge that they are working with a site that can be trusted and that will lead to successful task completion without the danger of fraudulent activity by a criminal third party. In this sense, customers may be highly dependent on an effective form of passive site-to-customer authentication.

Additional effort is being put into passive site-to-customer authentication. For example, VeriSign Inc. recently announced it is strengthening online transaction security by working together with Microsoft on mutual authentication solutions. Such solutions take advantage of a Microsoft technology codenamed 'InfoCard' through its Internet Explorer browser, as well as VeriSign Secured Sockets Layer (SSL) certificates and the newly launched VeriSign Identity Protection (VIP), to protect consumers and website owners against phishing, pharming and other forms of online IDTF. These complementary technologies allow both the destination site and the consumer to identify each other easily and positively.[1] Other technologies for multi-factor customer verification that have been adopted by credit card companies include Verified by Visa and SecureCode, which respectively help protect Visa and MasterCard credit cards against third-party fraud through customer use of personal passwords while shopping online.

Risk-based authentication is an approach that uses different authentication methods based on a risk analysis of a system, rather than by simply deploying user IDs and passwords on all the company's systems. The higher the risk, the stronger the authentication ought to be. When performing a risk assessment of a network or system, the following questions need to be considered by the company:

- Who has access to the system? Is it a small, restricted group of employees in one department, or thousands of customers? The larger the circle of users, obviously the greater the risk.
- What type of data does it hold? If it has sensitive customer information—names, addresses, Social Security Numbers and the like—the security level must be increased, including encryption of databases and transmitted information. If it is marketing data that can't be traced back to your customers or employees, lower the security level appropriately.
- Where are the servers hosting data located in your network? Are they publicly accessible web or application servers sitting inside your firewall?
- Is the application web based, and what does it do? For a catalogue with a shopping cart or a banking application, increase the security level. If it is simply information, the security level can be lower.

---

1 http://www.verisign.com/press_releases/pr/page_037034.html.

Once the level of risk is established, a decision can be made on the authentication method to be used and how to deploy it. For higher-risk applications, typically those with customer data access or with online financial applications, a two-factor authentication method may be in order. If the system is entirely within the organization's network where the risk is lower, user ID and password might be enough. For larger and distributed companies, it might be cost-effective to invest in commercial software that will support risk-based authentication (Anonymous 2009).

Summary

This chapter began with a brief discussion of organizational security and how important it is to adopt and adapt the appropriate internal controls to achieve a level of security consistent with the threat level to the organization. This cannot be achieved solely by technology; management must be a strong supporter and change management approaches must be used to encourage management and all employees to embrace security, if security threats are to be managed. We discussed Identity and Access Management systems, which provide centralized control of single sign-on approaches to simplify employee access to data and applications in firms of all sizes and complexities. Next, we described networks and how to protect them, ranging across both external and internal networks and the associated threats to firms and the various sources from which they arise. Finally, we discussed authentication issues in detail, including the various types of authentication and the threats to each type from a variety of attacks, including a model of mutual authentication and how it might help defeat these attacks.

As a final summary of authentication issues, mutual authentication can play an important role in online transactions, both in protecting customer trust and institutional reputations: 1) Mutual trust is vital in online consumer commerce. "At the core of performing online transactions is the need for mutually recognized identities.… Without this mutual trust, online transactions cannot be completed without significant risk of misrepresentation and fraud" (Voice 2005); and 2) Institutional reputations may be undermined by criminal attacks on online sites, as "18% of online banking users decreased or altogether stopped their use of online banking due to concerns about the security of their identity" (Entrust 2005).

References

Allen, J. H. 2004. *Building a Practical Framework for Enterprise-Wide Security Management*. Secure IT Conference.

Anonymous. 2005 (17 November). "Commissioner's Phone Records Access Puts Long-Standing Data Broker Problem in the Spotlight." *PrivacyScan*, Murray Long & Associates Inc. http://www.privacyscan.ca/November17,2005.pdf [consulted April 5, 2009].

Anonymous. 2009. "RSA Announces New Release of Adaptive Authentication Platform: Platform Provides Risk-Based, Transparent Authentication to Enterprises." *Information Week: Business Technology*. http://www.darkreading.com/securityservices/security/client/showArticle.jhtml?articleID=217201247 [consulted May 31, 2009].

Beaumier, C. M. 2006. "Multifactor Authentication: A Blow to Identity Theft?" *Bank Accounting & Finance* 19: 2: 33–37.

Bruno-Britz, M. 2006. "Online Authentication is a Two-Way Street." *Bank Systems & Technology*, 43: 10: 11.

Caloyannides, M. A. 2004. "The Cost of Convenience: A Faustian Deal." *IEEE Security & Privacy*, 84–87.

CMI. 2007. *Canadian Security Technology Readiness Intelligence Report*. Canadian Advanced Technology Alliance: 18. http://www.cata.ca/Media_and_Events/Press_Releases/cata_pr06070701.html [consulted July 3, 2009].

Cocheo, S. 2006. "Read This Before You Take the Multi-factor Plunge." *ABA Banking Journal*, 98: 5: 54–55.

Collette, R., and M. Gentile. 2006. "Countering the Phishing/Pharming Threat." *Computer Economics*, 28. http://www.computereconomics.com/article.cfm?id=1099 [consulted February 25, 2009].

Comodo. 2006. "Mutual Authentication for Online Banking: One Size Does Not Fit All." http://www.compliancehome.com/whitepapers/PCI/abstract10157.html [consulted May 30, 2009].

Crosbie, M. 2005. "Biometrics for Enterprise Security." *Network Security*, 11: 4–8.

Dhamija, R., and J. D. Tygar. 2005. *The Battle against Phishing: Dynamic Security Skins*. Symposium on Usable Privacy and Security. Pittsburgh: ACM Press.

Dreger, R. 2010. "Comply (and/or) die: Conforming with multiple regulations." *Global CIO*. http://www.informationweek.com/news/global-cio/compliance/222400141 [consulted May 4, 2011].

Dyck, T. 2003. "Managing Risk: Network Security Stakes, Complexities are Rising." *eWeek*, 20: 64–66.

Entrust. 2005. "Consumer Perspectives on Online Banking Security." Entrust Online Banking Survey, October 2005. download.entrust.com/resources/download.cfm/21961/Entrust_Internet_Survey_web.pdf/? [consulted February 25, 2009].

FDIC. 2005. "Putting an End to Account-Hijacking Identity Theft." Washington D.C.: Federal Deposit Insurance Corporation. http://www.fdic.gov/consumers/consumer/idtheftstudy/identity_theft.pdf [consulted July 3, 2009].

FFIEC. 2005. *Authentication in an Internet Banking Environment*. Arlington, VA: Federal Financial Institutions Examination Council.

Furnell, S., and L. Zekri. 2006. "Replacing Passwords: In Search of the Secret Remedy." *Network Security*, 2006: 1: 4–8.

Haugen, S., and J. R. Selin. 1999. "Identifying and Controlling Computer Crime and Employee Fraud." *Industrial Management & Data Systems*, 99: 8: 340–44.

Hiltgen, A., T. Kramp, et al. 2006. "Secure Internet Banking Authentication." *IEEE Security & Privacy*, 4: 2: 21–29.

Howie, J. 2006. "Authentication Options: Is It Time to Say 'So Long' to Username Password Authentication?" *Windows IT Security*, 1-6. http://windowsitpro.com/article/articleid/50550/authentication-options.html [consulted May 30, 2009].

Karygiannis, T., and L. Owens. 2002. "Wireless Network Security: 802.11, Bluetooth and Handheld Devices." *Special Publication 800-48*. Washington, D.C.: National Institute of Standards and Technology: 20–23.

Krebs, B. 2006. "Citibank Phish Spoofs 2-factor Authentication." *Washington Post* (Security Fix Blog). http://blog.washingtonpost.com/securityfix/2006/07/citibank_phish_spoofs_2factor_1.html [consulted March 20, 2011].

MasterCard. (2008). "News Release: MasterCard Brings Chip and PIN-based Internet Payments to over 2 Million European Homes." Paris, France: MasterCard. http://www.cartes.com/ExposiumCms/cms_sites/SITE_324050/ressources324050/cap_and_securecode_eur_rel110508.pdf [consulted February 25, 2009].

OPCC. 2010. "Legal Corner." Ottawa: Office of the Privacy Commissioner of Canada. http://www.priv.gc.ca/leg_c/index_e.cfm [consulted May 5, 2011].

Parr, F. 2006. "Chip & PIN? Is It as Safe as You Think?" *Credit Management*, May: 36–37.

Peterson, B. H., P. Smedegaard, et al. 2008. "Managing Multiple Identities." *Journal of Accountancy*, 206: 3: 38–42.

Phifer, L., and D. Piscitello. 2007. "The Sad and Increasingly Deplorable State of Internet Security, Revisited." *Business Communications Review*, June: 14–18.

Pulkkis, G., K. J. Grahn, et al. 2006. "Taxonomies of User-Authentication Methods in Computer Networks." *Enterprise Information Systems Assurance and Systems Security*. Edited by M. Warkentin. Hershey, PA: Idea Group Publishing, pp. 343–71.

Roussos, G., D. Peterson, et al. 2003. "Mobile Identity Management: An Enacted View." *International Journal of Electronic Commerce*, 8: 1: 81–100.

Sausner, R. 2006. "Site Security: Will Authentication in Reverse Become the New Norm?" *Bank Technology News*, 19: 42.

Schneier, B. 2005. "Two-Factor Authentication: Too Little, too Late." *Communications of the ACM*, 48: 136.

Schreft, S. L. 2007. "Risks of Identity Theft: Can the Market Protect the Payment System?" *Economic Review*, 92: 4: 5–40.

Sheward, S. 2006. *Man-in-the-Middle Phishing Attack Successful against Citibank's 2-factor Token Authentication.* Tricipher.

Sipior, J. C., and B. T. Ward. 2007. "Unintended Invitation: Organizational Wi-Fi use by External Roaming Users." *Communications of the ACM*, 50: 8: 72–77.

Thompson, C. J. 1992. "Fraud." *Internal Auditor*, 19–23.

Turner, D.-M., and S. Hazari. 2007. "Bring Secure Wireless Technology to the Bedside: A Case Study of Two Canadian Healthcare Organizations." *Web Mobile-Based Applications for Healthcare Management.* Edited by L. Al-Hakim. Hershey, PA: IGI Global, pp. 167–80.

VeriSign. 2005. "What Every E-business Should Know about SSL Security and Consumer Trust." *Verisign Business Guide*, Verisign, Inc. http://www.zdnet.co.uk/i/z5/wp/2009/verisign/What%20Every%20E-business.pdf [consulted March 29, 2009].

Voice, C. 2005. "Online Authentication: Matching Security Levels to the Risk." *Network Security*, 12: 15–18.

Wells, J. 1997. *Occupational Fraud and Abuse.* Austin, TX: Obsidian Publishing Company, Inc.

Williamson, G. D. 2006. "Enhanced Authentication in Online Banking." *Journal of Economic Crime Management*, 4: 2.

Chapter 12

Evaluating and Managing Organizational Readiness for Security and IDTF Risks

"Minds are like parachutes. They only function when they are open."

—Sir James Dewar

Introduction

Information security is in a constant state of change, and security methodologies have been unable to keep pace with the continuous appearance of new threats. With each advance in technology, new risks are exposed that could represent security exposures to the enterprise, both internally and externally. Newly developed applications may have exploitable flaws. Personal applications used by employees, like peer-to-peer file sharing applications (US-CERT 2007), may also expose enterprises to risks from inadvertent disclosure of sensitive business information over the Internet or risks of licensing or copyright violations. Employees may use removable media devices like laptops to introduce unwanted applications or to move sensitive data outside of corporate walls, with the risk of improper disclosure. Organizations with an immature approach to security are constantly playing catch-up by reacting to risks posed by evolving technologies. This will not defend successfully against a constant flood of threats and vulnerabilities. There are a number of ways for an organization to plan for and defend against risks from security vulnerabilities. First, we discuss organizational security management. Next, we introduce and describe in some detail a maturity model for organizational security management, followed by an alternative balanced scorecard approach. Finally, we describe organizational readiness to implement and support security needs at the executive level.

Organizational Security

An acceptable level of security is one where the investment in security protection strategies is commensurate with the risk of exposure to the assets being protected. An organization must mobilize in a coordinated and collaborative way to achieve desired security goals (Figure 12.1). These security goals are reached by implementing, monitoring and controlling the security requirements of critical assets, managing risks to these assets and using effective processes to do so (Allen 2004).

The organizational dependencies depicted in Figure 12.1 are expanded upon below:

Security Adoption Drivers

- Support by top management
- Strategic importance of ICT to the organization

Figure 12.1: Organizational Security and Confidentiality Management

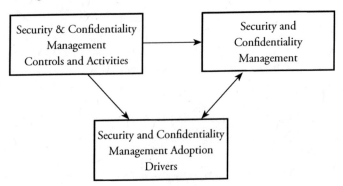

- Budget availability
- Availability of knowledgeable technical support
- Awareness of security and confidentiality issues
- Priority level for security and confidentiality measures
- Government and legal compliance regulations
- Contractual obligations
- Awareness of internal and external security threats
- External pressure from partners
- Manager(s) with designated responsibility for information security

Security and Confidentiality Management

- Planning
- Organizational team approach
- Change management
- Development of management policies
- Assignment of responsibilities

Security and Confidentiality Management Controls and Activities

- Adoption of ethical code of conduct
- Promotion of ethical code of conduct among employees
- Adoption of uniform procedures for managing and controlling security
- Management and employee education and training
- Monitoring databases and communications for security abuse
- Adoption of measures to counter abuse of security and privacy
- Adoption of measures for physical management of data
- Adoption of measures for virtual management of data

Organizational Maturity

Models of organizational maturity in managing security may assist in evaluating organizational performance in combating security threats. The level of organizational maturity should correspond to the level of computer security required to meet security threats. The resulting benefits for stakeholders include:

- Providing information that can be useful in the pursuit of an enlightened public policy
- Detection and reporting of trends in existing and new forms of IDTF
- Guiding organizational efforts to combat cybercrime
- Determining what types of IDTF are having the greatest social and economic impacts
- Relating levels of prevention to their impact on identity theft and fraud

The terms 'predictability,' 'control' and 'effectiveness' may be used to define organizational maturity (Harmon 2004). *Predictability* refers to the use of schedules, milestones and goals that are met. Immature organizations often create schedules, but then may miss milestones or goals by wide margins, and they only achieve their outcomes as a result of the heroic efforts of individuals using approaches that they create more or less spontaneously (Harmon 2004). Mature organizations create schedules and consistently achieve them. *Control* refers to the consistency with which organizations meet their goals. Mature organizations meet their goals over and over again with very little deviation. Immature organizations are never that sure which goals will be met and have little idea how likely it is that a milestone will be achieved within some particular interval. *Effectiveness* refers to achieving the right outcomes in an efficient manner. Mature organizations achieve the precise goals they commit to achieve. Immature organizations often achieve some but not all of their goals; moreover, in many cases, the quality may not be as good and the costs may be higher than acceptable. Basically, mature organizations have systematic processes and documented ways of doing things based on data from past efforts that are used to predict what will happen when similar efforts are to be undertaken.

The objectives of a security management maturity model are to enable organizations/enterprises to assess their capabilities with respect to the management and control of security and confidentiality and to provide organizations/enterprises with directions and steps further to improve their capabilities in this area. There have been several attempts to develop security management maturity models. For example, Thomson and Von Solms (2006) developed a maturity model to evaluate the extent that information security is embedded in the overall corporate culture of an organization. This model is useful but somewhat restrictive, as it addresses only employee and not necessarily other organizational behaviours with respect to information security practices. Based on the Conscious Competence Learning Matrix of Howell and Fleishman (1982), it describes four levels of employee maturity: unconscious incompetence, conscious incompetence, conscious competence and, finally, unconscious competence.

In another maturity model, Sharma (2006) focuses on the technical aspects of security through a three-level model: technical, process-centric and aligned. The Systems Security Engineering Capability Maturity Model Integration[1] (Abzug et al. 2003) is the most comprehensive security maturity model developed to date. Based on the original Capability Maturity Model Integration (CMMI) framework developed at Carnegie Mellon University, it includes maturity levels ranging from least mature (level 1) to most mature (level 5):

1. Performed informally
2. Planned and tracked

---

1 Copyright 1995 by Carnegie Mellon University.

3. Well defined
4. Quantitatively controlled
5. Continuously improving

When evaluating IT security governance, each level in the maturity model can be defined as a set of identified good practices, providing a basis for the next level. An organization cannot rise to the next level without first complying with the practices set for the previous levels.

Carbonel (2008) has applied CMMI to the ISO 17799:2005 standard for IT security. The meaning of each level determined from this transformation is shown in Table 12.1.

Table 12.1: IT Security Maturity Levels (adapted from Carbonel 2008)

CMMI Level	ISO 17799:2005 Standard Mapping
0	No security policy
1	Security policy is not formalized (process is unpredictable, poorly controlled and reactive)
2	Security policy is documented, validated and disseminated but may be incomplete or does not fit the organization (process is primarily reactive)
3	Security policy is documented, validated, disseminated and fits the organizational context (process is defined)
4	Controls are set up to assess application of the validated security policy document (process is measured and controlled)
5	Regular review process assesses validated document and enables regular updating (continuous process improvement)

Each level beyond Level 1 prescribes certain key processes, assumed to be repeatable, that must be in place before an organization can be said to have reached that level. Key processes implement a set of related activities that, when performed collectively, achieve a set of goals considered important for enhancing the organization's security and confidentially capability. These are cumulative as an organization progresses up through the maturity model levels. Organizations can improve their capabilities by implementing these key processes. A detailed description of the IT security maturity model levels follows, based partially on items derived from Harmon (2004), Sharma (2006), Szerszen (2007), Allen (2004) and Abzug (2003).

Level 1: Ad Hoc

Processes for security management are ad hoc. Few activities are explicitly defined and success depends on individual effort and heroics:

- Individual employee responsibility and management of files and passwords
- Individual management of web access and e-mail security (spam and anti-virus software)
- Ad hoc response to security and confidentiality threats and violations
- Ad hoc and reactive management of urgent software security patches
- No centralized enterprise security planning and management
- Backup and some limited security for centralized systems only
- Physical security for centralized systems only
- Excessive retrofitting to handle regulatory compliance, if undertaken at all
- No procedures for securing data on portable computers such as laptops
- No general employee awareness of need for security and confidentiality

- Security for outsourced systems left up to outsourcing organization

Level 2: Planned and Tracked

Organizations have now started to focus on processes and have defined some of the major ones. They can repeat some processes with predictable results, but other processes may not be well controlled. For example, the following might be in place:

- Vulnerability management becomes a standard process, providing the ability to detect weaknesses or flaws in software and software configurations and to take action to reduce the likelihood of exploitation
- Centralized content filtering for e-mail
- Centralized network and web access management, including firewall
- Physical security for the network and its operations
- Enterprise directory of applications and functions
- Centralized password management
- Encryption of sensitive data on ad hoc basis
- Confidential physical information shredding and disposal
- Confidentiality controls for customer files
- Controls in place for portable databases
- Individual responsibility for anti-spyware, anti-virus systems

Level 3: Defined

At this level, organizations have defined all basic security and confidentiality processes and have some degree of control over them. As an example, change management is critical to any security management process. Changes come from many sources: software updates including security patches, new applications, technology changes, configuration changes, etc. Business demands for change are high and frequent and thus can cause disruptions, delays or more serious impacts to service availability. In the absence of a change management process and appropriate controls, the IT operations group is often unable to respond effectively with a high change success rate. This is defined as the ratio of planned (authorized) to unplanned (unexpected, inadvertent) changes, so as organizations mature processes and controls that address the part of the change management problem space that they can control, this will free up resources to focus more attention and energy on the part of the problem that is unpredictable (Allen 2004).

At this maturity level, organizations have begun to emphasize the collection of data and use measures to help manage their processes, including the following:

- Established a policy framework setting forth an enterprise security posture, which enables the business and technical sides of the organization to work together to manage risk
- Policies and management of security developed and implemented for outsourced systems
- Regulatory security compliance at national level
- Centralized responsibility and inter-group coordination of security planning and management, including all network applications (including wireless networks)
- Inventoried all authorized and unauthorized network resources and how they are used, and determined whether they pose a risk to the enterprise
- Centralized content filtering for e-mail and webmail
- Developed process maps for security-sensitive applications
- Effective education program in place to increase employee awareness of the need for security and confidentiality
- Process for organizational change and enterprise-wide application of appropriate security tools

- Organized process for managing software security patches and updates
- Installed network security monitoring and intrusion detection and monitoring systems
- Security risk management focused on the security of key organizational assets, including a meta-directory of sensitive, at-risk functions and systems; risk mitigation undertaken on a priority basis
- Individual responsibility for sensitive data encryption and backup

Level 4: Managed

At this level, organizations proceed to emphasize the management of processes. They have good process measures and gather data consistently. Managers rely on measures and data when establishing goals or planning projects. There is a hierarchical alignment among project managers, so that the achievement of individual process goals contributes to the achievement of overall organizational goals. This might include

- Centralized identity management introduced, with automated systems where feasible (e.g., automated enterprise provisioning for authorizing and de-authorizing access)
- Enabled and promoted acceptable use of resources while preventing and reporting unacceptable ones that could put the enterprise at risk, such as the deliberate or accidental execution of unknown applications
- Consolidated logging and reporting on security and confidentiality levels relative to defined objectives
- Centralized content filtering for both incoming and outgoing e-mail and webmail
- Full regulatory security compliance at national level through a continual, organized process
- Converged IT (virtual security) and physical security

- Enterprise roles for security and confidentiality functions, including data encryption and backup of customer and HR data
- Employee training and responsibility assigned for handling specific security and confidentiality issues

Level 5: Incremental Optimization

At this level, employees have been educated about security and confidentiality processes and have been trained to support a continuous effort to refine and improve relevant processes, including the following:

- Full regulatory compliance at international level, as required
- Risk-based approach to identity management and security, continuous monitoring for new security rules and risks, and innovative solutions to problems that arise
- Routine, comprehensive reports developed to inform all policy stakeholders of the enterprise's security state on a continuous basis, escalating high-risk violations and providing a constant audit trail
- Security brought into a positive light by basing policy on only known 'good' and acceptable behaviours and resources, and by taking proactive measures to assess and remediate network and endpoint exposures
- Costs are challenged and reduced, and the focus remains on the organization's core business
- Employee experience, responsibility and attention to assigned security and confidentiality functions is continued
- Positive reinforcement of security and confidentiality activities is in place for employees and managers
- Risks are analyzed and mitigated for each new or existing sensitive process and application
- Identity federation is arranged with business partners

- Relevant national and international security requirements are monitored and managed

Determining Security Maturity Level

When determining the security maturity level in a medium to large organization, it is important to recognize that different groups within an organization may be at different maturity levels. When trying to assign levels to specific groups, the placement of boundaries around each such group is important to avoid disagreements in the level of each such group, since this will determine where further work is necessary to improve security maturity levels (Harmon 2004).

It is useful to determine the maturity level separately for each business unit based on the ISO standard, realizing that not all units within the organization are expected to reach full conformity with the standard, since not all standards apply to each unit (Carbonel 2008). Once the appropriate calculations have been completed, the results may be displayed in the form of a star chart for each unit, with its multiple dimensions showing measures like security incident management and physical security, as well as the calculated level of security maturity. This assists in identifying dimensions where units are performing at a lower level than other units. Displayed over annual time periods, this can assist in measuring progress in achieving an acceptable level for the organization.

Another approach by Allen (2004) to enterprise security management uses a framework that is tied to business objectives. This approach suggests that security belongs in an organizational and operational context not as a stand-alone discipline, and includes all of an organization's capabilities that need to be facilitated to select, execute and improve activities reliably to achieve and sustain a desired security state (see Chapter 7 for a related discussion). These capabilities include risk management, project management, enterprise security governance and audit. These need to be brought to bear in an integrated manner, much as we pointed out in an earlier chapter on handling IDTF risks. Security becomes the execution of a well-defined IT operational process, such as change management, within which security controls are articulated, defined and documented based on fundamental security requirements of confidentiality, availability and integrity. Components of each of these aspects can have a bearing on the level of organizational maturity in managing security issues and hence its performance in fending off breaches that can affect the organization, its employees, partners and customers. Using business objectives, organizations can then determine how far along the spectrum from current practice to high performing they need to be. In a 'high-performing' organization, operational excellence tends to produce appropriate security as a side effect, since it becomes one of the organization's operational requirements. Enterprise security management fits well with the concept of a security maturity model, whereby an organization can move from the lowest ad hoc level to one of several higher levels, depending upon the security requirements needed to meet the firm's objectives.

Balanced Scorecard

A commercial approach that uses the balanced scorecard methodology is another approach that might also be considered for identity management (AKS-LABS 2008). This concept can be used when the goal is to measure and control values associated with business performance. The balanced scorecard approach is relatively simple in concept but not necessarily easy to implement. It relies primarily on various performance measurement indicators. The goal of developing a balanced scorecard is basically to develop correct metrics that will indicate the organization's security performance and will assist in tracking its progress over time.

Implementation

Today's comprehensive security protection and control solutions elevate enterprise security policies to the top, enabling IT administrators, security professionals and business executives to share and interact at the policy level while automating critical aspects of policy, which include assessment, remediation and behaviour enforcement. The most effective policy models enable the enterprise management team to focus only on known, approved technologies and behaviours—a positive model, as opposed to 'negative models' based on legacy security solutions that focus more on identifying malicious technologies and behaviours (Szerszen 2007).

The most common approach to achieve executive-level attention to security is by appointing an executive-level Chief Information Security Officer (CISO), or an equivalent function like Chief Security Officer (CSO). The CISO is normally responsible for establishing and maintaining the enterprise vision, strategy and program to ensure information assets are adequately protected. The CISO directs staff in identifying, developing, implementing and maintaining processes across the organization to reduce information and information technology (IT) risks, respond to incidents, establish appropriate standards and controls, and direct the establishment and implementation of policies and procedures. The CISO is also responsible for information-related compliance.

Large companies and federal and state/provincial government agencies have led the way in appointing CISOs. Driven by bad publicity resulting from security breaches, more than 44% of larger corporations and federal and state/provincial agencies had appointed a CISO by 2009 (Hurley 2010). Moreover, companies with CISOs who manage the security function tend to focus on operational excellence in IT by implementing standardized procedures and controls, automating these procedures and controls and measuring, assessing and reporting on risks. This results in lower spending on audits, reduced data theft and higher customer retention (Hurley 2010).

The Chief Privacy Officer (CPO) is another relatively new position, which was created to respond to consumer concerns over privacy—particularly in medical data and financial information—and to ensure compliance with legislation such as the US Health Insurance Portability and Accountability Act (HIPAA) of 1996 and the Canadian Personal Information Protection and Electronic Documents Act (PIPEDA) of 2001. In Canada, for example, large healthcare institutions appoint CPOs to ensure continuing compliance with provincial privacy regulations that are closely linked with the equivalent federal PIPEDA regulations for firms and federal government agencies.

Summary

In this chapter we discussed briefly the needs and interactions in an organization that pertain to security and confidentiality needs. It is possible to evaluate the readiness of an organization by determining its security maturity level, through a five level model that is similar to maturity models used to evaluate the readiness of software development organizations. Knowing the maturity of an organization in managing security gives the organization an objective measure and a target to achieve when preparing its response to security threats. We also outlined another method based on the balanced scorecard, and describe how attention to security and privacy can be enhanced in organization by executive level appointments of chief information security officers and chief privacy officers, respectively.

References

Abzug, C., et al. 2003. *Systems Security Engineering Capability Maturity Model SSE-CMM*. Model Description Document Version 3.0. Pittsburgh: Carnegie Mellon University, p. 340.

AKS-LABS. 2008. "Balanced Scorecard Designer." AKS-LABS. http://www.strategy2act.com/solutions/develop-balanced-scorecard-metrics.htm [consulted July 21, 2009].

Allen, J. H. 2004. *Building a Practical Framework for Enterprise-Wide Security Management*. Secure IT Conference.

Carbonel, J.-C. 2008. "Assessing IT Security Governance through a Maturity Model and the Definition of a Governance Profile." *Information Systems Control Journal*, 2: 1–4.

Harmon, P. 2004. "Evaluating an Organization's Business Process Maturity." *Business Process Trends*, 2: 1–11.

Howell, W. C., and E. A. Fleishman. 1982. *Human Performance and Productivity: Information Processing and Decision Making*. Hillsdale, NJ: Erlbaum.

Hurley, J. 2010. "Want to Reduce IT Risk? Hire a CISO." *SC Magazine*. http://www.securecomputing.net.au/Opinion/171584,want-to-reduce-it-risk-hire-a-ciso.aspx/2 [consulted March 20, 2011].

Sharma, A. 2006. "Achieving Compliance through Identity Maturity." *Sarbanes-Oxley Compliance Journal*.

Szerszen, D. 2007. "Bringing Security into a Positive Light." *Infosecurity*, 46.

Thomson, K.-L., and R. Von Solms. 2006. "Towards an Information Security Competence Maturity Model." *Computer Fraud & Security*, 11–15.

US-CERT. 2007. "Risks of File-Sharing Technology." *Cyber Security Tip ST05-007*. Washington, D.C.: United States Computer Emergency Readiness Team. http://www.us-cert.gov/cas/tips/ST05-007.html [consulted March 20, 2011].

Chapter 13

A Research Agenda for Identity Theft and Fraud Risks

"If I have seen further than others, it is by standing upon the shoulders of giants."

—Sir Isaac Newton

Introduction

There are many possible aspects of IDTF and associated risks that can be explored by researchers wishing to contribute their expertise in the continuing battle against this growing problem. For example, a recent article by Romanosky et al. (Romanosky, Telang et al. 2011) discusses their findings on whether data breach disclosure laws actually reduce identity theft (they do). Many papers on a variety of IDTF topics continue to appear from time to time, ranging from management, political, social, policy and legal aspects to the more technical aspects of IDTF. Although there are few if any journals that restrict their coverage to IDTF, some of the journals that publish relevant papers from time to time include

Technical Aspects: *Journal of Computer Security, IEEE Security and Privacy, International Journal of Mobile Communications, International Journal of Information Security, Network Security,* etc.

Non-Technical Aspects: *International Journal of Electronic Finance, Journal of Policy Analysis and Management, Journal of Service Science, Information & Management,* etc.

Other Aspects: There are many published conference and workshop proceedings that address related issues. There are also a number of books available on a variety of IDTF and risk topics, including Camp (2010) and Taylor, Caeti et al. (2007). Many others are consumer 'how to' books that do not contribute much in terms of research background.

To accomplish meaningful results for analytical and/or policy studies, it is essential to have access to data and to overviews of existing work. Primary data is best for this purpose, since the researcher can specify exactly what data are to be collected. However, this is often expensive and time-consuming to collect, so secondary data should be used when and if it is available. The literature includes some excellent overviews of identity theft from a research perspective. For example, a team from the Economic Crime Institute at Utica College in New York state has identified critical issues and developed a research agenda that can address the many facets of the problem of IDTF. In an early publication, they give an overview of the problem (Gordon, Willox et al. 2004) and in 2006 Utica College formed the Center for Identity Management and Information Protection (CIMIP) to develop related research. After consulting with other academics, experts from the credit industry, law enforcement and other interested parties, CIMIP identified key challenges for identity theft research and developed recommendations for workshops and research projects that would address these issues (Gordon, Rebovich et al. 2007).

In 2005, the US Department of Justice commissioned a literature review to develop a research agenda aimed at identity theft prevention and enforcement (Newman and McNally 2005). In their report, Newman and McNally suggest that the main areas for research be categorized as offending, prevention and harm reduction. For the first area, they suggest that research consider the opportunity structure for identity theft by identifying specific acts or behaviours and the opportunities provided to offenders by the Information Age. A number of reasons are given for the vulnerability of current enrollment and authentication processes. Some of these reasons are (Newman and McNally 2005: viii)

- Low-tech identity documents that can be easily tampered with or counterfeited
- Lack of a universally accepted and secure form of identity document
- Authentication processes that rely on employees to make decisions
- Authentication processes that give employees access to personal information
- General availability of personal information on the Internet
- The ease with which electronic databases can be moved and transferred on the Internet

In this chapter, we describe contributions that can support a research agenda for IDTF. We begin with relevant theories from criminology, followed by a review of the various public sources of relevant information and advice, including: public-sector sources (US, Canada, UK, EU and Australia); private-sector-related sources (Liberty Alliance project, ID Analytics, victim reports and data breach reports); business sector research; and consumer surveys (consumer attitudes and behaviours, and prevalence and nature of IDTF).

Applying Theories from Criminology

In the study of criminology, routine activities theory suggests that, in order for a crime to occur, there must be motivated offenders, suitable targets and a lack of capable guardians. Situational Crime Prevention (SCP) builds on this theory by focusing on opportunity, place and guardianship as areas where crime prevention efforts should be focused. Both White and Fisher (2008) and Newman and McNally (2005) use SCP as a framework for their recommendations.

White and Fisher apply SCP to the problem by considering how identity theft "can be reduced or prevented by securing ... places, enhancing guardianship and thereby controlling the opportunities of motivated offenders" (White and Fisher 2008). Their recommendations for securing places where transactions occur or where identity information is exchanged include eliminating blind mailing, additional identification requirements when opening new accounts and a focus on online activities. Additional guardianship is recommended through more education, coordination, laws and reporting systems.

Newman and McNally show that information—and identity information specifically—is a 'hot' product, ripe for theft because it is 'CRAVED,' an acronym for *Concealable, Removable, Available, Valuable, Enjoyable and Disposable*. The systems within which information is housed are also 'hot,' or vulnerable to criminal attack, because they have the following 'SCAREM' characteristics: *Stealth, Challenge, Anonymity, Reconnaissance, Escape and Multiplicity*. In their perspective, SCP theory proposes specific techniques to reduce crime. These techniques fall under five general categories or aims:

1. Increase the effort
2. Increase the risks
3. Reduce the rewards
4. Reduce provocation
5. Remove excuses

Some of the specific techniques that Newman and McNally propose to reduce the incidence of IDTF are shown in Table 13.1.

Public-Sector Sources of Information and Advice

Various reports issued by public-sector organizations provide vast amounts of information, public surveys and advice for policy makers. Some of these sources, from the United States, Canada, the United Kingdom, Europe and Australia, are discussed in the following subsections.

Table 13.1: Techniques to Reduce Identity Theft

Technique	Applications
Increase the effort the offender must make to commit the crime	Harden targets Control access to facilities Deflect offenders Control tools
Increase the risks of getting caught	Extend guardianship Assist natural surveillance Reduce anonymity Utilize place managers Strengthen formal surveillance
Reduce the rewards from the crime	Conceal targets Remove targets Identify property Disrupt markets Deny benefits
Reduce provocations that might tempt offenders	Avoid disputes Reduce arousal and temptation
Remove excuses that offenders may use to justify the crime	Set rules Post instructions Alert conscience Assist compliance

(adapted from Newman and McNally 2005) *

* Note: Original framework is by Cornish and Clarke (2003). Newman and McNally (2005: 70) added specifics to apply their framework to IDTF.

United States

In most areas relevant to IDTF, the US government has taken the lead in identifying and responding to the problem. As a result, extensive amounts of information and numerous reports have been compiled to assist in the development of public policy. Many of these reports are available on the Internet.

In 1998, the Government Accountability Office (GAO) prepared a briefing report for congress on the problem of IDTF (GAO

1998). After consulting with many public- and private-sector organizations, they reported that there were no comprehensive statistics
on IDTF and no comprehensive estimates of its costs, although
there were indications that incidence rates were on the rise. Anec-
dotal evidence suggested that the increase might be linked to use
of the Internet and "computerized database services" (GAO 1998).
This report was the foundation for the Identity Theft and Assumption Deterrence Act, passed later that year. In 2002, the GAO gave
an updated report to Congress that concluded the prevalence and
cost of identity theft was still increasing (GAO 2002).

In 2006, President Bush assembled a task force of representa-
tives from all of the government organizations involved in protecting against identity theft co-chaired by the attorney general and
the chairman of the Federal Trade Commission. The task force
identified three stages in the lifecycle of IDTF, as follows:

1. The identity thief attempts to acquire a victim's personal
   information.
2. The identity thief attempts to misuse the information he
   has acquired.
3. The identity thief has completed his crime and is enjoy-
   ing the benefits, while the victim is realizing the harm.

The task force developed a strategic plan that included recommendations in four areas: data protection, avoiding data misuse,
victim assistance and deterrence (PresTaskForce 2007). Specific
recommendations under each of these areas are shown in Table
13.2. In 2008, the task force issued a report on its accomplish-
ments in its first two years of operation (PresTaskForce 2007).
Progress was reported on all of the recommendations. Numerous
workshops, communication plans and educational initiatives have
been organized and implemented, involving organizations in both
the public and private sectors. They believe that they have significantly raised awareness of the problem and provided guidance
to consumers, government agencies and businesses. Enforcement

efforts have also been increased, including civil suits against organizations that have violated various data security rules.

Canada

In 2005, the Office of the Information and Privacy Commissioner
of the Province of Ontario produced a report on IDTF with a
focus on information-handling practices. "The prevalence of identity theft comes about as a result of many complex factors. When
examined closely, however, we believe that the single largest cause
of identity theft is the existence of poor information management practices on the part of organizations" (Cavoukian 2005: 1).
The report expands on how the application of Fair Information
Principles can improve these practices. The five core principles
of privacy protection are 1) notice/awareness; 2) choice/consent;
3) access/participation; 4) integrity/security; and 5) enforcement/
redress (FTC 2007).

As the environment for IDTF evolves, the justice system must
also evolve to enact laws that can be used to monitor, arrest and
punish criminals responsible for IDTF. Unfortunately, legislation
often lags in this area, although it is updated from time to time.
For example, after extensive industry and justice system consulta-
tion and years of delay, the Canadian government finally enacted
legislation in October 2009 to update and strengthen the criminal
code on IDTF. The updated laws now specifically address identity
theft and provide police with the tools they need to help stop IDTF
crimes before they can be committed. "The new act creates three
new criminal code offences targeting the early stages of identity-
related crime, all subject to 5-year maximum prison sentences:

- Obtaining and possessing identity information with the
  intent to use the information deceptively, dishonestly or
  fraudulently in the commission of a crime;
- Trafficking in identity information, an offence that targets those who transfer or sell information to another

person with knowledge of, or recklessness as to, the possible criminal use of the information; and,

- Unlawfully possessing or trafficking in government-issued identity documents that contain information of another person.

A new power will be added permitting the court to order, as part of a sentence, that an offender be required to pay restitution to a victim of identity theft or identity fraud for costs associated with their efforts to rehabilitate their identity, e.g., the cost of replacement cards, documents and correcting their credit history. This provision will complement existing provisions which permit restitution to be ordered for actual economic or other property losses." (Department of Justice 2009a)

Several studies at the national level have surveyed consumer IDTF (Sproule and Archer 2008a; Sproule and Archer 2008b) and business fraud (Taylor-Butts and Perreault 2009). Self-reporting of consumer IDTF, including quarterly and annual reports of such activities, have been supported for some time through PhoneBusters, a joint effort by the Royal Canadian Mounted Police and the Ontario Provincial Police (Anonymous 2009). Unfortunately, because of methodological issues of self-reporting data, the rate of offenses recorded by this agency is far below the actual rate observed from consumer surveys. However, all surveys that are done on a regular basis can assist in determining the level of criminal activity, and adjustments can be made to the level of police activity as new types of IDTF are observed and linked to the impact of new laws introduced to prevent IDTF.

United Kingdom

In 2002, the United Kingdom Cabinet Office published a comprehensive report studying identity fraud in the United Kingdom (Cabinet Office 2002). This report estimates the minimum annual cost of identity fraud to the UK economy at £1.3 billion and

Table 13.2: Recommendations of the President's Task Force on Identity Theft

---

Prevention: Keeping Consumer Data out of the Hands of Criminals
Data Security in the Public Sector
- Decrease the unnecessary use of SSNs in the public sector
- Educate federal agencies on how to protect their data and monitor compliance with existing guidance
- Ensure effective risk-based responses to data breaches suffered by federal agencies

Data Security in the Private Sector
- Establish national standards extending data protection safeguards requirements and breach notification requirements
- Develop comprehensive record on private sector use of SSNs
- Better educate the private sector on safeguarding data
- Initiate investigations of data security violations
- Initiate a multi-year public awareness campaign
- Develop an online clearinghouse for current educational resources

---

Prevention: Making It Harder to Misuse Consumer Data
- Hold workshops on authentication
- Develop a comprehensive record on private-sector use of SSNs

---

Victim Recovery: Helping Consumers Repair Their Lives
- Provide specialized training about victim recovery to first responders and other organizations and individuals offering direct assistance to identity theft victims
- Develop avenues for individualized assistance to identity theft victims
- Amend criminal restitution statutes to ensure that victims recover the value of time spent in trying to remediate the harms suffered
- Assess whether to implement a national system that allows victims to obtain an identification document for authentication purposes
- Assess efficacy of tools available to victims

Law Enforcement: Prosecuting and Punishing Identity Thieves
Coordination and Information/Intelligence Sharing
- Establish a national identity theft law enforcement centre
- Develop and promote the use of a universal identity theft report form

- Enhance information sharing between law enforcement and the private sector

Coordination with Foreign Law Enforcement
- Encourage other countries to enact suitable domestic legislation criminalizing identity theft
- Facilitate investigation and prosecution of international identity theft by encouraging other nations to accede to the Convention on Cybercrime
- Identify the nations that provide safe havens for identity thieves and use all measures available to encourage those countries to change their policies
- Enhance the US government's ability to respond to appropriate foreign requests for evidence in criminal cases involving identity theft
- Assist, train and support foreign law enforcement

Prosecution Approaches and Initiatives
- Increase prosecutions of identity theft
- Conduct targeted enforcement initiatives
- Review civil monetary penalty programs

---

summarizes the use of identifying information, identity documents and IDTF legislation in a number of other countries. It recommends that the UK government adopt some of the authentication practices used in the private sector, primarily those that utilize a "historical footprint" consisting of extensive biographical data. It also recommends a central registry of stolen identities or identity documents.

Over the last few years, the United Kingdom has considered a controversial program to issue identity cards for all citizens. Public support for this plan has been mixed due to the inferences by some that this is a step further towards a 'nanny state' and 'Big Brother.'

European Union

In 2004, the Joint Research Centre of the European Commission commissioned a study to support policy development in the European Union (Mitchison, Wilikens et al. 2004). While it contains a survey of legislation in Europe and the United States, the study's primary focus and unique contribution is in its focus on

IDTF and technology development. The authors note that identity in the physical world is replaced by a 'nym' (a user ID) online. In the online world, we often use different nyms (or identities) for different roles, we use shared nyms (or identities) and have many partial identities, each consisting of a small subset of attributes. It is also easy to create new identities, and many would argue that it is sometimes necessary to falsify the information given for these new identities in order to protect one's privacy. The authors propose that all of these practices lead to a 'softening' of identity in the online world (Mitchison, Wilikens et al. 2004).

Another way that technological advancement has affected human identification is in the way that previously non-public pseudonyms (i.e., biographical information used as verifiers) have become public. An example is the availability of reverse directories, where a search on a telephone number will produce the associated address. The general availability of data poses a paradox, where access to different databases "enables the authorities to identify suspicious individuals more reliably and quickly; on the other hand, the increased linkages and vulnerabilities increase the risk of identity theft" (Mitchison, Wilikens et al. 2004: 17).

While UK policy has leaned toward the development of a centralized identification system, this paper recommends a very different approach. The authors say two ways to combat the problem are to make IDTF more difficult or to make it less profitable. Single-barrier systems, like a national ID card system, may indeed make IDTF more difficult. However, by creating a single point of vulnerability, they also make IDTF more profitable if the system can be breached. While single-barrier solutions are popular with users, multi-barrier systems, while not as user-friendly, are generally more secure (Mitchison, Wilikens et al. 2004).

The European Commission also sponsored two research projects associated with IDTF. The Roadmap of Advanced Research in Privacy and Identity Management (RAPID) was charged with developing research and expertise in the areas of privacy and identity management. Their work was completed in 2003 (RAPID

2003). The Future of Identity in the Information Society (FIDIS) is a 'network of excellence' program that brings together researchers from universities throughout the European Union.[1] FIDIS projects are organized around the following research topics:

- Identity of identity (definitions and concepts of identity, anonymity and pseudonymity, and identity management)
- Profiling
- Privacy and the legal-social content of identity
- Interoperability of IDs and ID management systems
- HighTech ID
- Forensic implications
- Mobility and identity

Some of the results of this research can be found in the journal *Identity in the Information Society*, which was founded by FIDIS to stimulate research and debate.

Australia

In 2003, the Securities Industries Research Centre of Asia-Pacific (SIRCA) published a comprehensive report titled *Identity Fraud in Australia: An Evaluation of its Nature, Cost and Extent* (Cuganesan and Lacey 2003). SIRCA is an independent, not-for-profit, university-owned research organization, and the report was commissioned by the Australian government's financial transactions reporting agency.

In conceptualizing the problem, the authors looked at the method, objective and context of identity frauds. Methods can involve the use of genuine documents, forged documents or no documents (in cases of exceptional circumstances or electronic registration). The objective of the fraud can be financial gain, to

---

1 www.fidis.net.

avoid financial losses or other subversive motives. Context refers to whether the fraud occurs in a new relationship or through the takeover of an existing relationship (Cuganesan and Lacey 2003).

In order clearly to outline what frauds the report will study, the authors operationalize the concept of context into three levels. A fraud at the first level involves a new relationship established in a fictitious, stolen or altered name. Frauds at the second level also include the appropriation of an existing relationship with an explicit act of impersonation, such as forging a signature or using an individual's PIN. Level three includes fraud where there is no overt act of impersonation, like skimming credit cards or theft of utility services through meter tampering. The data collected in the report includes frauds in the first and second levels only. The report also describes various Australian government documents used as proof of identity, and the circular, 'de facto' points-based system that is used for enrollment and authentication in these systems (Cuganesan and Lacey 2003).

In total, the authors estimated the organizational cost of identity fraud in Australia in the period from 2001–02 to be $1.1 billion. The study also includes responses related to the organizations' awareness of the problem, risk assessment, and prevention and detection programs. Using data from US studies, the cost of restoration to Australian victims was estimated at $61 million (Cuganesan and Lacey 2003), considerably less than 10% of the organizational cost.

Private Sector Research

Liberty Alliance Project

The Liberty Alliance Project was a global effort to develop open, standards-based specifications and to publish and promote best practices for managing identity information. Originally formed in 2001 with thirty members, it grew to include more than 150 organizations. Membership was available to both commercial and non-commercial organizations and members include major technology vendors, service providers, financial organizations, government agencies and non-profit organizations. As of April 2009, Liberty Alliance was superseded by the Kantara Initiative,[2] which includes identity organizations and their members, vendors and employees working in the identity sector, developers, open source communities, legal, privacy and business experts.

Two of the first white papers published by the Liberty Alliance Project were a paper on *Privacy and Security Best Practices* (Liberty Alliance 2003) and an *Identity Theft Primer* (Liberty Alliance 2005b). Both papers provide an excellent non-technical overview of the problem and potential solutions. More recently, Liberty Alliance was successful in developing and promoting the use of many standards that can be used in a federated identity management environment, including identity-based web services.

ID Analytics

ID Analytics is a commercial firm that uses a proprietary analytic technique and masses of identity information collected from client databases to provide real-time risk analysis related to identity fraud. Clients include organizations in the financial, telecommunications and retail industries. Using the identity data collected from these client firms, this firm has produced a number of white papers.

The first of these white papers was an analysis of fraud rings across the United States (ID Analytics 2005). The paper provides information about patterns of attacks and patterns of data manipulations that can be used to help detect fraudulent applications. A subsequent paper lists ID fraud 'hot spots' within the United States (ID Analytics 2007). ID Analytics has also published two studies that examine data breaches and the associated risks of fraud (ID Analytics 2006; ID Analytics 2007b).

---

2 http://kantarainitiative.org/wordpress/about/.

While the ID Analytics papers contain some very useful and insightful frameworks and classification systems, other researchers often note that the quantitative analysis is based on proprietary data and methods and cannot therefore be independently validated, and that the research cannot be duplicated by others.

Victim Reports

Most of the earliest data on IDTF came from US consumer advocacy groups who reported on the experiences of victims. In the 1990s, agencies like the California Public Interest Research Group (CALPIRG) had issued early warnings about the growing problem of IDTF. In 2000, CALPIRG teamed up with the Privacy Rights Clearinghouse to issue a report titled *Nowhere to Turn: Victims Speak Out on Identity Theft* (Benner, Givens et al. 2000). The report summarizes survey data from sixty-six victims who had contacted these organizations for assistance.

With growing public awareness of the problem, various other agencies began to act as advocates for victims. The Identity Theft Resource Center is a non-profit organization that provides victims with assistance, education and consulting services aimed at reducing the incidence and impact of IDTF. Its reports, *Identity Theft: The Aftermath 2003* and *Identity Theft: The Aftermath 2004*, offer a similar detailed analysis of 173 and 197 victim experiences respectively (Foley, Foley et al. 2003; Foley, Foley et al. 2004).

While victim surveys such as these contain rich detail, there are also a number of summary reports available from various agencies that take victim complaints. The US Identity Theft and Assumption Deterrence Act of 1998 directed the FTC to maintain a database of IDTF complaints and to use this information to encourage and coordinate law enforcement response. The FTC periodically reports on the cases in its registry. While the FTC uses this data to compile information on trends and direct education programs, it admits that the reported cases are not necessarily representative of the larger problem, as many cases are never reported to them. It also receives reports that when the victim first realizes that a theft or fraud has occurred, the full impact and awareness of consequences are rarely experienced at the time, and there is no follow-up with victims (FTC 2003; Consumer Sentinel 2005).

In the United States, the Federal Bureau of Investigation, the White Collar Crime Center and the Bureau of Justice Assistance together run the Internet Crime Complaint Center (IC3). The IC3 issues annual reports on a variety of Internet crimes, and identity theft is one of the crimes tracked (IC3 2007). PhoneBusters is Canada's fraud reporting agency, and its regular reports include a classification showing the IDTF reports received. However, its voluntary victim reports represent only a small minority of actual IDTF events.

Reports from all of these organizations are accumulated in the statistics reported by the Consumer Sentinel Network. This is a branch of the FTC that provides IDTF report data to law enforcement agencies throughout the United States and Canada. While victim reports, both detailed and summary, are useful for some purposes, this data cannot be considered to be representative of the true picture because the reporting rates for many types of IDTF are very low. Detailed reports from victim surveys also suffer from methodological problems associated with limited sample sizes and selection bias (White and Fisher 2008).

Law Enforcement Reports

There has been some research that uses data from law enforcement files to examine the characteristics of cases, victims and offenders. Police reports are often the only source of information that tie ID theft to ID fraud, since identification information often passes through many criminal hands between the original unauthorized access and its use in a fraud. However, law enforcement does not classify cases in a way that is easy to search for IDTF cases (Allison, Schuck et al. 2005; Gordon, Rebovich et al. 2007). Identity theft can also be associated with crimes other than those we are

classifying as identity fraud. For example, if a terrorist impersonates someone else in order to carry out his or her plans, the case
would be reported as a terrorism offense and would not likely be
flagged as identity theft.

A study done in a large police department in Florida found
that the incidence rate of identity theft showed an upward trend
compared to other types of fraud and theft crimes, while clearance
rates for identity theft were comparable to these other crimes. It
also examined differences between the demographic characteristics of victims, offenders and the general population (Allison,
Schuck et al. 2005).

A review of US Secret Service cases provided good information
about a certain class of serious ID fraud cases that would be referred to
the Secret Service. The study looked at characteristics of cases, offenders and victims, and offered recommendations as to how the results
can guide law enforcement policy (Gordon, Rebovich et al. 2007).
But again, because of the more serious nature of the cases referred to
the Secret Service, this study cannot be considered representative of
the larger groups of crimes included in our definition of IDTF.

Two Canadian researchers have examined offender characteristics by examining media reports, primarily from the US (Dupont
and Louis 2009), and another study of offenders was conducted
through jailhouse interviews. The jailhouse study explored offender
demographics, motivations, perceptions of risk and justifications.
It also looked at the various methods and skills employed in the
commission of these crimes. The authors suggest that the most
effective way to reduce the incidence of IDTF might be to remove
the 'excuses' that offenders use to justify their actions. However,
jailhouse interviews have their own methodological limitations,
which are outlined in the report (Copes and Vieraitis 2007).

Data Breach Reports

In the United States, most states have enacted some sort of mandatory disclosure of data breaches. The number and size of these

reported breaches can give a measure of the number of potential victims of identity fraud, but requirements for reporting differ from state to state. There is a considerable amount of data breach data available from various agencies. For example, the Privacy Rights Clearing House (PRC 2011) provides an annual report on US data breaches, and the Verizon RISK team combined with the US Secret Service and the Dutch High Tech Crime Unit to generate an analysis of 2010 data breaches (Verizon 2011). However, many of the reported cases involve loss of information rather than targeted theft, and there is no information to tie the loss or theft to cases of IDTF.

Business Sector Research

In general, businesses are reluctant to provide information about security breaches or fraud losses, fearing that such disclosures will damage their reputations and scare customers away. Published survey information of this type is therefore difficult to find. However, the Australian study referenced earlier in this chapter (Cuganesan and Lacey 2003) was able to estimate the organizational cost of identity fraud in Australia in the period 2001–02 to be $1.1 billion. The study also included responses related to organizational awareness of the problem, risk assessment and prevention and detection programs. In addition, a 2008 study of business fraud in Canada by a Statistics Canada "Survey of Fraud Against Businesses" (SFAB) focused on businesses in the retail, banking and insurance industries (Taylor-Butts and Perreault 2009). The purpose of SFAB was to provide data and information that could be used to assist in building a standard, more comprehensive picture of the prevalence and characteristics of business fraud in Canada. The report provides a national-level overview for the retail, banking and health and property insurance industries on issues like the prevalence and types of fraud experienced, how businesses respond to incidents of fraud, the monetary and non-monetary costs of fraud and fraud detection and prevention practices.

An interesting approach to accessing business IDTF information was used by Chris Hoofnagle of the University of California (Berkeley). He used the Freedom of Information law to force the US Federal Trade Commission to reveal the businesses mentioned in identity theft complaints received by the agency over three randomly chosen months in 2006. His analysis shows that some financial institutions have a greater incidence rate than others and that telecommunications firms were involved in a large proportion of the complaints (Hoofnagle 2008).

Business surveys are often used to gauge security practices within organizations and the general security concerns of their IT management (e.g., CMI 2007; Oltsik, McKnight et al. 2007; Ponemon Institute 2007).

Consumer Surveys

Surveys of Consumer Attitudes and Behaviours

Some consumer surveys examine consumer behaviours or attitudes with respect to IDTF. There are many surveys reported in the North American popular press that try to gauge consumer level of concern about these issues. Many of these are sponsored by firms in the financial sector. They typically ask about the general level of concern and whether the consumer's concern is increasing, decreasing or remaining at the same level. As pointed out in an earlier chapter, their definitions of identity theft and/ or fraud vary or are not even given to participants, so it is very difficult to develop objective comparisons of the results. It is interesting to note, however, that some of these surveys show that members of the group that tends to be least concerned about IDTF have been victims of credit card fraud. This derives from the fact that consumers are not held liable for such frauds in North America, provided they are reported as soon as they become apparent to the consumer.

Another set of studies asks people about their behaviours related to the prevention and detection of identity theft. These studies may also try to gauge how people's behaviours are changing. Examples of such surveys can be found in Milne 2003; Milne, Rohm et al. 2004; Winterdyk and Thompson 2008; and Sproule and Archer 2008b.

Surveys of Prevalence and Nature

Although all of the above methods can shed some information on the problem of IDTF, many of them are subject to the problems associated with clear definitions and none can be used to produce measures like incidence rates or to analyze the characteristics and nature of cases that are occurring in the general population.

In the United States, the primary source of longitudinal measurements of IDTF has been a series of consumer surveys originally developed and conducted by the FTC in 2003 (FTC 2003) and subsequently conducted on an annual basis by Javelin Strategy and Research (Javelin 2005; Javelin 2006; Javelin 2007; Javelin 2008), in addition to more recent surveys. These surveys place cases of ID fraud into three categories: 1) credit card fraud, 2) existing account fraud and 3) new account and other fraud. Because more than one type of fraud can occur in a single incident of ID theft, each case is counted in the category where the most serious fraud occurred. In 2004, the US National Crime Victimization Survey (NCVA) included questions about ID theft and ID fraud and also used these categories (Baum 2006). The full results of the FTC and NCVS surveys are available on the Internet. While the full Javelin survey results are only available for purchase, Javelin provides limited summary information on their website each year as the surveys are completed.

In Canada, a similar survey was conducted by the McMaster eBusiness Research Centre (MeRC) in 2008. In order that comparisons with the US could be made, this survey was modeled after the original FTC survey and used its categorizations of ID fraud.

An additional question about ID theft was included that asked if participants were aware of any situations where their personal data had been subject to unauthorized access (Sproule and Archer 2008b).

While the FTC, Javelin and NCVS surveys were Random Digit Dialing (RDD) telephone surveys, the McMaster survey was conducted by a commercial market survey firm using an online panel. Around the same time, Gartner Research conducted an online survey in the United States that was also modeled after the FTC/Javelin surveys (Litan 2007). Together, these surveys provide the best information available about the nature and prevalence of consumer IDTF. However, caution is advised in comparing data gathered with these two different methodologies because it is known that participants tend to perceive experienced incidence rates higher when surveyed through online surveys than they do when surveyed by telephone.

Summary

This chapter has identified a number of research contributions and data sources that can support a research agenda for IDTF. The work begins by describing several relevant theories from criminology. This is followed by brief discussions of public sources of IDTF information, with particular reference to sources in the US, Canada, the UK, the EU and Australia. Private-sector sources include the Liberty Alliance project, ID Analytics, victim reports and data breach reports, most of which are generally available online at no charge. Finally, there are other sources from business-sector research and consumer surveys that use survey information to measure consumer attitudes and behaviours and the prevalence and nature of IDTF.

References

Allison, S. F. H., A. M. Schuck, et al. 2005. "Exploring the Crime of Identity Theft: Prevalence, Clearance Rates, and Victim/Offender Characteristics." *Journal of Criminal Justice*, 33: 1: 19–29.

Anonymous. 2009. "PhoneBusters: The Canadian Anti-fraud Call Centre." Toronto: Competition Bureau of Canada. http://www.phonebusters.com/ [consulted January 2, 2010].

Baum, K. 2006. *Identity Theft, 2004: First Estimates from the National Crime Victimization Survey*. Bureau of Justice Statistics, US Department of Justice.

Benner, J., B. Givens, et al. 2000. *Nowhere to Turn: Victims Speak Out on Identity Theft (A Survey of Identity Theft Victims and Recommendations for Reform)*. CALPIRG/Privacy Rights Clearinghouse 2005.

Cabinet Office. 2002. *Identity Fraud: A Study*. London, UK: Cabinet Office. www.statewatch.org/news/2004/may/id-fraud-report.pdf [consulted March 14, 2011].

Camp, L. J. 2010. *Economics of Identity Theft: Avoidance, Causes and Possible Cures*. New York: Springer.

Cavoukian, A. 2005. *Identity Theft Revisited: Security Is Not Enough*. Information and Privacy Commissioner/Ontario.

CMI. 2007. *Canadian Security Technology Readiness Intelligence Report*. Canadian Advanced Technology Alliance: 18. http://www.cata.ca/Media_and_Events/Press_Releases/cata_pr06070701.html [consulted July 3, 2009].

Consumer Sentinel. 2005. *National and State Trends in Fraud and Identity Theft*. Federal Trade Commission.

Copes, H., and L. Vieraitis. 2007. "Identity Theft: Assessing Offenders' Strategies and Perceptions of Risk." *Technical Report*. Washington, D.C.: National Institute for Justice.

Cornish, D., and R. Clarke. 2003. "Opportunities, Precipitators and Criminal Decisions: A Reply to Wortley's Critique of Situational Crime Prevention." *Theory For Practice in Situational Crime Prevention: Crime Prevention Studies*. Edited by M. Smith and D. Cornish. Monsy, NY: Criminal Justice Press, 16: 151–96.

Cuganesan, S., and D. Lacey. 2003. *Identity Fraud in Australia: An Evaluation of its Nature, Cost and Extent*. Sydney: Securities Industry Research Centre of Asia-Pacific (SIRCA), pp. 1–126. "

Department of Justice. 2009a. "Tough New Laws Targeting Identity Theft Receive Royal Assent." Ottawa: Department of Justice. http://www.justice.gc.ca/eng/news-nouv/nr-cp/2009/doc_32447.html [consulted January 2, 2010].

Dupont, B., and G. Louis. 2009. *Les voleurs d'identité. Profil d'une délinquance ordinaire*. Montréal: Université de Montréal.

Foley, L., J. Foley, et al. 2004. *Identity Theft: The Aftermath 2004*. Identity Theft Resource Center.

Foley, L., J. Foley, et al. 2003. *Identity Theft: The Aftermath*. Identity Theft Resource Center.

FTC. 2003. *Identity Theft Survey Report*. Federal Trade Commission and Synovate.

FTC. 2003. *Overview of the Identity Theft Program*. Federal Trade Commission.

FTC. 2007. "Fair Information Practice Principles." Federal Trade Commission, http://www.ftc.gov/reports/privacy3/fairinfo.shtm [consulted May 5, 2011].

GAO. 1998. *Identity fraud: Information on prevalence, cost, and Internet impact is limited*. Washington, D.C.: US Government Accounting Office. FAO/GGD-98-100BR.

GAO. 2002. *Identity Theft: Prevalence and Cost Appear to be Growing*. US Government Accountability Office. GAO-02-363.

Gordon, G. R., D. J. Rebovich, et al. 2007. *Identity Fraud Trends and Patterns: Building a Foundation for Proactive Enforcement*. Center for Identity Management and Information Protection.

Gordon, G. R., N. A. Willox, et al. 2004. "Identity Fraud: A Critical National and Global Threat." *Journal of Economic Crime Management*, 2: 1: 1–47.

Hoofnagle, C. 2008. "Measuring Identity Theft at Top Banks." *Law and Technology Scholarship*. Berkeley, CA: Berkeley Center for Law and Technology.

IC3. 2007. "2007 Annual Report." Washington, D.C.: Internet Crime Complaint Center. http://www.ic3.gov/media/annualreport/2007_IC3Report.pdf [consulted February 10, 2010].

ID Analytics. 2005. "ID Analytics National Fraud Ring Analysis: Understanding Behavioural Patterns." ID Analytics.

ID Analytics. 2006. "National Data Breach Analysis." ID Analytics Inc., pp. 2–36.

ID Analytics. 2007. "US Identity Fraud Hot Spots." ID Analytics.

ID Analytics. 2007b. "Data Breach Harm Analysis." ID Analytics.

Javelin. 2005. *2005 Identity Fraud Survey Report (Complimentary Overview)*. Pleasanton, CA: Javelin Strategy & Research.

Javelin. 2006. *2006 Identity Fraud Survey Report*. Javelin Strategy and Research, co-released with the Better Business Bureau, sponsored by Visa USA, Wells Fargo Bank and CheckFree Corproation.

Javelin. 2007. *2007 Identity Fraud Survey Report: Identity Fraud Is Dropping, Continued Vigilance is Necessary*. Pleasanton, CA: Javelin Strategy & Research.

Javelin. 2008. *2008 Identity Fraud Survey Report: Identity Fraud Continues to Decline, But Criminals More Effective at Using All Channels*. Javelin Strategy & Research.

Liberty Alliance. 2003. "Privacy and Security Best Practices." Liberty Alliance Project.

Liberty Alliance. 2005b. "Liberty Alliance Whitepaper: Identity Theft Primer." Liberty Alliance Project.

Litan, A. 2007. *The Truth Behind Identity Theft Numbers*. Gartner, Inc.

Milne, G. R. 2003. "How Well Do Consumers Protect Themselves from Identity Theft?" *The Journal of Consumers Affairs*, 37: 2: 388.

Milne, G. R., A. J. Rohm, et al. 2004. "Consumers' Protection of Online Privacy and Identity." *The Journal of Consumer Affairs*, 38: 2: 217.

Mitchison, N., M. Wilikens, et al. 2004. *Identity Theft: A Discussion Paper*. Italy: European Commission, Directorate-General, Joint Research Centre.

Newman, G. R., and M. M. McNally. 2005. *Identity Theft Literature Review*. US Department of Justice. Document No. 210459.

Oltsik, J., J. McKnight, et al. 2007. *Research Report: The Case for Data Leakage Prevention Solutions*. Enterprise Strategy Group for Vericept.

Ponemon Institute. 2007. *Database Security 2007: Threats and Priorities within IT Database Infrastructure*. New York: Ponemon Institute LLC, sponsored by Application Security Inc.

PRC. 2011. "2011 Breach List." Privacy Rights Clearinghouse. http://www.privacyrights.org/data-breach [consulted April 29, 2011].

PresTaskForce. 2007. "The President's Identity Theft Task Force Report." Washington D.C., United States Government. http://www.ftc.gov/os/2008/1 0/081021taskforcereport.pdf [consulted February 10, 2010].

RAPID. 2003. *Roadmap for Advanced Research in Privacy and Identity Management—Final Report*. Information Society Technologies, under EC Contract IST-2001-38310.

Romanosky, S., R. Telang, et al. 2011. "Do Data Breach Disclosure Laws Reduce Identity Theft?" *Journal of Policy Analysis and Management*, 30: 2: 256–86.

Sproule, S., and N. Archer. 2007. *Defining Identity Theft*. Eighth World Congress on the Management of eBusiness, Toronto, IEEE.

Sproule, S., and N. Archer. 2008a. "Measuring Identity Theft in Canada: 2006 Consumer Survey. Working Paper #21." McMaster eBusiness Research Centre Working Paper Series. Hamilton, Ontario: McMaster University, p. 87.

Sproule, S., and N. Archer. 2008b. "Measuring identity theft in Canada: 2008 consumer survey." *McMaster eBusiness Research Centre Working Paper #23*. Hamilton, Ontario: DeGroote School of Business, McMaster University.

Taylor-Butts, A., and S. Perreault. 2009. "Fraud against Businesses in Canada: Results from a National Survey." Ottawa: Statistics Canada, 27. http://www.statcan.gc.ca/pub/85-571-x/2009001/aftertoc-aprestdm1-eng.htm [consulted January 2, 2010].

Taylor, R. W., T. J. Caeti, et al. 2007. *Digital Crime and Digital Terrorism*. Upper Saddle River, NJ: Prentice Hall.

Verizon. 2011. "2011 Data Breach Investigations Report." Verizon Corp. http://www.verizonbusiness.com/resources/reports/rp_data-breach-investigations-report-2011_en_xg.pdf [consulted May 5, 2011].

White, M. D., and C. Fisher. 2008. "Assessing Our Knowledge of Identity Theft." *Criminal Justice Policy Review*, 19: 1: 3–24.

Winterdyk, J., and N. Thompson. 2008. "Student and Non-student Perceptions and Awareness of Identity Theft." *Canadian Journal of Criminology and Criminal Justice*, 50: 2: 153–86.

Chapter 14

Monitoring Trends: Indexes of Identity Theft and Fraud

"Those who cannot remember the past are condemned to repeat it."

—George Santayana

Introduction

Throughout this book, we have outlined findings from various surveys and other sources on IDTF. In this chapter, we focus on findings discovered by collecting relevant data through government-mandated policies and by surveys that probed the consumer, business and government sectors. Finally, we point out the benefits that would be derived from a regular process of monitoring IDTF incidents and by organizing the results into an annual index.

What more can be done to combat the continuing threat of identity theft and fraud? One approach that would help involves the collection of data at regular intervals at the individual, organizational and national levels. Such information that is already collected, often sporadically, has been very useful in understanding the changes in levels and types of IDTF. Additionally, it has been used to plan how best to combat these criminal activities. Regular collection of such data could be used, for example, to monitor increases in certain types of IDTF and to check on whether certain security and/or educational campaigns have had an impact on the level of such attacks. In the United States, IDTF surveys of various types are taken on a regular basis (see Chapter 13), resulting in data that can be used to develop indexes that could be useful in proposing legislation and policies to reduce the incidence of IDTF through education, regulation and technology development. Although some US agencies regularly collect relevant data, the results are not always organized in a serial fashion to demonstrate how these criminal activities morph and grow over time. In this chapter, we present a brief introduction to the topic of monitoring such trends, and the types of information that would be required and collected either continuously or (regularly) through annual surveys. We also present some examples where serial data collection has been used to good effect to unearth useful information that cannot be found in individual one-off studies. Finally, we suggest how indexes could be developed that would provide standard measures (preferably on an annual basis) to assist businesses and government policy makers to make decisions on the best ways to combat the threats of IDTF.

In Canada, regular monitoring of IDTF is not done at the present time, and what is being done is poorly organized compared to indicators or indexes used in other fields like consumer prices, purchasing activity, quality of life, consumer confidence and stock markets. In each of these fields, trends are measured by means of a statistical compilation of a series of values of a ratio or other number that measures levels and changes over time. These trends are used extensively in decision making by organizations, government agencies and legislators alike in developing and implementing suitable policies. Various government agencies and private firms in the United States (e.g., IC3 2009; ID Analytics 2007b; Javelin 2009) undertake regular surveys that can be used to monitor changes in level and type of IDTF. These could easily be organized into a national index that might be used in developing government policy. In Canada, regular annual surveys are not currently available. For maximum effectiveness, surveys should be done at least on an annual basis, with the objective of comparing the past history of IDTF with the present, and perhaps predicting the future. Data collected regularly could be used to develop IDTF indexes for use by business organizations, government agencies, legislators and police forces. These indexes could play an important role in measuring changes in the activities measured, so responses to these activities could be organized to reduce their impact on business, government and society in general. Such indexes for tracking trends in identity theft and fraud in Canada do not yet formally exist.

It is the responsibility of individual organizations to monitor the impact of their own security and confidentiality provisions by measuring their impact on IDTF from both internal and external sources. Security breaches may originate externally or internally to an organization, and the only way to respond to the challenges posed by these threats is to take them seriously and create an internal structure that is devoted to combating the threats. Acceptance of improved organizational security can be increased through widely accepted metrics for characterizing security, or de facto standards of best practice. Developing such metrics, along with measuring the impacts of relevant public education, business prevention activities and law enforcement on suppressing IDTF, is important to organizations that take security seriously. Since the number and nature of security events change over time, the ability to monitor these events is invaluable to organizations or governments seeking to reduce IDTF and to measure the impact of new regulations, education and legislation.

What would be the benefits to society of tracking trends in IDTF? Those who wish to research the effect of changes in technological and organizational approaches to improved security and access will, of course, be the first beneficiaries. Policy makers who are interested in determining whether business and government investments in technologies, systems and education to defeat criminal activities improve the online environment for information and transaction exchange will also be interested. As in any complex system, however, it may be difficult to link actions with effects. It is certain that everyone can gain from measuring both defensive actions and outcomes in terms of observed levels of IDTF. This is only possible when data are gathered and analyzed regularly in order to examine both short-term and long-term outcomes.

Results from sequential studies can only be interpreted correctly if certain standards are followed in collecting and interpreting the data. This also means that definitions of what is being asked of survey participants must be made clear to the participants. For example, asking participants about their experiences of 'identity theft' without first defining the term carefully will elicit responses that depend upon the participant's definition rather than the survey's definition, increasing uncertainty in the results. A lack of clarity in definition also makes it difficult to compare surveys by different organizations and in different regions. As pointed out by Cheney (2005), there are three important definitional delineations that would help to develop effective solutions to IDTF: measuring the success (or failure) of efforts to fight this crime, educating consumers about the risks and responses to this crime and coordinating mitigation strategies across stakeholders and geographies.

It is well known that it is not possible to manage something that is not measured, and findings from past studies have had a direct impact on the development of legislation to combat the onslaught of identity theft and fraud. Sequential surveys can make a strong contribution over and above any one-off surveys, since trends can be more easily identified from such studies. When sequential survey data are organized into indexes, these indexes can serve as indicators of the growth or decline in risks associated with IDTF. This can in turn help determine government and business policies to address these risks through education, criminal and civil law, policing and mandated release of information about events that affect the population.

Previous Surveys

Consumers

- In their 2009 *Identity Fraud Survey Report*, Javelin Strategy & Research (Javelin, 2009a) analyzed trends in overall identity fraud amounts and incidence rates in the United States over the period 2004–08, and showed that fraud incidents have been increasing but are detected more quickly. In addition, the costs to consumers of IDF have declined substantially. The implication is that monitoring accounts and other actions taken to detect identity fraud has had a positive effect on containing and reducing costs from these criminal activities.

- In the same 2009 Javelin survey, it was found that the downward trend in consumer IDF over the annual surveys between 2004 and 2007 had suddenly been reversed. The greatest increase was in existing accounts, rather than in opening new fraudulent accounts. The implication from the survey is that the increase was due to the rise in economic misfortune in the population in 2008.

- Again from the 2009 Javelin study, low-tech methods were found to be the most popular for perpetrating fraud, totaling 43% of all incidents where the method of access was known.

- In two studies of consumer IDTF in Canada (Sproule and Archer 2010), it was found that between 2006 and 2008 there was a significantly heightened experience and concern among consumer victims about new account or other IDF and existing account IDF. Concern also rose for those who were not victims. In the same time period, there was little if any increase in concern about credit card IDF. The lack of concern about credit card IDF appears to be because credit card companies, not consumers, bear the losses from such crimes, provided they are notified promptly about card theft or loss. At the same time, however, 20% of participants reported that they had stopped or reduced their online shopping, while 9% had stopped or reduced online banking activities. It is critical to spot trends like this, since action may be possible to reverse them. For example, more spending on education and advertising about how to manage online accounts, credit cards and shopping could be effective in combating increases in online criminal activities that give rise to concerns such as this.

- In a 2006 study that compared rates in the first and second halves of the year, ID Analytics (2007) was able to find regional hot spots in the United States where IDTF was increasing most rapidly. The findings were based on actual and attempted frauds confirmed by businesses. The study found a substantial emergence of these crimes in more rural areas, indicating a trend toward popularization of the crime, and an indication that perpetrators were beginning to act more 'under the radar' in remote areas.

Business Organizations

- In Canada, it is difficult for independent researchers to collect comprehensive data on identity fraud in business organizations due the reluctance of these organizations to respond to external requests for this information. Federal or provincial governments are more likely to be able to command the attention of businesses to respond to these kinds of surveys. Until recently, business data were available only on self-reported events and from police agency prosecutions, which did not come near to uncovering the full nature of business fraud (of which identity fraud is just one component). In 2008, however, Statistics Canada, a federal government agency, conducted an initial Survey of Fraud Against Businesses (SFAB) (Taylor-Butts and Perreault 2009). The intent of SFAB is to provide data and information that could help to build a standard, more comprehensive picture of business fraud in Canada. This particular study focused on businesses in the retail, banking and insurance industries. One important finding was that frauds were more likely to be perpetrated in person than online. On the other hand, debit card fraud was the most reported criminal activity at banks. SFAB did not probe the growing issue of data breaches, which has been highlighted in recent years as a major problem in the United States (and is probably a serious problem in Canada). The Canadian study examined only one point in time, but it would be necessary to continue the survey, possibly with some adjustments, on a regular basis if trends in fraudulent activities were to be brought to light. This would enable governments and businesses to focus resources on the most critical issues related to fraud and thereby yield the best return on their investment. For example, should there be a legal requirement that organizations report data breaches publicly, as in the United States? What are the benefits and disadvantages of doing so?

- A Ponemon Institute study of the cost of data breaches in the United States (Ponemon 2009) found that this cost has increased every year during the interval 2006–09. In the most recent year (2009), the cost to companies averaged US$ 197 per compromised record ($145 in direct costs—abnormal turnover, or 'churn,' of customers—and $52 for direct costs). This clearly highlights the enormous costs to businesses that do not have adequate security provisions in place, costs of which could be far exceeded by major data breaches.

- The US Internet Crime Complaint Center (IC3) has been accessed by US citizens and businesses since 2000 to file complaints about Internet crime (IC3 2009). The Center does an initial investigation and then refers the complaint to law enforcement agencies for further investigation and prosecution. The reason that it receives such a large volume of complaints (over 275,000 in 2008) is probably due to the fact that such complaints may result in referral and prosecution of the offenders. The large number of reports received also makes this agency a good source of information on trends. For example, there was a spike of 33% in complaints they received in 2008, similar to spikes noticed by other crime monitoring agencies. As an example of data they reported, in 2008, e-mail (74.0%) and webpages (28.9%) were the two primary mechanisms by which fraudulent contact took place. The e-mail figure for 2006 was almost identical, but the webpages figure was 36%, indicating that this type of fraud is slowly becoming less prevalent in the United States.

- In 2009, Verizon prepared a second annual report (Verizon 2009) in which the company claimed that 285 million records were compromised in ninety confirmed US breaches in 2008, more than the previous four years combined. The financial services sector accounted for 93% of all compromised records, 90% of which involved groups engaged in organized crime. This enormous rise could not have been spotted without continuous recording of such events over a period of time. Collection of statistics on data breaches in the United States is greatly aided by the fact that almost all US states require businesses and other institutions to reveal data breaches to the public.

Indexes of Identity Theft and Fraud

Business Indexes

As pointed out in Chapter 7, identity management approaches are very useful for organizations to measure and track their own performance on identity management and related privacy and security measures, but an index model is needed for tracking national performance on such issues. To evaluate overall national organizational performance requires the development of indexes based on periodically gathering information such as security breach data, periodic national surveys of organizational readiness and experience, and periodic national surveys of consumer experience and perceptions of IDTF. Any IDTF events that organizations are required by law to report can provide information that can be used to follow trends in the nature of particular classes of offense. However, voluntary reporting has been found to provide less than complete data on the relative size and nature of IDTF problems (Taylor-Butts and Perreault, 2009).

Measures of the impact of IDTF in a specific organization can be derived by monitoring, tracking and reporting the following relevant information at regular intervals:

- Number, type, source (internal or external) and severity of known or attempted security breaches
- Costs of installing and maintaining security (includes systems, personnel, education and training, etc.)
- Costs due to loss recovery operations
- Direct and indirect losses due to fraud caused by security breaches
- Compensation paid to customers for losses due to security lapses
- Number of customers directly impacted by security breaches
- Number of employees personally affected by security breaches
- Number of partner organizations directly impacted by security breaches originating from the organization in question
- Confidentiality and/or privacy breaches

National reports from governments and other agencies (e.g., police forces) can also be useful in alerting responsible agencies, due to increases in the number of criminal activities that can appear in statistics collected on

- Number of identity fraud investigations
- Number of losses or theft of secure documents
- Number of counterfeiting investigations
- Number of credit card trafficking investigations

Consumer Indexes

There are three particular reasons why consumer IDTF events should be monitored by governments and other organizations affected by these events:

- To monitor growth or decline in specific types of events and to plan educational, deterrent and enforcement investments to counter growing threats
- To determine whether the nature and frequency of new identity theft activities are becoming significant enough to warrant greater attention
- To increase awareness regularly through public announcements of threats of identity theft to individuals, organizations the economy

Data that should be collected from consumer surveys and reported publicly in order to get a good understanding of the difficulties caused to consumers from IDTF are listed below. All of these data are useful in establishing sources and levels of IDTF and the resulting hassles to consumers when and if they become victims (Sproule and Archer, 2008b). Those measures marked with an asterisk could be used to construct a suitable national index of consumer IDTF:

Incidence rates:
- Credit card fraud *
- Debit card fraud *
- Existing account fraud *
- Mortgage fraud[1] *

---

1 Very few cases of mortgage fraud are detected in consumer surveys due to their low incidence rates.

- New accounts and other fraud *
- Other *

Costs:
- Fraud amount *
- Victim's hours spent resolving problems resulting from the fraud *
- Victim's out-of-pocket costs *
- Other *

Method of detection:
- Notification from victim's bank
- Monitoring accounts online
- Notification from credit card company
- Discovery on an account statement received in the mail
- Other

Time from event to its detection (days) *

Awareness of how the identity information was obtained (yes or no) *

How the information was stolen from the victim:
- Business transactions (in-person)
- Business transactions (online)
- Debit card compromise
- Credit card compromise
- Stolen wallets or purses
- Someone close to the victim
- Other

Identity of the perpetrator (if known):
- 'Stranger' fraud (someone not familiar with the victim)
- 'Friendly' fraud (someone known to the victim)

Non-monetary costs:
- Banking problems
- Problems with credit card companies

- Charged higher interest rates
- Contacted by debt collectors
- Turned down for loans
- Subject to criminal investigation
- Other

Reported incident to:
- Credit card company
- Bank
- Police
- Credit reporting agencies
- Other

Developing a Composite Identity Theft and Fraud Index

A composite index is an aggregation of several relevant indexes on the basis of an underlying model of the multi-dimensional concept being measured (multi-dimensional concepts cannot be captured by a single index). Given individual indicators, aggregation is built upon a logical framework (Nardo, Saisana, Saltelli and Tarantola 2005).

Below is a suggested approach to develop an overall index of a composite measure of the impact of IDTF, with separate indexes for consumers and organizations. Since no work has been done at this point, this is strictly a conceptual outline and it would very likely have to be modified as experience is gained in its application.

1. A theoretical framework is developed that provides for the selection and combination of single indicators into a meaningful composite indicator under fitness-for-purpose principles. This can include analytical soundness, measurability, coverage, relevance to the phenomenon being measured and relationships to each other. Proxy variables can be considered when data are scarce.

2. An exploratory statistical analysis should investigate the overall structure of the indicators, assess the suitability of the data set and explain the methodological choices, including the use

of weighting and aggregation. Determination of an appropriate weight for each indicator depends on the desired end result. An estimate of the overall economic impact of IDTF would suggest that the weights should depend on the economic impact of each of the factors to be aggregated.

3. Consideration should be given to different approaches for imputing missing values. Extreme values should be examined, as they can become unintended benchmarks.

4. Indicators should be normalized to render them comparable.

5. Indicators should be aggregated and weighted according to the underlying theoretical framework.

6. Analysis should be used to assess the robustness of the composite indicator in terms of: the mechanism for including or excluding single indicators, the normalization scheme, the imputation of missing data and the choice of weights.

7. Attempts should be made to correlate the composite indicator with other published indicators, as well as to identify linkages through regressions.

8. Composite indicators can be visualized or presented in a number of different ways, which can influence their interpretation.

9. Finally, composite indicators should be transparent and decomposable into their underlying indicators or values.

Summary

As previously pointed out in this book, it is not possible to manage or control well something that is not being measured. For this reason, monitoring IDTF activities is critical to countering these activities successfully. Serially collected data can provide information on trends not available through one-off studies, supporting projections of future levels of IDTF and assisting government and business to plan counter-measures. Monitoring can take the form of internally collected information in each particular business firm or other organization, with action taken by the organization's

Chief Security Officer (see Chapter 12), when necessary. At the national, provincial or state level, data should be collected at least annually through well-designed surveys to provide information that can be used to develop government policies and potentially to upgrade criminal laws that will support the prosecution of identity criminals. For consumers, regular annual surveys can be very useful in spotting trends and evaluating new threats, and supporting counter-measures (including new laws, if necessary) to dampen the growth of particular risks. National surveys of businesses and consumers can be used to create and report index measures on IDTF. These can be used to measure the results of efforts to fight IDTF, educating consumers about the risks and responses to these crimes and coordinating mitigation strategies across stakeholders and geographies.

References

Cheney, J. S. 2005. *Identity Theft: Do Definitions Still Matter?* Philadelphia: Payment Cards Center, Federal Reserve Bank of Philadelphia. http://www.phil.frb.org/payment-cards-center/publications/discussion-papers/2005/identity-theft-definitions.pdf [consulted February 19, 2010].

IC3. 2009. *2008 Internet Crime Report.* Washington, D.C.: Internet Crime Complaint Center.

ID Analytics. 2007. *U.S. Identity Fraud Hot Spots.* ID Analytics.

ID Analytics. 2007b. *Data Breach Harm Analysis.* ID Analytics.

Javelin. 2009. *2009 Identity Fraud Survey Report: Consumer Version.* Javelin Strategy & Research.

Javelin. 2009a. "Latest Javelin Research Shows Identity Fraud Increased 22 Percent, Affecting Nearly Ten Million Americans: But Consumer Costs Fell Sharply by 31 Percent." Javelin Strategy & Research. http://www.idsafety.net/Javelin2009IdentityFraudSurveyPressRelease.pdf [consulted February 18, 2010].

Nardo, M., M. Saisana, A. Saltelli and S. Tarantola. 2005. *Handbook on Constructing Composite Indicators: Methodology and User Guide.* No. STD/DOC(2005)3). OECD.

Ponemon, L. 2009. *Fourth Annual US Cost of Data Breach Study.* Traverse City, Michigan: Ponemon Institute. http://www.ponemon.org/index.php [consulted February 19, 2010].

Sproule, S., and N. Archer. 2008b. *Measuring Identity Theft in Canada: 2008 Consumer Survey.* Hamilton, Ontario: DeGroote School of Business, McMaster University.

Sproule, S., and N. Archer. 2010. "Measuring Identity Theft and Identity Fraud." *International Journal of Business Governance and Ethics*, 5: 1/2: 51–63.

Taylor-Butts, A., and S. Perreault. 2009. *Fraud against Businesses in Canada: Results from a National Survey.* Ottawa: Statistics Canada. http://www.statcan.gc.ca/pub/85-571-x/2009001/aftertoc-aprestdm1-eng.htm [consulted January 2, 2010].

Verizon. 2009. "Verizon Business 2009 Data Breach Study Finds Significant Rise in Targeted Attacks, Organized Crime Involvement." http://www.verizonbusiness.com [consulted February 19, 2010].

Chapter 15

Overview of the Book and a Glimpse of the Future

"I never think of the future—it comes soon enough."

—Albert Einstein

Introduction

The objective of this book is to highlight the risks of identity theft and fraud to consumers, businesses, governments and other institutions that are victims of the escalating level of these crimes, and to discuss methods that are being used to reduce the risks and to defend against related criminal activities. We also present statistics that show the extent of IDTF and data breach risks to society, and evaluate laws that can be used to prosecute related criminal activities. However, although the legal system is slowly adjusting to the realities of these threats, it is the responsibility of the various stakeholders to contain the threats of IDTF. We also suggest approaches to developing a research agenda for IDTF, including data sources, and propose the development of suitable indexes that can be used to track new threats and to evaluate progress in managing IDTF. We conclude with an attempt to give a partial glimpse of the future of a society that must continue to adapt and to deal with new risks that arise from IDTF, as much as that is possible to do in such an unpredictable environment.

Overview

Ready access over the Internet to a huge range of information, communications among individuals and organizations, and business transactions has revolutionized the world at an ever-increasing pace. Regrettably, this has been accompanied by a substantial increase in related risks, such as identity theft, fraud and cyber-extortion by criminals. Shielded from their victims by sophisticated electronic techniques, these criminals can work in anonymity from any country around the world. Accompanying the expansion in the availability of the Internet and other networked services is a massive increase in the amount of confidential information at risk, and a resulting rise in the potential for losses to organizations and consumers through IDTF.

Although most attention is paid to illegal activities by criminals intent on fraudulent use of personal identity such as credit or debit cards, a far more pervasive opportunity for privacy invasion and identity theft is the massive amount of consumer data collected by marketers, businesses and governments, as well as clinical health records that exist in paper or electronic form. These and many other databases represent opportunities for both marketing campaigns and illegal access to personal data for fraud or impersonation. Trying to balance individual privacy and public benefit through protective legislation represents a major public policy issue.

Individual perceptions of risk are also changing due to public reports of criminal fraud involving personal information, and an increase in terrorism. At the moment, the balance between the right to privacy and the need to preserve national and internal security appears to be shifting towards law enforcement as opposed to the rights of the individual. Links between individual risk perception and concepts of privacy represent dangers from increased privacy intrusion in the relationship between the individual and the state, as well as relationships between citizens (Rauhofer 2008). The balance between the two is currently not in equilibrium, but is actually in a state of flux due to changes in the level of perceived risks, whether these risks are real or imagined.

Identity theft, "the unauthorized collection, possession, transfer, replication or other manipulation of another person's personal information, and/or identification documents, for the purpose of committing fraud or other crimes that involve the use of a false identity," is a problem associated with the guardianship of personal information. On the other hand, identity fraud, "the use of stolen or bogus identities to commit fraud," is a problem associated with authentication. The stakeholder model introduced in Chapter 2 shows how the parties affected by IDTF interact. These include identity owners, identity issuers, identity checkers and identity prosecutors—and, of course, identity criminals. Successfully controlling IDTF requires continuing attention to guardianship and authentication, and each of the defending parties has particular responsibilities in combating IDTF.

Risk is an extremely important aspect of the process of protecting against identity theft, because the level of perceived risk from the threat of identity theft determines how much time, effort and money should be spent to reduce this risk. More resources clearly should be expended on mitigating the risk of high-likelihood and high-impact threats than on threats that have a low likelihood and/or low impact. Organizations must develop strong risk management policies and processes in order to reduce surprises or unexpected losses by avoiding, eliminating or mitigating risks from potential threats. Risk management policies need to be flexible and should be updated on a regular basis, and new processes, applications and procedures need to be analyzed thoroughly to identify and reduce potential risks before being implemented.

Perceptions of risk govern the behaviour of both consumers and organizations when viewing the possibility of certain events. Neither always behaves rationally when faced with choices involving risk. Each stakeholder has particular responsibilities in managing and mitigating IDTF risks. This includes consumers (ID owners), who must take precautions, for example, when shopping, and ID issuers, who evaluate the background and documentation of consumers. Trust plays an important role in everyday interactions of consumers with other entities, including banks, retail stores and personal physicians. These entities must earn and maintain a reasonable level of trust if continuing interactions of organizations and people are to lead to successful and productive outcomes.

Personal credit and finance revolves around the credit reporting system, which is intimately associated with identity and its management. The financial and credit industry therefore plays a substantial role in everyone's life. Identification is key to the successful management of this role. Personal credit depends extensively on the ability to identify an individual and that individual's financial situation. This has given rise to the credit reporting system upon which we all rely. Unfortunately, this system is designed to protect the interests of creditors, not individual consumers. Solutions to the problems of IDTF need to consider which of the stakeholders is best able to avoid the loss. In many cases, the individual identity owner is saddled with the loss even though creditors or credit reporting agencies were in the best position to avoid the loss. There is currently an imbalance in how losses are distributed between creditors, individuals and the credit reporting industry.

Criminals can obtain identity information electronically, through physical methods or through social engineering activities like phishing. Data breaches are a rapidly growing form of identity theft and, although the connection to identity frauds can be tenuous, the obligation to notify affected individuals is the subject of much discussion by policy makers. Legislation requiring notification has been introduced in many jurisdictions. To avoid over-notification (and resulting panic or de-sensitization of consumers to risk), most recent legislation includes measures of risks and specific risk thresholds associated with each breach.

A general model for managing data, identity theft and fraud risks was introduced in Chapter 7. The purpose of the model is to provide advice in how to contain and counter such risks in an organized manner. The model's concept is similar for organizations and consumers, although the details of the risks and how to manage them differ substantially between these two classifications. Small businesses also differ from large businesses in the approach they must take to manage IDTF risks, because they typically cannot afford to employ security specialists to do this, instead assigning an employee with the responsibility as just one among multiple responsibilities. The same conceptual model has also been adapted specifically for consumers. The model includes three phases: Anticipatory, where actions are taken to protect against threats from IDTF perpetrators; Reactionary, involving the management of IDTF attacks as they occur; and Remediation, to manage the process after an attack, including changes in policies and operations, and investigation and prosecution of guilty parties.

A lifecycle framework was also introduced (Chapter 8) for analyzing identity theft risks for entities responsible for the issuance, usage and maintenance phases of consumer identity documentation. The analysis shows that in each stage of the lifecycle there are vulnerabilities that can be exploited by identity thieves. The analysis revealed some differences in the risk of fraud between passports and credit cards. For passports, the physical booklet is the main medium that carries the owner's identity information, serving as the reference point when the passport is used to verify the owner's true identity. It lacks an online system for identity verification purposes. If identity thieves have the technologies to make fake passports with the same security features that authentic ones have, identity checkers would not be able to detect fraud. For credit cards, on the other hand, issuers usually have online systems for card verification purposes.

Organizations are the sites of identity information collection, use and storage, and employees are involved in all the stages of the identity management lifecycle. How they deal with information at hand will have a major impact on information security and ultimately identity theft. To prevent employees from mishandling critical identity information, organizations should consider implementing a number of measures, including 1) top management leading by example; 2) enforcement of accountability; 3) security education, training and awareness programs; 4) security behaviour as part of employee performance evaluation; and 5) involving users in security policy design.

It is important for an organization to adopt and adapt the appropriate internal controls to achieve a level of security that is consistent with the threat level to the organization. This cannot be achieved solely by technology; if security threats are to be managed, management must be a strong supporter and change management approaches must be used to encourage management and all employees to embrace security. Identity and Access Management systems provide centralized control of single sign-on approaches to simplify employee access to data and applications in firms of all sizes and complexities. Networks must be protected from threats to the firm that arise from a variety of sources. Issues associated with improved authentication processes and technologies, including multi-factor authentication and mutual authentication as described in Chapter 11. Mutual authentication can play an important role in online transactions, both in protecting customer trust and institutional reputations.

One approach to evaluating the readiness of an organization is by determining its security maturity level. This was outlined in Chapter 12 through a five-level model similar to maturity models used to evaluate the readiness of software development organizations. Knowing the maturity of an organization in managing security gives the organization an objective measure and a target to achieve when preparing its response to security threats. Another method, based on the balanced scorecard, is also described. Finally, how the attention of an organization can be focused on security and privacy is discussed, including how executive-level appointments of chief information security officers and chief privacy officers, respectively, can enhance improvements in both areas.

A number of literature overviews and data sources are provided in Chapter 13 that can help interested researchers to get started in this field. In 2005, the US Department of Justice commissioned a literature review to develop a research agenda aimed at identity theft prevention and enforcement (Newman and McNally 2005). In their report, Newman and McNally suggest that the main areas for research be categorized as offending, prevention and harm reduction. For the first area, they suggest that researchers look at the opportunity structure for identity theft, by identifying specific acts or behaviours and the opportunities provided to offenders by the Information Age. A number of reasons are given for the vulnerability of current enrollment and authentication processes.

There is an old axiom that you can't manage something if you can't measure it. However, there are many problems with identifying how IDTF affects its victims, and it is therefore difficult to find a basis for measurement. There are many indicators and various sources of information that can be collected, but there is much difficulty in compiling this information to arrive at a single estimate of cost. Throughout this book, we have outlined findings from various surveys and other sources on identity theft. There are many benefits that would be derived from a regular process of monitoring incidents of IDTF and from organizing the results into an annual index, separated for businesses and consumers. Details of how such an index could be developed are included in Chapter 14. For consumers, regular annual surveys can be very useful in spotting trends and evaluating new threats, and supporting counter-measures (including new laws, if necessary) to dampen the growth of particular risks. National surveys of businesses and consumers can be used to create and report index measures on IDTF. These can be used to measure the results of efforts to fight IDTF, educating consumers about the risks and responses to these crimes and coordinating mitigation strategies across stakeholders and geographies.

A Glimpse of the Future

The massive growth in the use of the Internet, SMS and smartphones for communicating, gathering and compiling information, as well as for business transactions, continues to result in innovative new applications. For example, ten years ago, who could have predicted the development of social media like Facebook and MySpace, or the evolution of smartphones with an unending stream of 'apps' that can be used for such a wide variety of useful applications? For this reason, we cannot pretend to predict the future when it comes to evaluating the risks that will need to be addressed as these innovations come on line. What we have indicated below are a few recent developments and the risks that have accompanied them.

Medical Data Networks

The Obama administration in the United States has allocated large sums of money to improve the use of digital systems and networks for recording and communicating patient clinical records. This is an important issue, because patients move from one healthcare entity to another in the process of being evaluated, diagnosed and treated for illnesses, and each entity generates clinical records about the patient. If these records are not always easily and quickly available to their primary care physicians, tests may have to be repeated and delays in diagnosis and treatment will result, with a general reduction in the likelihood of healthy outcomes. For patients being treated by a single entity, such as a Health Maintenance Organization (HMO), this is less of a problem, because HMOs generally have their systems networked together; so, once records are created they are available to all the healthcare providers in the HMO who have access permission. This is also the case for the US Veterans Health Administration's networked system, VistA, which covers veteran care for potentially up to a quarter of the nation's population. However, many of the regional healthcare systems ('natural referral areas'; see below) are not associated with networks that link their systems together, with the result that there are many isolated computer systems ('silos') that do not communicate either intra-regionally or externally to other regional systems because they do not adhere to common standards for storing and transmitting clinical data. There is a need to link these regional systems, as well as to upgrade and/or install systems in physicians' offices (fewer than 40% of US physicians currently have Electronic Medical

Record systems, or EMRs) so that individual patient records can be accessed readily when needed.

Healthcare funding, when used for carefully thought-out, standardized regional systems and networks, will be money well spent. European nations like Denmark and the Netherlands have successfully implemented such networks, which cover a very high percentage of their physicians and healthcare facilities, so this is entirely feasible. However, while these upgrades will greatly improve the healthcare system, they come with a cost in terms of patient and physician privacy that must be carefully managed through access controls and risk management of the sort discussed in Chapters 7 and 10. Privacy is a very sensitive issue in health-care, and any changes must always keep this issue front-and-centre throughout the planning and installation process. One way to prevent unnecessary problems is to restrict regular record sharing to within natural referral areas (geographical regions within which consumers live that cover a high percentage of the healthcare facilities ever likely to treat the consumer).

We can repeat the above story for medical systems and networks in Canada. In this case, the federal funding agency is Canada Health Infoway, which works in collaboration with provinces and territories to implement IT applications for healthcare. Upgrades or new installations are underway across Canada in the same manner as they are in the United States, and the same cautions mentioned above need to be observed concerning communications within and among regions.

Cloud Computing

Cloud computing is a model for enabling convenient, on-demand network access to a shared pool of configurable computing resources (e.g., networks, servers, storage, applications and services) that can be rapidly provisioned and released with minimal management effort or service provider interaction (NIST 2010). The wide-scale adoption of cloud computing is expected to result in more efficient computing. It may also improve ready access to a wider array of computing resources than current computing resource models, plus it eliminates user needs to acquire and maintain computer software and servers. However, many organizations must comply with regulations on data security and privacy in the jurisdictions in which they operate, and cloud service might not allow compliance with the required standards. For example, government-enforced regulations may demand the secure storing and handling of private data on servers located physically within the jurisdiction, and the use of cloud service could jeopardize compliance. Contracting for such services to handle highly secure computing and confidential data may therefore result in complex regulatory situations that may be difficult to resolve.

Social Media Use by Corporations

A recent survey of small and medium enterprise (SME) social media use by PandaLabs (Corrons 2010) found that many businesses have been using social media to communicate with customers and their target audience as they evolve toward collaborative environments where businesses engage in a dialogue with the user community. This has proven to be an efficient and cost-effective way to implement marketing, communication and customer service actions. Regrettably, the benefits of social media also expose companies to many risks and potential public relations disasters. Corporate security plans, whether for large or small businesses, must include contingency action plans in the event of public crises caused by any of these online platforms, which could result in reputation damage and financial loss. Companies involved in such activities are highly likely to be targeted by cyber-criminals, since each attack could realize greater results than attacks on individual users.

The PandaLabs survey involved 315 US companies with from fifteen to one thousand employees and found that most of these companies overlook the challenges posed by social media in terms of authenticity, security and privacy. The survey found that Facebook was cited as the top contributor to malware infection (71.6%) and privacy violations (73.2%). YouTube was also responsible for malware infection (41.2%), while Twitter contributed to privacy violations (51%). Companies suffering financial losses from employee privacy violations cited Facebook as the most common social media site where these losses occurred (62%), followed by Twitter (38%), YouTube (24%) and LinkedIn (11%).

The main security concerns expressed by companies in the PandaLabs survey included:

Identity theft. Administrators' computers could become infected and have their profile login data and passwords compromised, so anybody could take control of the corporate account to perform any actions, including scheduling events with malware links. Any malicious user that took control of an account could post information from a company's official profile with disastrous effects.

Infection risks. Attackers could take advantage of instant messaging applications or the timeline feature in micro-blogging platforms to send users information with hidden links to malware sites. This could result in targeted attacks specially designed to infect user computers and penetrate networks to access information. Followers could also post malicious links on profile walls and spread computer threats. Any of these actions could compromise brand integrity.

Platform vulnerabilities. There have been many security problems exposed in social networks like Facebook and Twitter, and these put users at risk. As more users join these sites, this will include hackers looking for security flaws.

Privacy. Corporate profiles are managed by administrators who may provide too much information to followers or visitors. This information could then be used by malicious users against the company itself, either online or offline, by posting corporate information about finances, practices and work processes. The study also showed that 27% of SME employees use social networking during working hours where they could share confidential information.

Social Media Use by Individuals

The current generation is growing up with casual everyday use of social networking websites such as Facebook and MySpace, where posting accounts of their lives for their friends and the wider world to see is the norm. They often display a general disregard that the information they post, like name, birth date and a list of their network of friends could be easily accessed and used against them for criminal purposes. When gathered and organized by technologies for compiling data, this information can be combined with data from other sources to create a dossier or a specific pattern of behaviour (Anonymous 2009b) leading to identity theft or worse. Thus, users are revealing far more than they might if they knew the potential for criminal activity. For example, people often post information about their whereabouts, such as being away for the weekend or on vacation, which is valuable information for burglars who may be 'friending' them. People often say that privacy is important to them, but at the same time they are engaging in behaviours that reflect a lack of concern. This behaviour indicates a major shift from the views of older generations concerning privacy, since many users do not appear to be concerned that the information can be used not only for legitimate business and recreational purposes, but unfortunately also to further the criminal goals of identity thieves and other online human predators.

There are clearly serious privacy and security problems with the unfettered use of social networking. These can be partly addressed by better security, but since users are directly responsible for the information they post, user education in the risks of using social networking is probably the best way to address these problems.

Database Breaches: Follow-up Attacks on Consumers

In one of the largest data breaches in US history, the names and electronic contact information of many millions of customers of some of the largest US companies and a large number of college students were hacked in a break-in at Epsilon, an online marketing unit of Alliance Data Systems Corporation in March 2011 (Spicer and Aspan 2011). An example of a follow-up attack followed soon after. This was an example of 'spear phishing,' where a phony Epsilon website appeared claiming to have an update from Epsilon in the form of a downloadable file that would tell users if their personal information had been stolen. Users who were concerned about whether they were victimized by the initial data breach might download and open the file, but the file contained a Trojan horse that would be installed on the user's system and would run malicious code to gain access to personal information on the user's computer. The clear lesson here to users, who have been notified of data breaches by organizations with whom they communicate, is to be extremely careful about follow-up communications. In this case, the URL of the phony website was not exactly the same as the actual Epsilon website, an indication to the user to avoid clicking on that URL.

Wikileaks

Wikileaks, a 2006 startup that gained notoriety by releasing large amounts of classified information to the public (e.g., a 2010 release of 392,000 classified Iraq War documents (Greenberg 2010)), is an example of insiders misusing access to confidential information. In this case, a single whistleblower with a conscience caused a lot of trouble for a very large organization (in this case the US Armed Forces). While the insider involved and the Wikileaks organization may have been motivated by altruism or other unknown reasons, a great deal of damage may have resulted to some of the individuals and organizations and their relationships with others identified in the documents released. It is very difficult for organizations to prevent such releases, even by employees they trust, and it is easy to set up websites to distribute such information. So, we can probably expect more of this to happen in the future. Any organizational evaluation of risks needs to take such possibilities into account (see Chapter 7) and to develop procedures to guard against such leaks, even by trusted employees.

Multi-factor Authentication

As database breaches become more common, along with events like Wikileaks disclosures, organizations concerned about confidentiality (healthcare providers, banks, etc.) are moving toward much stronger authentication processes. An example is the recent introduction of chip-and-PIN credit and debit cards in Canada, which use two-factor authentication (something you have and something you know). Currently, some companies in Europe and possibly soon in Canada will be adopting commercial three-factor authentication—for example: something you have (a device about the size of a credit card that is carried on one's person), something you are (three fingerprints stored on the authentication device) and something you know (a one-time password displayed on a computer screen after the user is authenticated). This system in essence accomplishes mutual authentication (see Chapter 11). With these levels of authentication, the system is particularly robust against most of the usual attacks such as phishing, pharming and spoofing. This particular system is described on the AXSionics website[1] (AXSionics 2011).

International Cooperation against IDTF

The majority of identity theft and fraud takes place over the Internet, and fraudsters frequently operate internationally. This makes it a global issue, so international cooperation in apprehend-

---

1 http://www.axsionics.com/tce/frame/main/414.htm.

ing IDTF criminals is essential and international efforts must continue to improve if the battle against such crimes is to be effective. International agreements, multilateral instruments addressing online IDTF, international agencies and informal networks are among the tools that can make this work. Specific agreements include the international Cybercrime Convention (Council of Europe 2001) and agencies like the OECD (2009) and Interpol (2010).

These are just a few of the innovations and technological advances that continue to pose new challenges in the battle against IDTF. This battle is important, as the threat of IDTF can eat away at the trust that consumers have in organizations and markets. Solutions to the problems of guardianship and authentication that lie at the heart of IDTF will only be found through the collective efforts of all of the stakeholders who collect, handle, store and transmit personal information about individuals.

References

Anonymous. 2009b. "Leaving 'Friendprints': How Online Social Networks Are Redefining Privacy and Personal Security." In *Knowledge@Wharton*. Wharton University. http://knowledge.wharton.upenn.edu/article.cfm?articleid=2262 [consulted April 16, 2011].

AXSionics. 2011. *AXSionics Internet Passport*. AXSionics: The Internet Passport Company. http://www.axsionics.com/tce/frame/main/414.htm [consulted April 16, 2011].

Corrons, L. 2010. "Social Media Risk Index for Small to Medium Sized Businesses." *First Annual Social Media Risk Index for SMBs*. Panda Security. http://prensa.pandasecurity.com/wp-content/uploads/2010/06/1st-Annual-Social-Media-Risk-Index-Slidedeck.pdf [consulted April 16, 2011].

Council of Europe. 2001. Convention on Cybercrime. http://conventions.coe.int/Treaty/EN/Treaties/Html/185.htm [consulted March 13, 2011].

Greenberg, A. 2010. "Wikileaks Reveals the Biggest Classified Data Leak in History." *Forbes Magazine*. http://blogs.forbes.com/andygreenberg/2010/10/22/wikileaks-reveals-the-biggest-classified-data-breach-in-history/

Interpol. 2010. *Payment Cards*. International Criminal Police Organization (Lyon, France).

Newman, G. R., and M. M. McNally. 2005. "Identity Theft Literature Review." In US Department of Justice Vol. Document No. 210459.

NIST. 2010. "Cloud computing." National Institute of Standards and Technology (Washington, D.C.). http://csrc.nist.gov/groups/SNS/cloud-computing/ [consulted on April 16, 2011].

OECD. 2009. *Online Identity Theft*. Paris: Organization for Economic Cooperation and Development, Directorate for Science, Technology and Industry.

Rauhofer, J. 2008. "Privacy Is Dead, Get Over It! Information Privacy and the Dream of a Risk-Free Society." *Information & Communications Technology Law*, 17: 3: 185–97.

Spicer, J., and M. Aspan. 2011 (4 April). "More Customers Exposed as Big Data Breach Grows." *Reuters US News*

Glossary[1]

Account hijacking *
The assumption of a customer's identity on a valid existing account.
Also known as 'account takeover.'

Account level breach *
The compromise of a consumer name in connection with a credit card account number and possibly additional information, such as account expiration date and Card Verification System (CVS) number.
See also 'identity level breach.'

Account origination
The process of identification, authentication and issuance of unique identifiers (ID numbers, passwords, PINs, documents, tokens, etc.) when a person first establishes a relationship with a business or organization.
Also known as 'enrollment.'

Account takeover *
The assumption of a customer's identity on a valid existing account.
Also known as 'account hijacking.'

ATM
Automatic teller machine.
Also known as 'ABM,' for 'automatic banking machine.'

---

1 Sources for the definitions of items marked with an asterisk can be accessed at http://www.business.mcmaster.ca/IDTDefinition/glossary/index.htm.

Attributed identity
Individual attributes given at birth, like parents' names, date and place of birth, and full name.

Authentication *
1. The process of validating and verifying a claimed identity. This includes establishing that a given identity exists; establishing that a person is the true holder of that identity; and enabling the genuine owner of the identity to identify themselves for the purpose of carrying out a transaction.
2. The process of verifying the identity of a person or entity. Authentication is typically dependent upon customers providing an 'identifier' like an ID card or number, followed by one or more authentication factors, or credentials, to prove their identity.
3. The techniques, procedures and processes used to verify the identity and authorization of prospective or established clients.
4. Authentication for the purpose of identification documents like the testimony of a court-certified document examiner, or in some cases the manufacturer, that a document is genuine and unaltered.
See also 'authentication factor,' 'multi-factor authentication,' 'single-factor authentication' and 'credentials management.'

Authentication factor
Secret or unique information linked to a specific person's identifier that is used to verify that person's identity. There are three types of authentication factors:
1. Something a person knows—commonly a password or PIN (*see 'Shared secrets'*)
2. Something a person has—most commonly a physical device referred to as a 'token'
3. Something a person is—most commonly a physical characteristic, such as a fingerprint, voice pattern, etc. *See also 'biometrics.'*
See also 'multi-factor authentication' and 'single-factor authentication.'

Balanced Scorecard Methodology
An analysis technique developed by Robert Kaplan and David Norton in 1992, designed to translate an organization's mission statement and overall business strategy into specific, quantifiable goals and to monitor the organization's performance in terms of achieving these goals.

Bill S-4

Federal law adopted by the Canadian parliament in 2009 to update relevant Canadian laws on identity theft and to give the justice system more power to apprehend and prosecute thieves involved in such activities.

Biographical identity attributes

Individual details that are accumulated over time, including life events like details of education or other qualifications, employment history, property ownership, marriages and other details such as benefits claimed, taxes paid, current and past addresses, etc.

Biometrics

A group of authentication factors based on physiological or physical characteristics unique to each individual, like fingerprints, DNA profile, hand geometry, facial structure, etc.

Breeder document

A document, such as a birth certificate, that is used by an identification issuer to establish the identity of an applicant.

Browsing

Not the normal use of a Web browser, but rather searching specifically for password or other access information.

Carding

A term used to describe the process of verifying the validity of stolen credit or debit card data. The carder (card data thief) presents the card information on a website that has real-time transaction processing. If the card is processed successfully, the thief knows that the card is still good. A website known to be susceptible to carding is called a 'cardable' website. Carding is typically used to verify credit card data obtained directly from victims by skimming or phishing.

Card not present

Transactions where purchases are made over the telephone, by mail order or through electronic commerce.

Chip-and-PIN cards

Payment cards that have a microchip instead of a magnetic strip, and for which a PIN number is used to verify the card owner's identity, rather than or in addition to a signature. The PIN is encoded on the chip, so the point-of-sale terminal can ensure that the PIN entered at the keypad matches the PIN encoded on the chip.

CISO

Chief Information Security Officer. The CISO is normally responsible for establishing and maintaining the enterprise vision, strategy and program to ensure information assets are adequately protected.

Also known as 'Chief Security Officer,' or 'CSO.'

Cloud computing

A model for enabling convenient, on-demand network access to a shared pool of configurable computing resources (e.g., networks, servers, storage, applications and services) that can be rapidly provisioned and released with minimal management effort or service provider interaction.

Corporate identity theft

The unauthorized collection, transfer, replication or manipulation of a business's identifying information for the purpose of committing fraud or other crimes. Such information can include the business's name, address, telephone number, corporate credit card information, bank account information, tax identification numbers, employer identification numbers, e-business Web sites, URL addresses, articles of incorporation and company profiles.

Also known as 'commercial identity theft' or 'business identity theft.'

Counterfeiting

For the purposes of identity theft, the illegal duplication of identity documentation.

CPO

Chief Privacy Officer. A management position created to respond to consumer concerns over privacy, particularly in medical data and financial information and to ensure compliance with government legislation.

Credentials management *
Authentication of the identity of parties accessing data.
Also known as 'authentication.'

Credit alert
An alert that credit reporting agencies attach to a credit file. When an individual with a credit alert on file attempts to open a credit account, the lender should contact the individual to verify that he or she wishes to open the new account. If no contact is possible, the credit account may not be opened. A creditor is normally not required by law to contact the individual if there is a fraud alert in place.
See also 'credit freeze.'

Credit freeze *
A security freeze that is placed on a consumer's credit file to prevent the file from being shared with anyone, thus forestalling new accounts from being opened in the consumer's name.
See also 'credit alert.'

Credit reporting agencies
Agencies that collect credit and personal information about consumers.
Also called 'credit bureaus.'

Cybercrime Convention
An international agreement ratified in 2001 by a group of Western countries led by the Council of Europe and including Canada and the United States. It deals with crimes committed via the Internet and other computer networks, including copyright infringements, computer-related fraud, child pornography and violations of network security. Its main objective is to protect society against cybercrime through appropriate legislation and international cooperation.

Cyberextortion
A crime in which payment is demanded in order to prevent or stop attacks on an organization's website, network or computer systems. A 2004 Carnegie Mellon study found that roughly one out of five cyberextortionists who threatened an attack but did not receive payment actually carried out their threats.

Data breach
An instance when personal information contained in a set of paper records or an electronic database is compromised by theft, loss or unauthorized intrusion. Breaches can be classified as account-level or identity level.
Also known as 'security breach' or 'privacy breach.'

Data brokers
Organizations that purchase personal identifying information from credit reporting agencies and other entities, combine it with information acquired from online public records, organize the information and resell it to companies or government agencies seeking to conduct background checks or otherwise to verify identities.

Document breeding
The process of using one or more identity documents to apply for and receive additional documents in the same name

Domain Name Service (DNS) poisoning
A method of collecting personal information by misdirecting consumers to a fraudulent website. A consumer may type in the correct URL, but a criminal may have surreptitiously changed some of the address information that Internet Service Providers store to speed up Web browsing.
Also known as 'pharming.' See also 'redirector.'

Drive-by download
Software that secretly and automatically installs on a computer when the user visits certain websites. The user is usually unaware that anything was installed until after the fact.

Dumpster diving
A method of collecting personal information by physically searching through trash. The information found in this way may be used to access accounts and perform account maintenance.

Eavesdropping
Listening to transmissions intended for others.

Electronic signature
Any sound, symbol or process attached to or associated with an electronic record by the person who has intended to sign the electronic record. For a digital signature to be legal, it must be permanently bound to the document by the use of appropriate software; this is the same requirement for physical pen-and-paper signing.

Encrypted payload *
Encryption of portions of transmitted data, while leaving headers and non-confidential data as plain text.

Encryption *
Any procedure used in cryptography to convert plain text into cipher-text in order to prevent any but the intended recipient from reading that data.

Enrollment *
1. The process of introducing the personal characteristics of a person into a biometric-based system. Samples of data from one or more physiological or physical characteristic are taken, converted into a mathematical model or template and registered in a database.
2. The process of identification authentication and the issuance of unique identifiers (ID numbers, passwords, PINs, documents, tokens, etc.) when a person first establishes a relationship with a business or organization. *Also known as 'account origination.'*

Enterprise risk management (ERM)
A comprehensive enterprise-wide risk management approach that is economically practicable and includes, among other things, the management of information security and privacy across the organization.

Existing account fraud
Debit card fraud, cheque frauds and frauds involving existing telephone, utility or online accounts. Credit card fraud is usually considered separately because of its particular characteristics and its relatively high rate.

Evil twin *
A wireless network that offers Wi-Fi connections like the kind commonly found in local coffee houses, airports and hotels, but is actually a ruse to steal consumer passwords and/or credit card numbers.

Fair Credit Reporting Act
A United States federal law, originally passed in 1970, that governs the collection, dissemination and use of consumer information, including the operations of credit reporting agencies. In 2003, it was supplemented by the Fair and Accurate Credit Transactions Act (FACTA).

Fictitious identity
A false identity that is not based on a real person's personal information. *Also known as a 'synthetic identity.'*

Firewall
A set of related programs, located on a private network gateway server, that monitors all network traffic entering or leaving the private network in order to protect the resources of the private network from users on external networks.

General trust
The belief that other people can be relied on.

Hacking *
Obtaining unapproved access into an organization's computer systems, databases or intranet with the intent of stealing confidential information.

Health Insurance Portability and Accountability Act (HIPAA)
A US law designed to provide privacy standards to protect patient medical records and other health information provided to health plans, doctors, hospitals and other healthcare providers.

Identity and Access Management (IAM)
An administrative process coupled with a technological solution for validating the identity of individuals and allowing owners of data, applications and systems to maintain central or distributed responsibility for granting access to their respective resources to anyone participating within the IAM framework.

ICT (Information and Communications Technologies)
All the technical means used to handle information and aid communication, including computer and network hardware, communication middleware and necessary software.

Identity checker
An individual or organization that verifies that the person presenting the identification document or credentials is the person to whom the identity belongs.

Identity crime *
Offenses involving the use of a false identity.

ID
Identity

IDF
Identity fraud.

Identity fraud (IDF)
The use of stolen or bogus identities to commit fraud.

Identity harvesting
A term used for the collection of personal information when the collection method targets a group of people. This would include methods like hacking, insider access, phishing, pharming, etc.

Identity information
Information that is unique to an individual or that can be used alone or in combination with other information to identify an individual or to allow access to goods, services, locations or benefits.
Also known as 'personal information' or 'means of identification.'

Identity issuers
Trusted institutions, public or private, who issue identity documents or other credentials.

Identity level information
Identity information that is difficult or impossible to change (e.g., name and address, biographical information like birth date or mother's unmarried name, and government-issued identity information like driver's license numbers, Social Security Numbers or Social Insurance Numbers,

health card numbers, etc. Identity level information is required to open new accounts or to commit other non-financial frauds.

Identity level breach
The compromise of a consumer name in connection with a Social Security Number (US) or Social Insurance Number (Canada), and possibly address, date of birth or associated phone numbers, as well. *See also 'account level breach.'*

Identity manipulation
The alteration of one's own identity.

Identity owner
Someone truly associated with identity information or identity documents.

Identity protectors
Individuals or organizations involved with protecting identity owners, issuers and checkers against IDTF.

IDT
Identity theft.

IDTF
Identity theft and fraud.

Identity theft (IDT)
The unauthorized collection, possession, transfer, replication or other manipulation of another person's personal information and/or identification documents, for the purpose of committing fraud or other crimes that involve the use of a false identity.

Identity thief
An individual or organization involved in illicitly obtaining personal information, developing false identities or committing crimes using a false identity.

Insiders
Employees or other participants in transactions or with authorization to access systems and/or places where personal information is stored.

ITADA (Identity Theft and Assumption Deterrence Act)
A federal law adopted by the United States in 1998 bringing identity theft and fraud into the criminal code: "Whoever knowingly transfers or uses, without lawful authority, a means of identification of another person with the intent to commit, or otherwise promote, carry on, or facilitate any unlawful activity that constitutes a violation of federal law, or that constitutes a felony under any applicable state or local law [commits identity theft.]"

Keyboard logger *
Software designed to permit an attacker to record all keystrokes made on a computer keyboard and transmit the information to another location.

Malware
Short for "malicious software," it refers to any harmful software. Malware includes computer viruses, worms, Trojan horses and spyware.

Masquerading
Unauthorized access using a legitimate user ID.

Man in the middle *
An attack in which a perpetrator is able to read, insert and modify at will messages between two parties without either party knowing that their communication link has been compromised.

Means of identification *
Any name or number that may be used, alone or in conjunction with any other information, to identify a specific individual.
Also known as 'personal information' or 'identity information.'

Multi-factor authentication *
1. A process that uses two or more authentication factors to verify customer identity.
2. Combining two or more authentication techniques together to form a

stronger, more reliable level of authentication. This usually involves combining two or more of the following types:

- Secret—something the person knows
- Token—something the person has
- Biometric—something the person is

Mutual authentication

A process whereby customer identity is authenticated and the target website is also authenticated to the customer.

Natural referral area

Used in healthcare to describe the geographical region within which a consumer lives that covers a very high percentage of the healthcare facilities that will ever need to treat that consumer.

New account fraud

Fraud that occurs when an identity thief steals personal information and opens one or more new credit card accounts, loans or other accounts under the victim's name.

Non-repudiation

The assurance that someone cannot deny something.

One-time password (OTP) *

A unique pass code generated by an electronic password–generating token or contained on a scratch card. OTP tokens are often used in multi-factor authentication schemes.

Organizational maturity model

A set of structured levels that describe how well the behaviours, practices and processes of an organization can reliably and sustainably produce required outcomes, as in, for example, the management of organizational security.

Out-of-band authentication *

Any technique that allows the identity of an individual to be verified through a channel different from the one being used to initiate the transaction.

Peer-to-peer file sharing application

An application that uses peer-to-peer (P2P) networking. A peer-to-peer network allows computer hardware and software to function without the need for special server devices. P2P is an alternative to client-server network design, and helps P2P client applications upload and download files over P2P network services.

Personal information

Information unique to an individual or that can be used alone or in combination with other information to identify an individual or to allow access to goods, services, locations or benefits.
Also known as 'identity information' or 'means of identification.'

PATRIOT Act (Providing Appropriate Tools Required to Intercept and Obstruct Terrorism Act)

A law passed by the US Congress in 2001 to deter and punish terrorist acts in the United States and around the world, and to enhance law enforcement investigatory tools. It is often invoked to gather information in the investigation of money laundering and financing of terrorism, to scrutinize various classes of international transactions, etc.

PIN (Personal identification number)

A PIN is a unique personal password that is keyed into a website, ATM or computer to verify the identity of the person keying it in.

Personally identifiable information *

In information security and privacy, any piece of information that can potentially be used to identify, contact or locate a single person.
Also known as 'personal identifying information.'

Pharming

A method of collecting personal information by misdirecting consumers to a fraudulent website. The consumer enters the correct URL, but the criminal has surreptitiously changed some of the address information that Internet Service Providers store to speed up Web browsing.
Also known as 'Domain Name Service (DNS) poisoning.'

Phishing *

1. The act of sending an e-mail to a user falsely claiming to be an established legitimate enterprise in an attempt to scam the user into surrendering private information to be used for identity theft.
2. The criminal creation and use of e-mails and websites designed to look like e-mails and websites of well-known, legitimate businesses, financial institutions and government agencies in order to deceive Internet users

into disclosing bank and financial account information or other personal data like usernames and passwords.
See also 'vishing,' 'smishing,' 'pharming' and 'spear phishing.'

Phonebusters
A joint effort by the Royal Canadian Mounted Police and the Ontario Provincial Police for the purpose of receiving self-reported incidents of consumer identity theft and fraud from the victims of these crimes.

Piggybacking
Unauthorized signals added to communications messages.

PIPEDA (Personal Information Protection and Electronic Documents Act)
Beginning in 2001 and implemented in stages through to 2006, a Canadian federal act that applies to organizations in the private sector, except when provincial laws exist that are substantially similar to PIPEDA.

Pretexting *
The collection of information about an individual under false pretenses (the 'pretext'), usually done over the phone (e.g., calling a bank) while posing as a customer to find out personal information.

Privacy Act
A Canadian federal government law passed in 1983 that covers the public sector.

Privacy breach
An instance when personal information contained in a set of paper records or an electronic database is compromised by theft, loss or unauthorized intrusion. Breaches can be classified as account-level or identity level.
Also known as 'security breach' or 'data breach.'

Privacy Impact Assessment (PIA)
A privacy analysis tool used to ensure that new technologies, information systems and initiatives, or proposed programs and policies meet basic privacy requirements, thus addressing the potential for loss of privacy. It also helps to anticipate public reaction to privacy implications of a proposal, and, as a result, can prevent costly program, service or process redesign.

Red Flags Rules
Part of the US Fair and Accurate Credit Transactions (FACT) Act of 2003. A directed program to identify and mitigate IDTF risks, to detect and report violations when they occur (i.e., 'Red Flags') and to take corrective action when needed to update the program.

Redirector *
Crimeware code designed with the intent of redirecting end-user network traffic to a location where it was not intended to go. This includes crimeware that changes host files and other DNS-specific information, crimeware browser-helper objects that redirect users to fraudulent sites and crimeware that may install a network-level driver or filter to redirect users to fraudulent locations.
See also 'pharming' and 'DNS poisoning.'

Risk
A state of uncertainty where some of the possibilities involve a loss, catastrophe or other undesirable outcome.

Risk mitigation
An attempt to reduce to an acceptable threshold one or both of the probability of an event's occurrence or the impact of an adverse risk event. Especially for high-risk events, this is usually far more effective than trying to repair the damage later that results from an actual adverse event.

Risk perception
A publicly held view that may be very different (either more or less so) than actual risk.

Routine Activities Theory
A criminology theory that holds that, in order for a crime to occur, there must be motivated offenders, suitable targets and a lack of capable guardians. Situational Crime Prevention (SCP) builds on this theory by focusing on opportunity, place and guardianship as areas where crime prevention efforts should be focused.

Salami techniques
Diverting rounded-up financial data to illicit accounts

Scraping
A practice that involves automated software that roams the web recognizing and collecting data from web pages. Scraping was originally developed for spammers to collect e-mail addresses, but it can also be used to sniff out Social Insurance Numbers or other identifying information.

Secure Sockets Layer (SSL) *
The leading Internet security protocol. Developed by Netscape, SSL is used to do two things:
- Validate the identity of a website
- Create an encrypted connection for sending data

Security alert
A statement added to one's credit report when a credit bureau is notified that the consumer may be a victim of fraud. It remains on file for ninety days and suggests that creditors should request proof of identification before granting credit in that person's name.

Security breach
An instance when personal information contained in a set of paper records or an electronic database is compromised by theft, loss or unauthorized intrusion. Also known as a 'privacy breach' or 'data breach.' Breaches can be classified as account level or identity level.

Shared secrets
Information elements that are known or shared by both the user and the authenticating entity.

Shoulder surfing
A method of collecting PINs, user IDs, passwords or other personal information by eavesdropping, looking over someone's shoulder or otherwise standing in close proximity as they operate an ATM, telephone, computer or other data collection device.

SIN
See Social Insurance Number (Canada).

Single-factor authentication
A process that uses only one authentication factor to verify a customer's identity. An example is the use of only a password to gain access to a computer system or website.
See also 'multi-factor authentication.'

Skimming *

The act of producing unauthorized copy of an electronic security device while it is being used for its intended purpose. Originally skimming meant making an illegal copy of a credit card or a bank card when the original was being used correctly. Typical methods of skimming involve use of a modified reader that reads and stores all the information that the original card contains.

SMEs

Small and medium enterprises, usually defined as companies with five hundred or fewer employees.

Smishing *

A version of phishing in SMS (Short Message Service) messaging (text messaging) systems, which sends a cell phone message directing victims to a website that downloads malicious spyware (e.g., a Trojan horse) to the victim's cell phone or computer.

Social engineering *

A method of collecting personal information that involves exploiting human nature. An identity thief can often get information simply by asking for it, pretending they are someone in authority who has a right to request it.

Social Insurance Number (SIN)

In Canada, a nine-digit number used to identify individuals for the administration of government programs, including income tax, pensions, employment insurance, etc. These numbers are issued and managed by Human Resources and Development Canada, a federal government department.

Social Security Number (SSN)

In the United States, a nine-digit number issued by the federal government's Social Security Administration Department and used to identify individuals. An SSN is required to get a job, file tax returns or claim benefits. It is often used as an identification number by businesses or other institutions for billing or filing transactions. The SSN cannot be regarded as a unique identifier, so the theft of one number can affect more than one individual. A recent study found that, out of 280 million SSNs issued, more than twenty million Americans have more than one SSN associated with their names; and more than 100,000 have five or more SSNs associated with their names. These duplications may be due to identity theft, or just bad memory, data input errors or mistakes in record keeping.

Spam
Unsolicited commercial e-mails. Some of these come from legitimate companies, but many also come from questionable businesses.

Spear phishing *
The technique of using harvested personal information to mount more convincing phishing attacks on users.
See also 'phishing.'

Spoofing
A fraudulent website or e-mail that appears to be from a well-known company and attempts to get the user to provide, update or confirm personal information. Similar to 'pharming.'

Spyware *
Computer software that collects personal information about users without their informed consent.

SSN
See Social Security Number (US).

Swift trust
To trust and to be trustworthy within the limits of a temporary system, rather than wait while experience gradually shows who can be trusted and with what.

Synthetic identity
A false identity that is not based on a real person's personal information.
Also known as a fictitious identity.

Token
A physical device that may be part of a multi-factor authentication scheme. Examples are ABM cards, USB token devices, smart cards and password generating tokens.

Transport Security Layer (TSL)
A security protocol from the Internet Engineering Task Force (IETF) that is based on the Secure Sockets Layer (SSL) 3.0 protocol.

Trapdoor
Surreptitiously installed software that allows bypassing normal computer access controls.

Trojan horse
A Trojan horse contains or installs malicious programs that can run on a computer autonomously, masquerading as useful programs, or hack into the code of an existing program and execute while that program runs.

Trust
The willingness to make oneself vulnerable to another based on a judgment of similarity of intentions or values.

Trusted third parties (TTPs)
TTPs usually combine technical and social domains. They help to manage relationships by acting as trusted intermediaries between human and technical domains.

URL (Uniform Resource Locator)
The clickable website link that opens up the page in question when clicked.

Validation *
1. The process of determining that a specific identifier exists.
2. A process that determines if data (e.g., address, phone or SSN) are real. At this level, there are two concerns:
   • Do the specific personal identifiers (e.g., address, phone or SSN) exist?
   • Are the elements in the appropriate format as identified by the issuer of the data (e.g., driver's license number and Social Security Number)?
3. Validation for the purposes of ID documents is the process of adding the legal attribution and registration number by the document issuer to the surface of a genuine ID document blank at the time of issue.

Verification *
1. The process of determining that a specific identifier belongs to the person who is presenting or claiming it as their own.
2. A related but separate process from that of authentication. Customer verification complements the authentication process and should occur during account origination. Verification of personal information may be achieved in three ways:

- Positive verification to ensure that material information provided by the applicant matches information available from trusted third-party sources.
- Logical verification to ensure that information provided is logically consistent (e.g., do the telephone area code, ZIP code and street address match?).
- Negative verification to ensure that information provided has not previously been associated with fraudulent activity.

3. A process that determines if data belong together and determines if information supplied is the best available information.

- As an example, can the name, address, telephone number and SSN be confirmed together in multiple databases through parallel searching/matching?
- Are there keying errors?
- Is data accurately based on the best available data?

4. Verification for the purpose of ID documents is the process of confirming with the ID document issuer that a document was issued to a person with the personal identifiers and registration number provided.

VPN (Virtual Private Network)
A network that uses a public network, like the Internet, to provide remote offices or individual users with secure access to their home organization's network.

Viruses
Malicious programs with the ability to replicate and install themselves on or 'infect' a computer without the computer user's knowledge or authorization. Viruses are often unintentionally downloaded when the user accidentally clicks on a link to a website containing a virus.

Vishing *

A version of phishing that uses a combination of e-mail and telephone, or just telephone; the victim is urged to resolve an account issue by a criminal posing as a financial institution, and is thereby prompted to provide personal information.

VoIP (Voice over Internet Protocol)

An Internet protocol telephony term for a set of facilities used to manage the delivery of voice information over the Internet.

Wardriving

Physically finding and marking the locations and status of (improperly protected) wireless networks.

Worms

Computer viruses that can self-replicate by resending themselves via e-mail or network messages.

Index

A

acceptability, as human identifier, 59
Access, Privacy and Security, Service Alberta, 141
access to information, 70, 78, 79–80
account level information, 88
account takeover, 21, 111, 330
accountability, 193, 199
Acquisiti, A., 50
active authentication, 252
Affiliated Computer Services, 92
Alberta, 78, 127, 139, 141
Allen, J. H., 270
American Data Recovery Association, 137
American Health Information Management Association (AHIMA), 211
Amerprise, 191
anticipatory phase of risk management, 124–134, 140–143, 144–148
Anti-Phishing Working Group, 83
asset, vulnerability and threat, 155–156
ATM cards. *see* debit cards
attributed identity, definition, 15, 331
Australia, 118, 286–287
authentication
    active, 252
    approaches, 240–241
    basic layer, 248–250
    biometric identity, 244–245
    credit cards, 176, 178–179, 181, 254
    customer-to-site, 241–245
    definition and concept, 236, 331
    identity fraud, 39–40
    multi-factor, 16, 241, 327, 340–341
    mutual, 237, 247–255, 341
    online attacks, 237–239
    passive, 252–253
    passports, 165–166, 167–168, 171
    processes, 16, 240–241
    risk-based, 254
    single-factor, 236, 241, 242, 345
    site-to-customer, 245–247
    technical issues of security, 235–255
    three-factor, 327
    two-factor, 236, 241
    vulnerability, 277
AVT approach, 155–156
awareness and education, 147–148, 194, 198–199

B

Bagby, J. W., 48
balanced scorecard, 271, 331
bank account information. *see also* financial information
    existing accounts, 109, 111–113
    fraud examples, 109
    new accounts, 109, 113–115
    sale of, 89–90
Bank of America, 248
banking sector, 103–104. *see also* financial institutions
basic layer of authentication, 248–250

Bell Canada, 92
Bill 152 (Ontario), 209
Bill C-29 (Canada), 78
Bill S-4 (Canada), 29, 39, 332
biographical identity, definition, 15,
  332
biometric authentication, 244–245,
  332
biometric identity, 15, 59, 247
British Columbia, 127, 209
British Medical Defence Union,
  211–212
brokers. *see* data brokers
Brown, A., 132
Bush, President, 280
business sector research, 292–293
businesses. *see also* institutions;
  organizations
      fraud, 292, 293, 304–306
      indexes of IDTF, 306–308, 320
      risk management, 125–140
      surveys, 304–306

C
California Public Interest Research
  Group (CALPIRG), 289
Caloyannides, M. A., 230
Canada
      bank account fraud, 111–112
      business fraud, 292, 304–305
      business surveys, 304–305
      consumer protection, 31–33
      consumer surveys, 294–295,
        302–304
      costs of identity fraud, 116
      credit bureaus, 63
      credit card fraud, 108–110
      data breach legislation, 97–99,
        135, 139, 140, 143
      data breaches, 78, 215–216
      database storage, 143
      debit card fraud, 112
      incidence of identity fraud, 106
      legislation, 19, 28–30, 31–33,
        34, 281–282
      legislation, data breach, 97–99,
        135, 139, 140, 143

      medical fraud and data,
        210–211, 212–214, 322
      monitoring data for IDTF,
        300–301
      mortgage fraud, 207, 208–209
      other identity frauds, 115–116
      passports, 165, 166
      privacy, 127, 141, 273, 281
      Privacy Impact Assessments
        (PIAs), 133
      research, 281–282
      shopping, 206
      Social Insurance Number (SIN),
        5, 346
Canada Health Infoway, 322
Canada Post, 220–221
Canada Revenue Agency, 91
Canadian Bankers Association, 108
Canadian Canola Growers
  Association, 93
Canadian Health Care Anti-Fraud
  Association (CHCAA), 213
Canadian Internet Policy and Public
  Interest Clinic (CIPPIC), 9, 29–30
Canadian Privacy Commissioner, 9
Capability Maturity Model
  Integration (CMMI), 263–264
Carbonel, J.-C., 264
card not present (CNP), 108–110,
  174–175, 332
carding forums, 20
cellular phones, 21, 233
Center for Identity Management and
  Information Protection (CIMIP),
  86, 87, 276
certification authority, 242
certification programs, to build trust,
  55
Chadwick, D. W., 214
Cheney, J. S., 302
cheques, fraud, 111, 113
chief information security officers
  (CISO), 272
chief privacy officer (CPO),
  272–273, 333
chief security officers (CISO), 272,
  333

chip-and-PIN cards, 111, 236, 327, 333
ChoicePoint, 73, 91, 128–129
CIBC, 79
Clarke, Roger, 14, 58–60, 62
cloud computing, 322–323, 333
CMI, 215
collectability, as human identifier, 59
composite index of IDTF, 310–311, 320
computer crimes, 229
confidence, 52–53. *see also* trust
confidentiality management, 260–261
Conscious Competence Learning Matrix, 263
Consumer Measures Committee (Canada), 31–32
consumer protection, legislation, 30–33
Consumer Reports, 54–55
Consumer Sentinel Network, 290
consumer surveys for research, 282, 293–295, 302–304, 308
consumers. *see also* personal information
  actions against IDTF, 146–147
  attitudes and behaviours, 293–294
  education and awareness, 147–148
  follow-up attacks on, 326
  framework to combat IDTF risks, 144–150
  identity, 5–8, 17–19
  indexes of IDTF, 308–310, 320
  losses, 71–72, 317
  tips against identity theft, 144–145
contracts, electronic, 34–35
Copes, H., 82
costs of information. *see also* sale of information
bank account, 68, 89–90
credit cards, 68–69, 89–90
  data breach, 99, 123, 305
  financial, 68–69, 99, 123, 305
  in IDTF, 7–8, 116–119, 218–220
  privacy, 8
counterfeiting, 20–21, 110, 166–167, 333

credit bureaus, 62–63, 70
credit cards
  account takeover, 111
  authentication, 176, 178–179, 181, 254
  AVT approach, 155–156
  chip-and-PIN cards, 111, 236, 327, 333
  counterfeiting, 110
  dangers of, 3–5
  data security risks, 179
  fraud, 108–111, 173–174
  issuance stage, 173–174, 176–177
  maintenance stage, 175, 181–183
  new account fraud, 113
  renewal and updating, 181
  risk analysis of lifecycle, 173–183, 318
  risks, 175, 183–184
  sale of stolen information, 68–69, 89–90
  skimming, 81–82
  usage stage, 174–175, 178–180
credit reports, 30–31, 33, 63–65
credit status, 32–33
credit-reporting systems, 62–64, 317
crime and criminals
  computers, 229
  definition, 37, 339
  detection and report of, 103–105
  false identity and, 23–25
  prevention, 277–278
  profiles, 86–88
Criminal Code (Canada), 28–29
criminal organizations, 87–88
criminology theories, 277–278
customers, 236, 253. *see also* consumers
customer-to-site authentication, 241–245
cybercrime, international aspect, 35–36
Cybercrime Convention, 36, 328, 334

D
data breach
  agents, external and internal, 94–95, 138–139
  ChoicePoint, 73, 91, 128–129

CIBC, 79
costs of, 99, 123, 305
definition, 67, 90, 335
disclosure, 97–98
examples, 91–93
follow-up attacks, 326
information about, 90
investigation steps, 137–138
legislation, 68, 78, 135, 317
legislation, Canada, 97–99, 135, 139, 140, 143
legislation, United States, 97, 135, 139, 143
link to fraud, 96–97
management model, 122, 317–318
notification of, 77–79, 97–99, 138, 139
in organizations, 94–96, 215–218
prevalence, 95–96
prevention, 138
reported breaches and exposed records, 93–94
reports used for research, 291–292
risk, 98–99, 215–218
TJX, 79
use of data, 67–68
data brokers, 66–67, 72–73, 335
data collection
control of, 69–73
identity information, 2, 17–19
by marketers, business, governments, 8, 315
for monitoring IDTF, 299–301, 308
for research, 276
data dissemination, control of, 69–73
data protection, legislation, 33
databases, 6–7, 9–10, 66–67, 68–69
DataLossDB, 90, 93–94
debit cards, 82, 111–113, 173
Department of Housing, Education and Welfare (US), 69–70
Department of Veterans Affairs (US), 91
detection, 103–105, 116, 230
deterrance, 132–133

digital dossiers, 66
digitization, role in ID theft, 6–8
disclosure, 97–99
disposal of electronic goods, 222
document breeding, 21, 39, 335

E
eBay, 113
education and awareness, 147–148, 194, 198–199
electronic contracts, 34–35
electronic signatures, 34–35, 336
e-mail, 34–35, 68, 83–85, 235, 238. see also phishing
employee mishandling of information, 187–189
    categories, 189–191
    factors, 191–197
    prevention, 197–200
employees
    accountability, 193, 199
    behaviour causing identity theft, 189–190
    identity assets, 187
    insider attacks, 130–132, 135–136
    security and, 191–197, 200
    SETA programs, 194, 198–199
    unethical use of company information, 11
enrollment, 15–16, 21, 277, 336
Enron, 11
enterprise risk assessment and management, 125–127
enterprise risk management (ERM), 123, 336
enterprise thieves, 87–88
Epsilon, 326
Equifax Canada, 32, 63
E-Sign (US), 34, 35
European Union, research, 284–286
exclusivity, as human identifier, 59
Express Scripts, 216

F
Facebook, 9, 212, 324
Fair and Accurate Credit Transactions Act (FACTA) (US), 30–31, 67, 128

Fair Credit Reporting Act (US), 30, 337
Fair Information Practices, 69–71
Fair Isaacs Organization, 4
false identity, 17, 18, 19–22, 23–25
false positive and negative, 63–65
familiar fraud, 86–87
Federal Trade Commission (FTC) (US)
    consumer surveys, 294–295
    identity fraud, 79, 106
    identity theft, 280, 289–290
    IDTF complaints, 2
    legislation, 26
    notification, 135
FICO credit scoring, 4
fictitious identification, 18, 22–23
financial information, 68–69, 148.
    see also bank account information
financial institutions, 84, 127–128,
    215–216, 240–241
Fisher, C., 277–278
Fleishman, E. A., 263
Forrester Research, 219
fraud. *see also* identity fraud
    other, 109, 115–116
fraud rings, 288
friendly fraud, 86–87
Frontline/World, 222
Future of Identity in the Information
    Society (FIDIS), 286

G
garbage, as source of information, 81
Gartner Research, 106, 137, 295
Government Accountability Office
    (GAO) (US), 117, 217–218, 279–280
Ghana, 222
Gill v. Bucholtz (British Columbia), 209
Gonzalez, Alberto, 93
government, identity theft control,
    139–140
Government Accountability Office
    (GAO) (US), 96
Gramm-Leach-Bliley Act (US), 33
grid cards, 242, 243

H
Hannaford Bros., 93

Health Insurance Portability and
    Accounting Act (HIPPA) (US), 33,
    272, 337
Health Maintenance Organization
    (HMO) (US), 321
Hearthland Payment Systems, 93, 129
Hoofnagle, C. J., 66, 70, 293
Howell, W. C., 263
human identification, 14, 58, 60–62
"Human Identification in
    Information Systems" (Clarke), 14
human identifier, 58–59

I
ID Analytics, 96–97, 288–289, 304
identification. *see also* human identifi-
    cation; identity information
    characteristics, 60–62
    concept, 14–16
    errors in, 63–64
    personal participation, 65
    process, 15–16
identifier, 16, 68
identity
    concept, 14–16
    forms of, 15
    online, 285
    sale of, 89–90
identity and access management
    (IAM), 231–232, 319, 337
identity assets, 154–156, 187
identity checker, 38, 39, 49, 157, 338
identity fraud. *see also* identity theft;
    identity theft and fraud (IDTF)
    authentication, 39–40
    categories, 107
    costs, 116–119
    definition, 2, 17, 23–25, 39,
        316, 338
    detection and report of,
        103–105, 116
    examples, 109
    incidence, 105–107
    knowledge of, 78, 79
    legislation (Canada), 28–30
    legislation (US), 26–27
    link to data breach, 96–97

loss allocation rules, 70
management model, 122, 124
physical acquisition, 81
research, 286–289
roles, risks, responsibilities of
    stakeholders, 49
stakeholder model, 36–38, 316
victims, 64, 79

*Identity Fraud in Australia: An
Evaluation of its Nature, Cost and
Extent* (Cuganesan and Lacey),
286, 292

Identity Fraud Steering Committee
(ISFC) (UK), 118–119

Identity Fraud Survey Report (Javelin),
302–303

identity harvesting, definition, 19, 338

identity information. *see also* identification; personal information
collection of, 2, 17–19
definition, 338
electronic acquisition, 85–88
physical acquisition, 81–82

identity issuer, 37–39, 49, 157, 338
identity level information,
    88–89, 338

identity management
issuance stage, 157–159, 160
lifecycle, 156–164, 183–185, 318
maintenance stage, 157, 161–164
usage stage, 157, 159–161, 162

identity owner, 37–38, 39–40, 49,
157, 338

identity protector, 38–39, 49, 157, 338

identity theft. *see also* identity fraud;
identity theft and fraud (IDTF)
definition, 2, 17, 23–25, 26,
    103, 316, 339
examples, 109
in financial markets, 68–69
guardianship, 38–39
identification and, 64–65
legality, 21–22
legislation (Canada), 28–30
legislation (US), 26–27
management model, 122
methods, 79–88

obtention of information, 67
organizations and, 188–189
risk, 155
roles, risks, responsibilities of
    stakeholders, 49
safeguarding, 77
services provided to, 63
signs of, 149
social media, 324
stakeholder model, 36–38, 316
tips against, 144–146
victims, 77–79

Identity Theft and Assumption
Deterrence Act (ITADA) (US),
26–27, 39, 67, 280, 289, 340

identity theft and fraud (IDTF). *see
also* identity fraud; identity theft
definition, 1–2, 17, 302
history, 3
lifecycle stages, 280
process model, 17–23
rates, 2
risks from, 2–3

Identity Theft Penalty Enhancement
Act (US), 26–27

Identity Theft Resource Center
(ITRC), 90, 150, 189, 289

identity thieves. *see* crime and criminals

impersonation, 27–28, 85, 343

indexes for monitoring IDTF,
300–301, 306–311, 320

indispensibility, as human identifier, 59

infection risks, 324

information and computing technologies (ICT), 221–222, 337

insider attacks, 130–132, 135–136

institutions. *see also* businesses;
organizations
insider attacks, 130–132, 135–136
risk mitigation, 48, 50–51
threat from IDTF, 9–11

intentional theft by employees,
189–190

internal control systems, 230, 318–319

international cooperation against
IDTF, 327–328

Internet
    role in identity theft, 6–8
    threats, external and internal, 232
Internet Crime Complaint Center
    (IC3), 290, 305–306
IS (information systems) security, 135
ISO 17799:2005, 264
issuance stage
    credit cards, 173–174, 176–177
    employee mishandling of infor-
        mation, 188
    identity management, 157–159,
        160
    passports, 165–167, 168

J
Jamieson, R., 124
Javelin Strategy & Research, 79, 85,
    106–107, 294–295, 302–303
Joint Research Centre of the
    European Commission study,
    284–285
journals about IDTF, 275

K
Kantara Initiative, 288
Kim, D. J. et al., 148

L
law enforcement, 283–284, 290–291
legislation
    in borderless world, 35–36
    Canada, 19, 28–30, 31–33, 34,
        281–282
    Canada, data breach, 97–99,
        135, 139, 140, 143
    collection of information, 19
    consumer protection, 30–33
    data breaches, 68, 78, 135, 317
        (see also Canada, data breach;
        United States, data breach)
    data protection, 33
    electronic signatures, 34
    identity theft, 21–22
    impersonation, 27–28
    notification and disclosure, 97–98
    privacy, 33, 134–135

    United States, 25–28, 30–31,
        33, 34
    United States, data breach, 97,
        135, 139, 143
lenders, losses, 72
Liberty Alliance Project, 287–288
logins, sale of, 90
logos, 247
LoPucki, L., 60–65, 70
loss allocation rules, 70, 72
losses prevention, 70–72
loyalty cards, 72–73

M
mail, 81, 110, 220–221
maintenance stage
    credit cards, 175, 181–183
    employee mishandling of infor-
        mation, 189
    identity management, 157,
        161–164
    passports, 169–172
malicious software, 237
man-in-the-middle attacks (MITM),
    235, 239, 340
maturity of security, 262–271, 319
    levels, 264–271, 319
    models, 263–264, 319
McMaster eBusiness Research Centre
    (MeRC), 294–295
McNally, M. M., 27, 276–278, 279,
    319–320
measurement
    IDTF, 102–105, 301–302, 307,
        320
    risk, 43–44, 46–47, 51
medical data networks, 321–322
medical identity theft and fraud
    (MIDTF), 209–214
mobile phones, 21, 233
mobile services, identity manage-
    ment, 230
monitoring of IDTF, 300–301,
    306–311
mortgage fraud, 114–115, 206–209
multi-factor authentication, 16, 241,
    327, 340–341

multiple identities, 22–23
multi-purpose identification schemes, 60
Mundy, D., 214
mutual authentication, 237, 247–255, 341

N

name, 16. *see also* identifier
National Crime Victimization Survey (NCVA) (US), 294–295
networks, security of, 129–130, 216, 232–234, 319
Newman, G. R., 27, 276–278, 279, 319–320
newspaper announcements, 67, 239
non-malicious handling by employees, 190–191
notification, data breach, 77–79, 97–99, 138, 139
nyms, 285

O

Obama administration, 321
Office of the Information and Privacy Commissioner of the Province of Ontario, 281
one-time password (OTP), 244, 341
online payment systems, protection, 139
Ontario
    data breaches legislation, 78
    medical fraud, 210, 213–214
    mortgage fraud, 115, 208–209
    research, 281
Organization for Economic Cooperation and Development (OECD), 70
organizational security. *see also* employee mishandling of information
    absence of, 214–215
    dependencies, 260–261
    goals, 262–263
    implementation, 271–273
    maturity, 262–271, 319
    maturity levels, 264–271, 319
    officers, 272
    recommendations, 197–200

response to threats, 220–221
    technical issues, 226–231
organizations. *see also* businesses; employees; institutions; organizational security
    accountability, 199
    confidentiality management, 260–261
    costs of IDTF, 218–220
    data breach, 94–96, 215–218
    identity theft, 188–189
    internal control systems, 230, 318–319
    monitoring of IDTF, 301
    outsourcing of ICT, 221–222
    privacy officers, 272–273
    risk, 214–218
    risk management, 122–125, 316
    risk mitigation, 48, 50–51, 316
    SETA programs, 194, 198–199
    social media use, 323–325
    top management's role, 192, 197–198
other fraud, 109, 115–116
out-of-band layer, 250
outsourcing of ICT, 221–222
over-notification, 98

P

PandaLabs, 323–324
paper documents and signatures, 34–35
passive authentication, 252–253
passports
    counterfeiting, 166–167
    issuance stage, 165–167, 168
    maintenance stage, 169–172
    risk analysis of lifecycle, 165–171, 318
    usage stage, 167–169, 170
password, 16, 90, 242, 244. *see also* verifier
password-generating tokens, 242, 244
PayPal, 113
peer-to-peer (P2P) threats, 238
permanence, as human identifier, 59
Personal Health Information Act (PHIPA) (Ontario), 78

personal identity, 5–8, 17–19
personal information
    access to, 70, 78
    consumer behaviour, 146–147
    definition, 342
    ease of access, 79–80
    methods of access, 80–81
    sale of, 68–69, 89–90
    types, 88–89
Personal Information Protection Act
    (PIPA) (Alberta), 78, 127
Personal Information Protection
    and Electronic Documents Act
    (PIPEDA) (Canada)
    compliance, 228
    data breaches, 78, 97, 135
    description, 33, 343
    notification, 97
    organizations and, 273
    privacy, 127
personalized keypad, 246, 248
pharming, 235, 342
phishing, 83–84, 235, 237–239,
    245–246, 251–253, 326, 342–343
PhoneBusters, 282, 290, 343
PIN (personal identification num-
    ber), 112, 342
point-of-sales terminals, skimming, 82
police. see law enforcement
policy formulation, 126–128
Ponemon Institute, 305
precision, as human identifier, 59
President's task force (US), 280–281,
    283–284
pretexting, 27–28, 85, 343
prevention
    crime, 277–278
    data breach, 138
    of IDTF, 132–133, 279, 283
    of losses, 70–72
    by organizations, 197–200
privacy
    breach, 134–135, 343
    Canada, 127, 281
    compliance with regulations, 141
    data brokers, 66
    legislation, 33, 134–135

    market value, 8
    medical information, 322
    officers in organizations, 272–273
    in outsourcing of ICT, 221
    risk and, 133, 315
    security and, 48–50
    in social media, 8–9, 324–325
Privacy Act (Canada), 33, 343
Privacy Impact Assessments (PIAs),
    133–134, 343
Privacy Rights Clearinghouse, 68,
    90, 289
private sector research, 287–292
prosecution of criminals, 29, 218–219
public information, danger of, 80
public-sector sources for research,
    278–287
purses, 81

Q
Quebec, 127

R
Rauhofer, J., 8
reactionary phase of risk manage-
    ment, 124–125, 126, 134–136,
    143, 148–149
real identity and fictitious identity, 22
recognition-based user authentication,
    241
Red Flags Rules, 31, 127–128, 139,
    210, 344
reduction of IDTF, 131–133, 279
remediation phase of risk manage-
    ment, 125, 126, 136–140, 143,
    149–150
research
    areas and sources, 275–277,
        319–320
    business sector, 292–293
    consumer surveys, 282, 293–295,
        302–304
    criminology theories, 277–278
    data about IDTF, 276
    journals about IDTF, 275
    private sector, 287–292
    public-sector sources, 278–287
retailing sector, identity fraud, 103–104

risk
    assessment, 128–131, 154–155
    authentication and, 254–255
    AVT approach, 155–156
    consumers and, 48, 144–150
    data breach, 98–99
    definition, 43, 344
    disposal of electronic goods, 222
    identification phase, 155
    identity theft, 155
    MIDTF, 209–214
    mortgage fraud, 206–209
    perception, 43–45, 50–52, 54, 315–316, 344
    prediction, 320–321
    privacy and, 315
    probability and measurement, 43–44, 46–47, 51
    reduction, 131–132
    in shopping, 205–206
    trust and, 54
risk analysis
    credit card lifecycle, 173–183, 318
    identity management lifecycle, 156–164, 183–185, 318
    passport lifecycle, 165–171
risk assessment, 128–131
risk management
    anticipatory phase, 124–134, 140–143, 144–148
    by businesses, 125–140
    definition and approaches, 154–155
    identity asset, 154–156
    IDTF, 122–125
    need for, 10, 46
    in organizations, 122–125, 316
    policies, 51, 316
    reactionary phase, 124–125, 126, 134–136, 143, 148–149
    remediation phase, 125, 126, 136–140, 143, 149–150
    SMEs, 140–143
risk mitigation
    definition and concept, 47–48, 344
    in organizations, 48, 50–51, 316
    phase, 155
    privacy and security, 48–50
    SMEs, 142–143

risk perception, 43–45, 50–52, 54, 315–316, 344
risk reduction, 131–132
risk-based authentication, 254–255
Roadmap of Advanced Research in Privacy and Identity Management (RAPID), 285–286
robo-signing, 207
Romanosky, S., et al., 275

S

sale of information, 20, 68–69, 89–90. *see also* costs of information
Sarbanes Oxley Act (US), 33
Sausner, R., 247–248
Schneier, B., 44, 241
Schreft, S. L., 139, 216
scraping, 80, 345
Secret Service (US), 291
secure sockets layer (SSL), 246, 248–250
Securities Industries Research Centre of Asia-Pacific (SIRCA), 286
security. *see also* organizational security; security maturity
    authentication, 235–255
    data breach, 67
    diagrams, 232, 234
    employees and, 191–197, 200
    end-users and, 200
    goals, 262–263
    identity and access management (IAM), 231–232
    implementation, 271–273
    management, 10
    of networks, 129–130, 216, 232–234, 319
    outsourcing, 221
    President's task force (US), 283
    privacy and, 48–50
    regulations, 228
    technical issues, 226
    wi-fi and cell phones, 129–130, 233–234
security education, training and awareness (SETA) programs, 194, 198–199

security impact model, 193
security maturity, 262–271, 319
    levels, 264–271, 319
    models, 263–264, 319
sensitive information, availability, 80
shared digital image, 246, 248
Sharma, A., 263
Sheward, S., 241
shopping risks, 205–206
signatures, 34–35, 336
SIN (Social Insurance Number), 5, 346
single-barrier solutions, 285
single-factor authentication, 236,
    241, 242, 345
Siponen, M. T., 196
site-to-customer authentication,
    245–247
situational crime prevention (SCP),
    277–278
skimming, 81–82, 112, 346
small and medium entreprises
    (SMEs), 140–143, 323, 346
smart cards, 242, 243–244
smishing, 83, 346
Smith, S., 124
social benefits, theft of, 9
social engineering, 82–85, 346
Social Insurance Number (SIN), 5, 346
social media, 8–9, 323–325
Social Security Number (SSN), 5,
    25–26, 62, 115, 346–347
Solove, Daniel, 65–66, 69–70
'something an online site knows,' 246
'something an online system has,'
    246–247
'something an online system is,' 247
'something you are,' 241, 244–245
'something you have,' 240–241,
    242–243
'something you know,' 240, 242
Sovern, J., 70
spear phishing, 84, 326
SSN (Social Security Number), 5,
    25–26, 62, 115, 346–347
stakeholder model for IDTF, 36–38,
    316
Statistics Canada, 292, 304
storability, as human identifier, 59

Survey of Fraud Against Businesses
    (SFAB), 292, 304–305
swift trust, 53, 347
symmetric authentication mecha-
    nism, 251–255
synthetic identity, 22, 347. *see also*
    fictitious identification
Systems Security Engineering
    Capability Maturity Model
    Integration, 263

T
technical issues
    authentication, 235–255
    identity and access management,
        231–232
    network security, 232–234
    organizational security, 226–231
telephone frauds, 84
theft. *see* identity theft
thieves. *see* crime and criminals
Thomson, K.-L., 263
threats, definition, 50
three-factor authentication, 327
title fraud, 207–208
TJX, 79, 90, 91–92, 130
transport security layer (TSL), 249, 348
TransUnion Canada, 32, 63
trends in IDTF, tracking, 301
Trojan horse, 237, 326, 348
true name identity, 22
trust, 52–55, 316–317, 348
trusted third parties (TTP), 53–54, 348
Twitter, 324
two-factor authentication, 236, 241

U
UK tax and custom service, 92
uncertainty, 43, 54
uniform resource locator (URL),
    247, 348
unintentional error by employees, 190
unique identifiers, 15–16
uniqueness, as human identifier, 59
United Kingdom
    cheques, 113
    costs of IDTF, 118–119
    credit cards, 111, 173–174

data breaches, 217–218
medical fraud, 211–212
organizational security, 214–215, 217–218
research, 282–284
shopping, 206
United Kingdom Cabinet Office report, 282–284
United States
authentication, 240
banks' security threats, 215–216
business fraud, 293, 305–306
class-action suits, 216
consumer protection, 30–31
consumer surveys, 294
costs of IDTF, 116–118, 218–220
credit bureaus, 62–63
credit card fraud, 108
data breach legislation, 97, 135, 139, 143
data breaches, 135, 215–216, 291–292, 305–306
data collection, 299–300
debit card fraud, 112
incidence of identity fraud, 106
law enforcement, 283–284, 291
legislation, 25–28, 30–31, 33, 34
legislation, data breach, 97, 135, 139, 143
management of identity theft, 127–128
medical fraud and data, 210, 321–322
mortgage fraud, 207
motor vehicle information, 67
other identity frauds, 115–116
passports, 166
President's task force, 280–281, 283–284
prevention of identity theft, 283
research, 279–281, 283
shopping, 205–206
Social Security Number (SSN), 5, 25–26, 62, 115, 346–347
victims, 283, 289–290
universality, as human identifier, 59
US mail, 221

usage stage
credit cards, 174–175, 178–180
employee mishandling of information, 188
identity management, 157, 159–161, 162
passports, 167–169, 170
USB token device, 242–243

V
value of information. see costs of information
Vance, A., 196
verifier, 16, 285
Verisign, 253
Verizon, 306
Veterans Health Administration's networked system (VistA) (US), 321
victim recovery, President's task force (US), 283
victims
connection to thief, 86–87
demographics, 106–107
identity fraud, 64, 79
identity theft, 77–79, 283
notification of breaches, 78–79
reports used for research, 289–290
Vieraitis, L., 82
vishing, 83–84, 350
VoIP, 83–84, 350
Von Solms, R., 263

W
wallets, 81
Wang, W., et al., 188
website communication layer, 250
White, M. D., 277–278
Wikileaks, 326–327
Williamson, G. D., 240
Wired Equivalent Privacy (WEP), 130n1
wireless network (wi-fi), security, 129–130, 233–234
wireless telephone acccounts, 114
World Privacy Forum, 212

Y
YouTube, 324